Edward Lewine is a freelance journalist for the *New York Times*. It was during a holiday to the continent that he began his love affair with Spain. He lives in New York with his young family.

www.booksattransworld.co.uk

Death and the Sun

A MATADOR'S SEASON
IN THE
HEART OF SPAIN

Edward Lewine

Doubleday

LONDON · TORONTO · SYDNEY · AUCKLAND · JOHANNESBURG

TRANSWORLD PUBLISHERS
61–63 Uxbridge Road, London W5 5SA
a division of The Random House Group Ltd

RANDOM HOUSE AUSTRALIA (PTY) LTD
20 Alfred Street, Milsons Point, Sydney,
New South Wales 2061, Australia

RANDOM HOUSE NEW ZEALAND LTD
18 Poland Road, Glenfield, Auckland 10, New Zealand

RANDOM HOUSE SOUTH AFRICA (PTY) LTD
Endulini, 5a Jubilee Road, Parktown 2193, South Africa

Published 2005 by Doubleday
a division of Transworld Publishers

A catalogue record for this book is available from the British Library.
ISBN 0385 605269

Typeset in 11/13½pt Minion

Printed and bound in Great Britain by
Mackays of Chatham plc, Chatham, Kent

1 3 5 7 9 10 8 6 4 2

Papers used by Transworld Publishers are natural, recyclable products
made from wood grown in sustainable forests. The manufacturing processes
conform to the environmental regulations of the country of origin.

BRINDIS:

THIS BOOK GOES FOR YOU, MEGAN,

WHO MADE EVERYTHING

POSSIBLE.

Neither the sun nor death can be looked at steadily.

— Francois, duc de La Rochefoucauld, Maxim 26

Contents

Third Third: All the Roads Home

A Short Note on Morality

THE SUBJECT OF THIS BOOK is a controversial one. In a formal Spanish bullfight six large mammals are put to death for the afternoon's entertainment of a paying crowd. The central moral question raised by such a spectacle is whether it is right for people to kill animals for pleasure. Various human activities raise this question. No one in the modern world has a life-or-death need to eat red meat, wear leather, hunt and fish, or attend bullfights. People continue to do these things because they like to. Are carnivores, leather wearers, sportsmen, and bullfighting aficionados behaving in a moral way? That is an excellent and complicated question. But it is not the topic of this book. This is not a book of moral philosophy. It does not tell the reader how the world should be. This is a book of journalism. It tries to show the reader how the world is.

This book tells the story of a single bullfighting season in the life of a Spanish matador, and through that story attempts to reveal a few things about the strange and violent subculture of the bullfight and about Spain. But even though the story is told from the point of view of people who are biased in favor of bullfighting and earn their living from it, this book is not designed to convert the reader into a bullfighting fan or to argue that bullfighting is a good thing. The goal here is to try to explain bullfighting as it is, by taking a hard look at things that are hard to look at, like death and the sun. After finishing this book, some readers may find themselves more sympathetic toward bullfighting, and others more resolved in their dislike of it. Either way, that is for the readers to decide.

Prologue: Fran

Pozoblanco, September 26. The afternoon of the bullfight broke clear and cold under a blue sky etched with gray clouds. Autumn chilled the air. The shadow cast by the falling sun had split the arena in two when a trumpet blast heralded the beginning of the day's show. It was six-thirty P.M. The bullring was a neat, whitewashed wheel. Twenty-five rows of seats led down to a circular space covered in sand. This was the arena floor, where the action would take place. The sanded floor was about seven feet beneath the first row of seating and encircled by a five-foot-tall red-painted wooden fence. A narrow passageway, formed between fence and stone, ran around the circumference of the ring. In the terminology of bullfighting this passageway is called the *callejón*. It is where the bullfighters stand when they are not in action.

Pozoblanco is a town of some fifteen thousand residents, situated in a high mountain valley in the southern Spanish province of Córdoba. Most of the time nothing much of interest happens there. This bullfight was an exception. It was a national news story. Print reporters, photographers, and television crews had been pouring into town for days and were conspicuous throughout the bullring. As always, the bullfighting press was on hand, but there was also a strong contingent of people from mainstream media outlets as well as members of the "pink press," the *prensa rosa,* which is what tabloid magazines and TV shows are called in Spain. A flock of still photographers crowded the *callejón.* They pushed and shoved, craning their necks, anxious to get their first glimpse of the man everyone had come to see.

A small brass band, seated up in the last row of seats, clashed to tinny life, kicking into one of those somber military marches called *pasodobles* that are always played at bullfights. A gate in the wooden fence swung open and the bullfighters stepped out of the dark hole and into the light. They looked like emissaries from a more vivid world, dressed in their costumes of deeply colored fabric decorated with gold tracery and studded with baubles and frills, the sun glinting off the gold, sending darts of light to play upon the dull sand and stone. The first matador had a square head of heavy blond hair and a big grin. His name was Manuel Díaz, but like many bullfighters he performed under a nickname — in his case, El Cordobés (the Man from Córdoba). Next came a tall, knock-kneed fellow named José Luis Moreno. He stepped into line next to El Cordobés.

Then there was a pause . . . and the third matador came into view. Francisco Rivera Ordóñez trotted out to where his colleagues stood, dragging his toes in the sand like a child unwilling to face an angry parent. Fran stood less than five feet nine inches. He was muscled yet limber like a gymnast, and most of his power was in his legs and buttocks. His hair was thick, oily, and wavy, the color of good espresso beans. His skin was smooth and caramel-colored. It looked fine against the ivory tuxedo shirt he wore underneath his gold-encrusted, chocolate-brown matador's uniform. His face was striking in a matinee-idol sort of way, but it was a matinee idol reimagined as a Gypsy prince: the eyes shone dark and deep above sharp cheekbones; the straight nose ran down to an even mouth of healthy teeth and the strong chin below it. Fran was twenty-eight years old and as good-looking as any man has a right to be.

When Fran appeared the photographers jumped over the wooden fence and rushed at him. Soon they had him surrounded. Fran stood his ground, eyes forward, face stern, trying to preserve the dignity of the moment. Eighteen years before, to the very day, a bull had fatally wounded Fran's father in this same Pozoblanco ring, and the bulls Fran was about to face came from the breeder that had produced the killer animal. During the course of an eight-year career Fran had never appeared in Pozoblanco on the anniversary of his father's death, much less with bulls from the same ranch. The other two matadors stood next to Fran, but the photographers ignored them. They were not part of the afternoon's story. By the established professional etiquette of the bull-ring, when the matadors first appear the press photographers have a minute to take pictures and then disappear. But many of the shooters that afternoon had never worked a bullfight before, and they kept on clicking. The crowd began to whistle. Finally someone called in the police and they cleared the ring.

The ring was empty. The audience applauded. The matadors saluted one another with hands outstretched, silently giving the classic bull-fighting benediction: "God send us luck, one and all." They crossed themselves once, twice, three times, kissing their thumbs at the end of each gesture. Then they stepped out, stepping out on their right feet for good luck, walking across the ring at a measured pace, walking to the music, their teams of assistant bullfighters on foot and horseback in three neat rows behind them. When the procession reached the opposite end of the ring, the bullfighters stopped, took off their hats, and bowed their heads.

Each year, just before the September 26 bullfight in Pozoblanco, they observe a moment of silence. Fran stood with his weight on his right leg, his left leg bent. His hat was in his hand, and his head was against his chest, eyes down. Everyone in the ring was watching him, wondering what he was thinking, a state of affairs Fran was used to. He had been a prince of bullfighting from birth. Fran's great-grandfather was Cayetano Ordóñez, nicknamed El Niño de la Palma, a star matador in the 1920s and the model for the bullfighter in Ernest Hemingway's *The Sun Also Rises*. Fran's grandfather Antonio Ordóñez starred in his own Hemingway book, *The Dangerous Summer,* and is thought by many to have been the best matador of the second half of the twentieth century. Fran's father, Francisco Rivera, called Paquirri, died on the road from Pozoblanco and became a tragic legend in Spain. Fran added to the family history by his excellence in the ring and by marrying Eugenia Martínez de Irujo, the duchess of Montoro, the daughter of one of the most titled aristocrats in Europe, the eighteenth duchess of Alba.

The moment of silence ended. The bullfighters bowed to the president of the bullfight, a local dignitary who stood in a flag-draped box midway up the stands. The bullfighters touched their right hand to their forehead, much as the gladiators did in the ancient Roman arenas, and you could almost hear them say, "We who are about to die salute you," and all that. The audience applauded. The band continued to play. Fran's face was blank as he went over to the wooden fence and accepted his bullfighting cape, which was handed over to him by his manservant Nacho. Fran skipped backward a few steps into the arena and made some easy, fluid practice passes, watching as an imaginary bull came across his body, painting giant clamshells in the sand with the sweep of his cape. A trumpet blew. The music stopped. Someone swung open a gate. The first bull appeared, lifted its great head, and trotted into the light.

The Challenge Accepted

MARCH

The bullfight is not a sport in the Anglo-Saxon
sense of the word, that is, it is not an equal contest or an attempt at an equal contest between a
bull and a man. Rather it is a tragedy.

— ERNEST HEMINGWAY, *Death in the Afternoon*

1

A Man, a Bull, a Small Town

Pozoblanco, September 26, 1984. They couldn't see more than a few feet ahead of them. Within the obsessive compass of the headlights the black road uncoiled, split by the white line, stretching and bending with the land. The BMW sedan was bone white, built heavy, well suited to drone out the thousands of miles a top matador must travel from town to town, from bullfight to bullfight, from February to October, through the eight-month marathon of the bullfighting season. Sometime early that morning—later documents would differ on the exact time—the car pulled into a small town and stopped before a building with the words *Hotel Los Godos* spelled out over the doorway. The driver got out, opened one of the rear doors, and prodded the shoulder of the man who lay asleep in the back seat.

"Paco," the driver said. "We've arrived."

His full name was Francisco Rivera y Pérez, but he was best known as Paquirri, a variant of Paco, which is a nickname for Francisco. This Paco, Francisco, Paquirri, whatever you wish to call him, was a bullfighter—in Spanish, a *torero*. More precisely he was a matador, the category of bullfighter who stars in the bullfight, employs a team of five assistant bullfighters, and finishes each performance by facing the bull alone, playing it with a red cape, and killing it with a sword. The most successful matadors are rich and famous entertainers, like professional athletes or movie stars. It is a hard trade. The elite minority of matadors who work regularly tend to end up in the hospital for a few weeks each season, but at least they work at their chosen profession. The rest of Spain's matadors spend their time in cafés, waiting for their cell phones to chime with an offer of a bullfight somewhere.

Paquirri never had that problem. He spent many years at the top, as a sought-after performer who by the end of his career commanded ten thousand dollars a bullfight, more than any other matador of the time. Paquirri was also a celebrity to nonbullfighting fans, thanks to two high-profile marriages: the first to Carmen Ordóñez, daughter of the legendary matador Antonio Ordóñez; the second to Isabel Pantoja, a curvy pop star. Paquirri drove the women crazy. He was dark, with ice-blue eyes, high cheekbones, and dimples. He was also a classic tough guy. He could be private, stern, quiet, independent, and full of pride, but he also took pleasure in horses and running and open fields, and was a fierce and loyal friend. He adored each of his wives in her time and always adored his sons: Francisco and Cayetano from his first wife, and Francisco José from his second.

Paquirri's life was a constant struggle. He was born poor in a small town at the southern tip of Spain, near the port city of Cádiz, and was given his nickname by his father, a failed torero who encouraged his sons to fulfill his bullfighting dreams. Lacking the natural grace that has been the basis of so many matadors' careers, Paquirri worked and studied and bled, literally, until he had forged himself into a technical master of his craft. He took the *alternativa*—the ceremony that elevates an apprentice matador to full rank—on August 11, 1966, and sweated for years to gain and then maintain the respect of the small cartel of bullring operators, talent agents, and newspaper critics who control bullfighting, until the mid-1970s when his career came together and he rose to be Spain's leading matador for six or seven years.

By 1984, however, Paquirri was slowing down. He would appear in just forty-six bullfights that season, a full twenty-six fewer than the most active matador of that year; he was not contracted for a number of the top bullfighting festivals, and to make matters worse he was starting to look fat. His own father had told him he was too heavy to be safe in the ring. "Next year I'm retiring to my ranch," Paquirri had begun to say. "Then I'm going to invite my friends and cut the pigtail." (Until the 1920s most matadors grew a small pigtail at the base of their skulls as a professional mark. Today they wear fake pigtails on bullfight days, but cutting the pigtail is still the final symbolic act of the matador's career.)

Paquirri had not planned to end the 1984 season in Pozoblanco. He was supposed to finish up the day before in the city of Logroño. Then in midsummer the promoter of the Pozoblanco ring called him up and twisted his arm and Paquirri agreed to appear there. As it turned out, the bullfight in Logroño on September 25 went well, and Paquirri drove all night to reach Pozoblanco and tumbled into his hotel bed. He awoke about noon and wandered down to the lobby, where he invited his assistant bullfighters for lunch. This was unusual. Paquirri tended to keep to himself before bullfights, but he was in an uncharacteristically good mood that morning. The work and worry of the season, and maybe of his career, were about to end. "What a great season we've had," Paquirri was overheard saying. "Not one injury among us!"

The bulls used in bullfights are descended from an ancient strain of wild bull that roamed Spain in prehistoric times. They are bred for beauty, size, strength, speed, and ferocity, and raised semiwild on special ranches whose names and reputations are well known to bullfighting fans. The six bulls used in Paquirri's bullfight in Pozoblanco came from the respected Sayalero y Bandrés ranch, but they were a scrawny group, the end-of-season dregs of the herd. One of them in particular looked awful. This bull's name was Avispado, and twice that season it had been shipped to a bullfight somewhere, only to be rejected by local bullring veterinarians for being too small and too ugly to appear in a professional bullfight.

Like most bulls who fail to make it into a bullfight during their fourth year of life, Avispado was headed for the slaughterhouse. Until Paquirri called looking for some animals for a last-minute gig he'd accepted in Pozoblanco. Normally the bullring promoter selects the bulls. But when there is a star matador involved, he also has a say, and Paquirri liked Sayalero y Bandrés bulls because he'd performed well with them in the past. So Avispado and five others were set aside. Then, a few weeks before the bullfight, the Pozoblanco mayor's office intervened. Pozoblanco's bullring was city-owned, and town officials had to approve all bulls presented there. But when the officials visited the Sayalero y Bandrés pasture they were displeased by the look of the bulls, declined them, and reserved animals from a different breeder.

There were many ways that Paquirri and Avispado might have avoided each other. Paquirri might have refused the Pozoblanco contract, or chosen other bulls, or allowed the officials to turn down the bulls he had chosen. Avispado might have been killed in an earlier bullfight or sent to the slaughterhouse. Instead Paquirri said that either he got the bulls he wanted or he wasn't going to perform. So little Avispado and his fellow Sayalero y Bandrés bulls were shipped to Pozoblanco. The morning of the bullfight, representatives of the three matadors performing that day met at the corrals to divide the bulls. Each bull had a number branded on its side, and the men wrote these numbers on slips of paper, balled the papers up, and tossed them into a hat. This was when the last piece of luck fell into place. Paquirri's assistant reached in and pulled out the piece of paper with the number 9 on it, Avispado's number.

Pozoblanco begins all of a sudden out of the rolling plain at the center of a valley called Los Pedroches. The twisted medieval alleyways of the older part of Pozoblanco are lined with the one- and two-story white-washed dwellings that are typical of southern Spain. Up a hill is the newer section of town, which has wider and straighter streets and modern buildings. The main highway runs through here, heading south across the Los Pedroches plain and down out of the mountains into the big city of Córdoba, about fifty-five miles away as the crow flies. In recent years the government has spent millions to make this route easier to drive; in Paquirri's time it was a hellish mountain road of hairpin turns, unnerving to traverse by day, terrifying by night.

There is now a hospital in Pozoblanco, but in Paquirri's day the only medical facility was the bullring infirmary, a rough room with two tables, a sink, and a shrine to the Virgin Mary. It may seem odd that Pozoblanco should have its own bullring, but many small Spanish towns and even some villages do, and those that don't can rent a portable ring or close off a public square for bullfights. One way or the other, many places in Spain of any size or importance will hold at least one bullfight or bull event a year, usually during the local *feria*. A *feria* is like a civic festival or celebration. The Spanish are mad for local traditions of this sort and maintain them with a fervor that is unmatched in Europe, and there is a *feria* somewhere in Spain most days of the year. *Ferias* differ from region to region, but most are dedicated to a local patron saint, and most include religious processions, an outdoor market, and some kind of bullfight or bull-related event.

By the time Paquirri arrived in Pozoblanco, the town was well into its *feria*. The municipal fairground on the outskirts of town was full of people eating, drinking, dancing, shrieking on amusement park rides, and riding horses. As afternoon became evening a crowd began to assemble at the town bullring, and by six P.M. the ring was packed under a strong evening sun. A trumpet sounded, the bullfighters marched in, and the festivities began. The first half of the bullfight went smoothly and each of the three matadors killed his bull with minimum fuss. Then it was time for Paquirri to face his second and final bull of the day. The gate opened and Avispado spilled into the ring. Paquirri came out, planted his feet, and swung his cape, using the cloth to lure the bull into charging back and forth across his body, and each time the bull chugged safely past Paquirri's legs, the crowd chanted *"Olé!"* in approval.

It was after the first series of passes that something went wrong. It might have been a miscalculation on Paquirri's part, or it might have been the bull that tripped or swerved unexpectedly. But as Avispado charged past Paquirri one more time, it bumped into him, spinning him around, sending his hands, still holding the cape, into the air. As long as Paquirri had the cape between himself and the bull he was relatively safe. Suddenly he found himself unprotected and with his back to the bull. He staggered around to face the bull again and yanked the cape out of the air, sliding it over to get it in front of his legs. Had he been a beat quicker he might have gotten the cape down before the bull had a chance to react to it. But Avispado was following the cape, and as Paquirri swung it over, the bull pursued the cloth straight into the matador's right thigh, sinking the horn deep into the flesh.

Somewhere in the audience a woman shrieked. Avispado thrust its head upward, flipping Paquirri feet-first into the air, the horn still in the leg. Four bullfighters ran up to Avispado, but the little bull was too fast and too strong and all they could do was watch. Avispado rushed forward. In a desperate attempt to extricate himself, Paquirri swung himself upright, which only made matters worse, causing his full weight to bounce up and down on the horn, producing more damage. After nine full seconds, Avispado wheeled, lowered its head, and Paquirri fell away. He stood for a moment, then collapsed. Several bullfighters picked him up and ran him from the ring. A matador named José Cubero, El Yiyo, stepped onto the sand. By law it was now his responsibility to kill Avispado.

As soon as Paquirri was tossed, Dr. Elíseo Morán left his place in the *callejón* and rushed to the bullring infirmary. Dr. Morán had a thriving surgical practice in Córdoba, but he spent summer weekends as the chief of the medical team in small bullrings around the province. By the day of Paquirri's goring, Morán had treated dozens of horn injuries, and was confident he could open and clean Paquirri's wound, stop the blood flow, and stabilize Paquirri so he could be taken to the hospital in Córdoba, where the proper facilities existed to help doctors reattach any severed blood vessels and close the wound. "Let's go," Dr. Morán told his fellow surgeons when he saw Paquirri in the air. "We've got a big one."

The infirmary was silent as the doctors scrubbed up, laid out needle, thread, anesthesia, and bags of blood. "Where are the toreros?" they asked themselves. "Why haven't they arrived yet?" No one spoke, and their eyes flicked to the room's glass doors. Then the doors flew open, shattering the glass. In came Paquirri, borne on a litter of hands and arms, and in his wake a small crowd of bullfighters, entourage members, and gawkers. They laid Paquirri out on the operating table. His thigh was sliced open like a Sunday roast and blood pooled on the table beneath it. The doctors trained their strong surgical lights on the wound and cut Paquirri's pant leg off, exposing his leg to the hairy genitals.

Among the people at the periphery of these events was a video cameraman from TVE, Spain's national network. Shooting under the surgical lights, he was able to capture a few minutes of Paquirri's agony. This footage would be shown again and again around the country in the weeks, months, and years that followed. As one writer described it, this video footage would become the Spanish equivalent of the Zapruder film, which captured the second when the bullet struck John F. Kennedy. The film begins with the camera at Paquirri's feet. Then the camera pans up his ruined thigh, his torso, to his face. Paquirri flinches now and then, but he is calm. His voice is firm, his face impassive. He takes control of the room, making sure everything is done right. This is his ninth serious goring.

"A moment please, Doctor, I would like to talk with you," Paquirri says. "The goring is a deep one. It has two trajectories. One through here and one through there." Paquirri gestures up and down, showing the paths of the horn inside his body. "Open me where you need to open me," he continues. "I place my life in your hands." The din in the room increases. "Quiet, please," the matador says. "Please wet my mouth with water." He drinks and then spits. The tape ends.

Out in the arena, El Yiyo killed Avispado. Then bullring servants attached chains to the bull's horns and a mule team dragged Avispado's carcass from the ring and into the bullring butchery, across an alley from the infirmary where Paquirri was being treated. A short time after the butchers had turned Avispado into cuts of meat for local markets, about eight o'clock, Paquirri was carried to a waiting ambulance, and the big white Citroën pulled out of town, siren yowling, and flew down the highway, careening along the twisting mountain roads. Around fifteen miles from the gates of Córdoba, Paquirri cried out, "Help me, I can't breathe." The ambulance screeched to a stop and a doctor worked on him by the side of the road. When Paquirri looked a little calmer, he was put back in the ambulance, which reached the hospital shortly after nine o'clock. It had taken less than an hour to get to Córdoba, but Paquirri was all but dead on arrival. He was thirty-six years old.

In the weeks that followed, Paquirri's death would remind many writers and commentators of some lines in "The Song of the Rider," a short poem written in the 1920s by Spain's best-known poet, Federico García Lorca, who was himself a bullfighting aficionado.

> Through the plain, through the wind,
> Black pony, red moon.
> Death is watching me,
> from the towers of Córdoba.
>
> Oh what a long road!
> Oh my brave pony!
> Oh that death awaits me,
> before I arrive in Córdoba!

Spain plunged into frenzied mourning for Paquirri. Newspapers picked over the grisly details of the goring and the race to Córdoba until the entire story took on the quality of legend. Many people second-guessed the doctors, wondering whether they had handled the wound in the right way. Strangely, amid all the fuss, it was never made clear just what had killed Paquirri, shock, loss of blood, or something else. The funeral took place in Sevilla. The prime minister was unable to attend, but sent his wife. The crowd that assembled in front of the apartment building where the body was laid out stretched for five miles. When the coffin was brought out, the massive throng wouldn't let it be placed in the hearse. Instead Paquirri was carried to Sevilla's bullring, where it was marched around and around to chants of a single word, "Torero." In certain parts of Spain there is no greater compliment.

Paquirri was buried in the cemetery of San Fernando, where his tomb faces the mausoleum of José Gómez Ortega, Joselito, perhaps the best bullfighter of all time, who was killed by a bull on May 16, 1920. Buried with Joselito is his brother-in-law, the matador Ignacio Sánchez Mejías, who killed the bull that killed Joselito. Fourteen years later, another bull killed Sánchez Mejías. Killing a murderous bull had brought bad luck to Sánchez Mejías (or so it was said), and this same misfortune pursued those who performed with Paquirri in Pozoblanco. In 1985, a bull gored El Yiyo in the heart, killing him instantly. He was twenty-one. In 1988, a gunman marched into the office of Avispado's breeder, Juan Luis Bandrés, and shot him to death. That case was never solved. In 1994, the third matador on the card that day, Vicente Ruiz, El Soro, injured his right knee. It ended his career, leaving him with a deformed leg.

Though it might have been bad for his fellow performers, Paquirri's death was a good thing for bullfighting. By the mid-1980s the bullfight had been losing ground as a popular spectacle for years, to soccer, television, and movies, in part because people believed bullfighting was fixed, that the matadors weren't really risking their lives. Paquirri's death changed that. Not only did it legitimize bullfighting as a serious thing, but it brought newfound admiration for matadors. Paquirri wasn't the first prominent matador killed by a bull. But he was the first one killed during the television age, and what was seared into the Spanish consciousness was not so much his death as the composure and humble bravery he showed in the infirmary video.

In the 1990s bullfighting would undergo a strong revival, driven in part by a new generation of young matadors who remembered Paquirri's death as a formative event. One of these was his own son, a ten-year-old named Fran, who went to bed that night thinking he had a father and was fast asleep when his mother came in to tell him he no longer did. Fran says he can't recall how he responded to this news. His mother remembered, however, and so did another person who was in the house that night. Apparently, when Fran heard what had happened, he looked up at his mother and said, "I am going to be a bullfighter."

2

The Former Phenom

Las Majadillas, March 12. It was all over the news. Eugenia Martínez de Irujo, the duchess of Montoro, and her matador husband, Francisco Rivera Ordóñez, were separating. You could read the gossip magazine headlines at every newsstand across Spain. "Eugenia Breaks Her Marriage," blared the cover of *Semana* magazine. "End Point: Fran and Eugenia Break Their Marriage after Various Attempts at Reconciliation," screamed *Lecturas.* "Fran and Eugenia: How It All Went Wrong," said *Diez Minutos.* The pink press worked the story from every angle. There were timelines of the couple's courtship, reports and photographs of the alleged love affairs that had broken up the marriage, hackneyed laments about a fairy-tale romance gone wrong, and unattributed quotes from so-called friends and family.

Eugenia was hiding from the press behind the walls of La Pizana, the seventeenth-century monastery-turned-villa she had shared with Fran just outside Sevilla. Fran's mother-in-law, the duchess of Alba, had fled to Paris. Fran's mother, Carmen Ordóñez, was giving interviews left and right. But no one knew where to find Fran. He had disappeared with an army of tabloid reporters on his trail. In fact, he was on an estate named Las Majadillas (Little Barns), in an empty countryside of squat oak trees thirty miles west of Sevilla. The estate, laid out on a hillside overlooking a winding valley, comprised a whitewashed mansion, a courtyard with a fountain, a stable full of sleek horses, and a parking lot filled with snazzy SUVs. The rest of the estate was devoted to the raising of bullfighting bulls. The owner was a rich man's son, a friend of Fran's who, like many Spanish aristocrats and millionaires, dabbled in bull breeding.

The afternoon was sunny and fresh and the air smelled of wood smoke. The bullfighting season had just begun, and up north the city of Valencia was holding the first important bullfighting festival of the year. At Las Majadillas young calves were being put to the test, a process that can also serve as practice for toreros. The private bullring was made of whitewashed cement. There was no seating, but there were two raised platforms, one opposite the other, at twelve and six o'clock. The breeder, his wife, and a few friends visiting from Mexico stood on these. Around the ring stood tough, sunburned men wearing tweed caps and oilskin coats. They were ranch hands and bullfighting professionals, hard country folk who smelled of earth and sweat and were not invited to sit with the rich people. They had come to see Francisco Rivera Ordóñez perform with live animals, something a big crowd would be paying to see a few days hence in Valencia.

A female calf stood in the center of the ring. It was two years old and about half the age and size of a full-grown bullfighting bull, meaning it weighed some six hundred pounds and had the same dimensions as a motorcycle. The little cow was in a state of shock. It had been released into the ring just moments before and had been confronted by a mounted horse covered in padded armor. Following its instinct, the cow had charged the horse, and just as the cow had dug its horns into the horse's protective padding, the man riding the horse had shot a metal-pointed spear, which Hemingway referred to as a pic because there is no single Spanish word that describes it, into the cow's withers. This was part of the test. If the cow had broken away from the horse at the pain of the pic, there would have been a mark against it, and it might have been sent to the slaughterhouse for meat. But this cow had ignored the pain and charged the horse again. As long as it performed well with Fran, it would be released into the fields, where it would mate with seed bulls to produce cattle for the ranch.

"Hey! Hey!" Fran stalked toward the cow, speaking to it as he came. He wore the bullfighter's standard practice uniform: leather boots, skintight trousers that rose to his breastbone and were fastened with braces, a white button-down shirt, and a dusty sweater. His head was bare. He held a bullfighting cape in his right hand. This type of cape is called a *muleta*, which means "crutch." The *muleta* consists of a half-circle of heavy red cotton twill lined with yellow fabric. The cloth is folded over and tacked onto a short wooden stick, from which it hangs like a curtain from a rod, except the stick is so short that half the cape falls limp at one end. A *muleta* may be any size, but most matadors prefer the fabric of the cape to be long enough so that the end of the cloth will brush the ground when the matador holds the *muleta* belt-high.

Fran gripped his *muleta* by the stick with his right hand, keeping the limp end of the cloth away from his body. He also held a lightweight practice sword in his right hand, positioned behind the cape so that its blade spread the limp end of the cloth to its full size. Cherry-red blood pooled in the gnarled black hair of the cow's back at the place where the horseman's spear had injured it. The cow waited, watching Fran approach. When he came within a few feet of the cow, he stopped. He was just to the left of the cow's left horn, outside the line the animal would take if it charged straight. Fran shuffled across the cow's face, keeping both feet on the ground, making sure his movements didn't provoke the cow, until he'd worked himself between the cow's horns. At this point, Fran stepped toward the cow with his left leg, so that the leg was in the direction of the cow and between the horns, while his right leg was farther from the cow and just outside its left horn.

Fran offered the cape and shouted, "Hey!"

The cow lowered its head, raised its tail, and sprang forward. Fran put the *muleta* in the cow's face, and at this moment a kind of magical transformation happened. The flimsy cloth hanging from the stick seemed to stop the cow in its tracks. It was as though the cape had a magnetic energy that held the cow in place. Then Fran swept the cape back and the cow was tugged along, its mad charge ratcheted down to a slow-motion trot by the cape. Fran kept the red fabric just ahead of the wet muzzle and pulled the cow through a slow, slower, ever slowing and deepening arc, taking the cow past his left leg, across his belly, brushing the cow past his outthrust right leg, twisting his wrist at the end to angle the cape and bring the cow behind his back, leaving the cow as far behind him as he could make it go. This was the first pass.

"*Bien, torero!*" growled the crusty types around the bullring in their tobacco-ravaged voices. Well done, bullfighter!

Fran kept the cape in the cow's face, holding the cow in place. He pivoted on his left foot, spinning around so that he faced the animal once again and was in the same position as before: left leg toward the cow and between the horns, right leg farther back and outside the left horn, the *muleta* in the right hand extended to the cow. Fran jerked the cape again, shouted, and put the cow through another slow, smooth journey around his body. He stood motionless as the animal brushed past him. His feet were fixed to the ground. His shoulders, arms, and torso moved the cape in a calm, easy fashion, and he leaned into the cow so that the cow had to step around his outthrust right leg, and the cow's blood painted a smudge on Fran's belly. Then Fran curved his wrist, sending the animal behind his back. That was the second pass.

"*Bien!*" came the audience's approval. "*Bee-yen!*"

At the end of the third pass, Fran did not spin around again. Instead he stayed in place, shook his cape, and brought the cow back the way it had come. As Fran finished this reverse pass, he lifted the cape upward, and as the cloth rose so did the cow, jumping out of the slowness of the pass like a plane taking off, shuddering, fighting gravity, and then shooting into a heart-compressing lift. The cow landed away from Fran, spun, and stared at him with hot betrayed eyes. The cow would not be in the mood to charge just then. It had been fixed in place by fatigue, disillusionment, and the brusqueness of the upward lift of the pass, which had jarred its neck muscles.

Fran was born on January 3, 1974, in Madrid. But soon his family moved to Sevilla so that Fran's father could be near La Cantora, the ranch he'd purchased some years before, an hour south of the city, in the province of Cádiz. The Rivera-Ordóñez household was not an easy one to grow up in. Fran's mother, Carmen Ordóñez, was just eighteen when Fran was born; she was a famous beauty distracted by nightlife and her ever-increasing role as a star of the gossip magazines. Fran's father, Paquirri, was a celebrated torero and a man who expected a lot from his sons. Once when Fran was still a little boy he begged his father to let him cape a calf. So Paquirri took Fran's hand and led him to La Cantora's ring, where a calf was waiting. But when Fran saw the little animal, he burst into tears and refused to go near it, an act of toddler cowardice that enraged his father. "Go back up to the house with the women, you faggot!" shouted Paquirri, and Fran ran up the hill to the house.

"That was my father," Fran recalled with a laugh.

Paquirri divorced Carmen when Fran was about six. A few years later Paquirri married the singer Isabel Pantoja in a nationally televised ceremony. Less than two years after that came Paquirri's death and the national hysteria that followed. In its aftermath Carmen took Fran and his brother back to Madrid, which might not have been the best place for her boys. Madrid was Spain's media capital and Fran had become a celebrity, a kind of JFK Jr. stand-in for his martyred father. It was a lot to put on a child, but Carmen seems to have loved the attention, and as the years progressed she became the undisputed queen of the pink press, the most covered, adored, and reviled figure in the country, someone who was said to earn good money by selling exclusive stories about herself to tabloid news outfits.

Following his father's death, Fran continued to talk about becoming a matador, and at the same time displayed a sustained contempt for academics, getting expelled from four schools in five years. Fran wasn't a bad kid, just an inattentive student with a taste for practical jokes. He could be polite, poised, and well put together if he was called upon to accept an award for his dead father or do an interview with his mother, but he could also play a wild prank on a friend or chase a pretty girl across a nightclub dance floor. In a mild sort of way Fran had two personalities, and these followed him into adulthood. The dominant one was the prince, an elegant, mild-mannered, distant, and proper fellow with a nice word for everyone. But every now and then a delinquent, unruly, needy, naughty, sometimes playful, sometimes sad, boy peeked out from the princely exterior.

In an effort to rein him in, get him away from the pressures of Spain, and cool his desire to become a bullfighter, Carmen sent Fran and his brother to Camp Kennebec, in Belgrade, Maine, for a few summers. The camp's director, Joel Lavenson, remembered Fran as a remarkable athlete who fit in with the other kids despite his almost complete lack of English. Lavenson knew Fran's story and tried to give the boy a little extra attention. But Fran — in full prince mode — put him off, and Lavenson realized there would be no getting through to the soft-voiced, painfully proper twelve-year-old who had suffered a heavy loss and was an ocean away from home, but who never complained, nor cried, nor fussed, but took a red cape to the baseball field at dusk and practiced bullfighting moves after dinner.

"He was like a deer in the headlights," Lavenson said. "He was going on autopilot. He wasn't homesick. He wasn't sad if he lost a game. He was in survival mode. He was in a state of shock. He just couldn't allow himself to let me comfort him."

After Fran's final school expulsion in Spain, Carmen sent him to the Culver Military Academy, in Culver, Indiana, hoping this would knock the bulls out of his mind for good. At Culver Fran marched around in uniform, learned to speak English, and developed a taste for basketball, American football, rap music, and Kim Basinger, and was expelled in the middle of his second year for leading a late-night foray into the dormitory of a local girls' boarding school. When Fran got back to Spain he was fifteen years old and had shown no inclination to do anything other than bullfight. So his mother took him to see his grandfather.

As Fran tells it, he walked into the room and there was Antonio Ordóñez, the most revered living matador in Spain, and for a moment Fran was mute with anxiety. Then he told his grandfather he wanted to be a matador. "My grandfather told me it would be hard for me," Fran said. "He said, 'It will not be easy to fight with your names, and it is not going to be easy for you, because if you fight, you must be the best. I can't have you be mediocre.' I said, 'I understand.' And he told me, 'If you are worth it, I will help you. If not, I will tell you. And if you insist, I will break your legs.' "

Fran spent the next two years living on ranches, learning to become a torero under his grandfather's tutelage. As Fran remembers it, his grandfather was not much of a teacher. Like many a gifted artist or athlete, Antonio Ordóñez had a hard time explaining how he did what he did, and Fran was left to figure things out for himself, something that probably came to hurt him down the line. Fran premiered as a bullfighter in 1991 and spent the following three seasons appearing in *novilladas,* which are bullfights that feature apprentice matadors and young bulls. During this time Fran's performances did not cause much of a stir with the fans or the critics, but Antonio decided that his grandson should take the *alternativa* and become a full matador in the April *feria* of Sevilla.

It was a huge gamble. Fran was an untested kid and the Sevilla *feria* is one of the most important bullfighting fairs in the world. Whatever he did there would be magnified many times over. If Fran succeeded he was on his way, but if he failed he might never dig himself out of the hole. As if the pressure weren't enough, Fran was mugged a few days before his debut, suffering a hard blow to his genitals. By the afternoon of the bullfight he was almost too swollen to walk, but he took a numbing needle in the groin, went out, and against all expectations had a total, absolute, utter, and dramatic success. "What Emotion!" raved a headline in the following day's edition of *Diario 16.* "No one expected the appearance of so much bullfighter so soon. It was so hard to believe, you had to rub your eyes."

The rest of that year was like one long victory lap, with Fran racking up triumph after triumph while the nation's bullfighting critics and fans went nuts. "Rivera was like an earthquake," said *Diario 16* in its season-end wrap-up. "Just four days after taking the *alternativa* in Sevilla, he was already a star, and the season was immediately turned upside down." For the next two seasons Fran was one of the two or three top matadors in Spain, paid tens of thousands of dollars a bullfight and featured in all the major *ferias*. He was brave, talented, and had what political consultants would call name recognition. Spanish men use the last names of both their parents, and Fran's surnames — Rivera and Ordóñez — conjured all the heartbreak of his father and the majestic performances of both his great-grandfather and grandfather. It was as though a new opera prodigy had come along and he was named Luciano Pavarotti Caruso.

But, looking back on it all, it seems almost preordained that Fran should suffer the decline that overtook him in his fourth season as a matador. He had gone further on less experience and training than just about any matador in history, and it is a truism of bullfighting that all successful young matadors suffer some kind of crisis after their first explosion onto the scene. The crisis can be internal, as the satisfactions of fame and money begin to cool the ambition that propelled the young phenom forward. Just as often the crisis comes from without, as the fickle bullfighting public turns its attention to the next young hero. Whatever the crisis, the young phenom — now a former phenom — must either find a way to overcome what ails him and go on to long years of achievement or watch his career ebb away.

The crisis hit Fran in the late 1990s, a time when he'd become distracted from bullfighting by the planning for his wedding — an event so large it merited four hours of live coverage on national television — and by the death of his beloved grandfather Antonio from cancer. Fran's performance in the ring deteriorated, and fans and critics were as vocal in their condemnation as they had been in their praise. When Fran was on top, his family background had made his victories seem bigger. When he started to sink, however, his famous names magnified his failures. Where once Fran had triumphed, he now had disasters. Where once he heard cheers, he now heard whistles and jeers. By the start of his eighth full season as a matador, the same bullfighting experts that had once called him the man who would save bullfighting were denying he'd ever been good. Fran was a pretty boy, they said, who worked as a matador because a certain ignorant segment of the public would always pay to see a bullfighter who appeared in the gossip magazines.

"Rivera Ordóñez is sustained by his family history," said Juan Posada, the respected critic for the newspaper *La Razón,* "and by his agreeable face and by the favors that are done for him by the pink press. He had much promise but he hasn't advanced. He hasn't moved on from what he was eight years ago, and that has hurt him."

Fran finished his practice session with the cow and trotted over to the grandstand to see whether any of the breeder's guests would like to cape the animal. This is a tradition at calf testings. When the professional toreros have had their workout, guests may come down and try a few passes. This can be dangerous, and many people have been badly hurt or even killed during these amateur hours. But Spain is a country that has never succumbed to the wear-your-seatbelt mentality prevalent in the United States and other English-speaking countries. Anglo-Saxon cultures fear death and avoid the very thought of it, to the extent that it is seen as unnatural, an insult to the living. By contrast, Spaniards view death as a natural consequence of life, and knowing they are going to die anyway, they see no reason not to stay out all night drinking, indulging in rich food, smoking cigarettes, and driving like fiends.

After some discussion, a tall, heavyset man dressed in blue jeans and a button-down shirt ambled into the ring. He was a lawyer and had no bullfighting experience. Fran smiled at the lawyer, offered him the cape, and pointed him toward the cow. The man advanced on the cow with unsure steps, dragging the cape on the ground in front of him. He was not gentle or careful in his movements the way Fran had been, and the cow became agitated, raising its head as this clumsy creature moved into view. When the lawyer had shuffled to within a few yards of the cow, the animal lost its composure and charged.

The lawyer then did two things that were natural under the circumstances but were two of the worst things he could have done. First, he stepped backward. Big mistake. Bullfighting bulls and cows charge at motion. Fran had controlled the cow by standing still and catching its attention with the movement of the cape, but the lawyer did just the reverse. His body moved all over the place while the cape hung lifeless in his hands. Second, as the cow bore down on the lawyer, he brought the cape in front of his legs in a reflexive, defensive gesture, which had the unfortunate effect of drawing the cow's attention directly to the lawyer's legs.

The cow barreled into him, flipping him in the air. He landed with a grunt on the sandy floor of the bullring. In an instant Fran was there. Fran had no cape, but he waved his hands in the cow's face and ran away from the lawyer, drawing the cow after him. At the same time, two ranch hands dashed in, lifted the lawyer up, and carried him to safety. The lawyer was going to have a deep bruise for a souvenir, nothing worse, and everyone had a good laugh. After that, no one else wanted to give the cow a try, until a child shouted down from the grandstand.

"*Papá, Papá*," the child said, "I want to bullfight." Fran smiled. He'd moved out of his house and the demands of the bullfighting season lay ahead, so he savored this spare time with his daughter.

"Come down, my love," Fran said. Cayetana Rivera was less than three years old. She was chubby, with her father's face in miniature framed in a pageboy of sleek brown hair. Fran picked her up and gave her a big kiss. Then he cradled her against his right side and carried her out into the ring—just the way Paquirri used to carry Fran. With the child in his right arm, Fran executed a casual series of passes with his left, and the cow grazed little Cayetana's legs as it charged back and forth, and Cayetana shrieked with delight as the sun made its way westward over the hills toward Portugal.

3

A Tragedy in Three Acts

Most non-Spaniards think of the bullfight as a sport, but it is not a sport. A sporting event is a competition between two or more parties in which the outcome is in doubt. The pleasure in watching a sporting event is to see who will win, to root for one side and perhaps place a wager. The Spanish love to gamble. They even gamble on poetry readings in the Basque Country. But there is no gambling on bullfighting, because everyone knows the outcome. The bull will die. If the bull should disable the matador, another matador will come out and kill the bull. If all the matadors are disabled, then the bull is taken out back and dispatched by an assistant bullfighter or a bullring butcher. The bull has no chance.

Bullfighting fans know this. So the crowds that come to the bullfights are not paying their money to see a fight or contest, nor are most of them coming for the pornographic pleasure of watching a public execution — though this may be the motivation for some viewers. Instead the majority of the crowd comes to see two things. First, they want to examine, analyze, and revel in the beauty and power of the bulls. This may not make much sense, since corridas are organized bull killings, but bullfighting fans admire bulls with the same fervor that horseracing fans admire thoroughbreds. Second, they want to see a man stand still and use his cape to make a bull run where the man wants it to, and do so in a graceful manner. In Spanish, these three qualities are named *parar, mandar,* and *templar.*

Parar (to stop) is usually defined, in bullfighting terms, as standing still while the bull charges. That may sound easy, but it's almost impossible to do. Humans are hard-wired to flinch at danger, and most people cannot control this impulse, but to be a professional bullfighter you must be able to stand without moving while a bull hurls itself at you. The capacity to keep your feet quiet, under the constant pressure of bodily harm and under the other stresses of a long season, is what separates even mediocre professional bullfighters from normal people.

Mandar (to command) means to use the cape to force the bull to charge in the direction of the bullfighter's choosing, and send it where the matador wants it to go. Any fool with raw courage can wave a cape in a bull's face and hope to survive the experience. A professional bullfighter has the skill to use the cape to dominate and control the animal.

Templar (to avoid extremes) refers to the man's capacity to smooth out and slow his movements and those of the bull, so that each and every pass is done in an unhurried manner, giving the impression that time and motion have been brought under the bullfighter's dominion. To put it another way, *templar* is what distinguishes the brute thrust of the long jumper, which is designed to do nothing more than move the athlete as far forward as possible, from the leap of a ballet dancer, which is meant to please the eye because it is done in such a way that the effort of the leap is hidden and all that remains is the impression of weightlessness.

As the theater critic Kenneth Tynan once observed, when bullfighting is done properly it doesn't look like much. All you see is a guy standing in a ring making a bull run around after a cape. Yet this is the essence of what the Spanish call the art of bullfighting, because — and this is very important — the Spanish view bullfighting as an art. In Spain, great matadors are addressed as Maestro, just as great musicians are. Bullfights are not covered in the sports section of newspapers but in their own special section. Journalists who write about bullfights are called critics, because they are thought to cover an art form, in the same way that journalists who cover music, theater, and dance do.

The Spanish have no word that means "bullfight." They refer to bullfighting as the *fiesta de los toros* (festival of the bulls), or the *fiesta nacional* (national festival), or the *fiesta brava* (wild festival), or simply *los toros* (the bulls). What a bullfighter does with a bull is usually translated into English as "to fight," but the Spanish word for this is *torear*, which takes the word for bull and creates a verb out of it, "to bull." The art or craft of bullfighting is called *toreo*—"bulling." A bullfighter is a *torero,* a "buller." (The word *toreador* is never used; it's best known from the opera *Carmen,* which was written by a Frenchman.) A single bullfight involving full-grown bulls is called a *corrida de toros,* or a running of bulls—not to be confused with the "running of the bulls" in the city of Pamplona, where people run in the streets with bulls. The act of holding a *corrida* is indicated by the verb *celebrar,* as in, "Yesterday they celebrated a corrida."

The word *matador* does mean "killer" in English, and the word *lidiar* (to fight) is often used in bullfight journalism. But the fact that the matador kills the bull makes bullfighting no more a sport or a fight than a butcher's killing a chicken makes butchery a sport; the word *lidiar* in a bullfighting context usually refers to the strategy the matador uses to control the bull and make art with it. There is little sense of conflict or sport or fight in most Spanish bullfighting terms, and for this reason it makes sense to avoid the confusing English word "fight" when writing about bullfighting. The only time "fight" will appear in this book is when someone else uses it in a direct quotation in English.

Nevertheless, bullfighting does retain an element of sport, because the bullfighter is an artist who must dominate and conquer his medium in order to use it. A paintbrush rarely seeks to kill the painter; an oboe does not resist the musician with violence. But there is a dangerous wildcard in every corrida, and that is the bull. To paraphrase Tynan again, the bull makes bullfighting such a difficult art that there are only forty or fifty people in the world at any given time who possess the guts, physical prowess, and knowledge of bulls to bullfight *poorly* on a regular basis, much less do it well. In truth, no one bullfights well on a regular basis for very long, not even the big stars. It can't be done without suffering dire consequences.

The Spanish corrida itself is a strictly choreographed and formal spectacle, and the order and ceremony of it never changes. Everything the men do in the ring—where they stand, when they wear their hats, what direction they walk—is subject to rules and regulations. Some of these rules are written in the bullfighting codes of Spain's national law, and some are nothing more than traditions, but every corrida unfolds the same way, and the structure and regulations of the corrida are enforced by a president—usually a local politician or police captain—who sits in a box in the stands and controls the action with a series of signals made with handkerchiefs of different colors. The only thing that makes one corrida different from another is the behavior of the bull and the specific things the toreros do to bring that bull under control and make it submit to the preordained logic of the bullfight.

The bullfight opens with the appearance of two *alguaciles,* horsemen dressed in plumed tricorn hats and black smocks, in the fashion of bailiffs in the time of the Hapsburg kings of Spain. The *alguaciles* lead a parade of the matadors, followed by the matadors' teams of assistant bullfighters, then the bullring attendants who help the mounted bullfighters — the so-called *monosabios* (wise monkeys), named after a traveling troupe of animal performers that appeared in Madrid during the nineteenth century — then the mule teams that drag the dead bulls out of the arena, and finally the bullring servants who sweep the sand. This parade is accompanied by music played by a live band. The parade is the only consistently enjoyable part of a corrida. To see the toreros come out in all their finery and march across the sand of a great bullring with the sun high in the sky and the band playing is always dramatic and moving. Often it is the best part of the proceedings.

In the typical corrida three matadors kill six bulls, the bulls drawn from the same breeder. The matadors appear in order of seniority, dating from their first bullfight as a matador. The senior man kills the first and fourth bulls, the next in seniority kills the second and fifth bulls, and the junior man dispatches bulls three and six. When a bull is released into the ring, the matador responsible for killing it is in control of events, and is assisted by his cuadrilla, or team of five assistant bullfighters: two picadors on horseback and three banderilleros on foot. The other two matadors and certain members of their cuadrillas are also required to be present in the ring at various times, to lend a hand.

Each bull spends about twenty minutes in the ring, and what happens to it during that time never varies. The process the bull undergoes is divided into three acts, which the Spanish call *los tres tercios,* or the three thirds. As the writer Angus Macnab has pointed out, each third, or act, is based on giving the bull a different lure to charge at: first a horse, then a man holding two wooden sticks, then a man holding the small red *muleta* cape. Each of these acts has an artistic and a technical purpose. In other words, each act is an opportunity for the bullfighter to do something beautiful with the bull and also a way to prepare the bull for the act that follows. One of the great satisfactions of watching a good corrida is to see how the toreros accomplish the technical tasks of preparing the bull while performing in an artistic manner. In that sense, good bullfighting offers pleasures similar to those of good architecture: both combine art and function in a pleasing way.

The first act of the corrida is the *tercio de varas,* the third of the lances, and it too is divided into three parts: the opening passes, the pic'ing, and the *quites.* Part one, the bull enters the arena and the matador passes it using a *capote,* the cape used by matadors in the first third and by their assistants throughout the bullfight. The *capote* is a circle of silk and rayon — magenta on one side, yellow on the other — with a wedge about one fifth the circumference cut out of it and a small collar sewn into the open wedge. The matador holds the *capote* at the ends of the cutout and swings it using both arms, sometimes letting go with one hand to create special effects. The *capote* weighs between seven and nine pounds and will stand upright like a pyramid when it is placed on the ground the right way.

The matador's opening passes allow him to ingratiate himself with the crowd and teach the bull to follow the cape. If the passes are well made — using *parar, mandar,* and *templar* — the matador will hear shouts of *"Olé!"* from the audience. The origin of this word is unclear, but it may derive from the Arabic "Allah," meaning God. A sizable portion of Spanish words come from Arabic, which was introduced to Spain during the Middle Ages, when the so-called Moors — Muslims from North Africa and the Middle East — controlled vast tracts of the country.

In the second part of the first third of the corrida, two picadors — bullfighters riding horses draped in padded armor — enter the ring and the matador draws the bull over to charge one of them. When the bull hits the horse's padded flank, the picador thrusts his pic, a long wooden spear with a three-quarter-inch metal point and a cross-guard some two inches down, into the large hump of muscle just behind the bull's neck. The ferocity of the bull's attack shows the audience the quality of the animal, and the horse provides the bull with an encouragingly solid target to hit. The resulting wound lowers the bull's head and causes bleeding that weakens the animal. The bull will usually be pic'd one to three times, depending on how strong it is. The person who decides this is the president, in consultation with the matador, although by law, bulls used in the top bullrings in Spain must receive a minimum of two pics each.

After the first pic comes the third element of act one, the *quite* (pronounced *key-tay*). In the *quite* the matador lures the bull away from the horse and tries to impress with a few more passes. After another encounter between bull and horse, the matador who is next in line to kill a bull will do a *quite* and try to outshine the *quite* of the first matador. If the bull is pic'd a third time, the third matador will have his chance.

A trumpet sounds and it is time for the second act of the bullfight, the *tercio de banderillas*. A banderilla is a wooden stick, about two feet long, decorated with bits of colored paper, and with an A-shaped barb at one end. The torero takes one banderilla in each hand and runs at the bull. When bull and man meet, the bull will lower its head to sink in the horn, and as it does, the man aims the sticks over the horns and plants them in the bull's shoulder, jumping away to let the bull trot safely past. Three pairs of banderillas are usually placed. Many matadors leave this job to their assistants on foot, which is why these assistants are called banderilleros, or banderilla placers. Most assistant banderilleros try to get the sticks in with a minimum of fuss, doing no more than whetting the audience's appetite for the work of the matador in the third act. There are also some matadors who place their own sticks, and when a great matador does this, it can be a fantastic show and is accompanied by music in most rings.

Then another trumpet sounds to begin the final third of the corrida, the third of the *muleta* and death. In this third, the ring is cleared. The matador comes out alone with *muleta* and sword — most often a lightweight, dummy sword, to spare the matador's wrist from wear and tear — and attempts to construct a coherent performance of linked *muleta* passes that is called the *faena* (work). During the *faena*, the matador will make his passes with the cape in both his left and right hands (though the sword stays always in the right hand), varying the type, speed, and position of the passes to build short series.

The basic *muleta* pass made with the right hand, with the sword held behind the cape to spread it out, is called the *derechazo* (right). The basic *muleta* pass with the cape in the left hand is the *natural*. The *natural* is the most dangerous and moving, and therefore most important, kind of pass a matador can perform, because the cape hangs limp, offering the least protection to the man. Besides the *derechazo* and *natural*, there are many other common *muleta* passes.

If the matador makes his passes slowly and gracefully, bringing the bull toward his body and out behind his back, then spinning to link the first pass with the next one in the series, he will hear shouts of *"Olé!"*

and the band may play music to accompany his work. It is this *faena* with the *muleta* on which modern matadors are principally judged, and everything that happens to the bull beforehand is meant to prepare it to perform well during the *faena*.

When the matador decides that the *faena* is complete — usually within seven to ten minutes — he will go over to his manservant and exchange the fake sword for the real one. Then he will stand in front of the bull and run at it, using his left hand to distract the bull with the cape and his right hand to thrust the sword into the flesh between the bull's shoulder blades. Sometimes the bull is killed with one thrust. More often the matador must run at the bull a few times to get the sword in the right spot. Even then, the bull doesn't always die right away and the matador must deliver a final blow with a special sword called a *descabello*, which is jabbed into the back of the bull's neck, severing its spinal cord and killing it in a jerky instant. The death of the bull is the simple means to end the performance, but the way the matador kills can be dramatic and aesthetically pleasing.

When the bull dies, the crowd may whistle, remain silent, applaud, or shout, to indicate its attitude toward the performance of the bull. This is done not for the bull's benefit, but rather for the benefit of the breeder and of the ring's management, which purchased the bull. When the bull has been taken from the arena, the crowd will do the same for the matador. If the fans judge that a matador has performed beautifully and killed quickly, they will wave white handkerchiefs to insist that the matador be awarded one of the bull's ears, two ears, or both ears and the tail, according to how well the audience thinks he has done. These gruesome rewards may have grown out of the eighteenth-century practice of tipping a successful matador with the valuable meat of the bull he'd just killed. The awarding of such trophies is subjective, but audiences in the larger, more important bullrings are stingier with their bull appendices than audiences in little towns. So one ear cut in Madrid is a greater honor than two ears cut in the provinces.

Since bullfighting is not a sport, there is no objective way to judge a matador's performance. Audiences rate what they see in the ring on a kind of sliding scale that takes into account the relative difficulty presented by the bull (some bulls are harder to work with than others); the amount of danger the bullfighter exposed himself to (some bullfighting techniques are more dangerous than others); whether the performance was aesthetically pleasing; and whether it was in keeping with bullfighting tradition and fitting for the bullring in question (some rings are more prestigious than others, and their audiences expect a more classical, refined style).

Newcomers to bullfighting often assume that the violence they are seeing is meant to taunt, humiliate, and therefore enrage the bull. In fact, the reverse is true. The passes, pics, and banderillas are used to slow the bull down, calm it, and focus its anger on the cape, so the matador can do a great *faena*. Spanish bullfighting bulls are bred to charge at the slightest provocation, and most bulls need little encouragement to act on that programming. Bulls are territorial creatures by nature and live in herds. When a bull is faced with danger it will first try to escape. If it cannot escape, it will do what it can to defend its turf and the cows it is mating with. So when a bull is separated from its herd and put into an enclosed space where it cannot escape, it will lash out, charging at whoever walks into what it perceives to be its space until that space is cleared. In that sense, the charge of the bull is really a running away in reverse.

The matador uses the opening passes with the *capote* to teach the bull to follow the cape. The horse provides a solid, confidence-building target for the bull to hit, and the picador's lance tires the bull and lowers the carriage of its head, lowering its horns and making it less dangerous to work with. The banderillas slow the bull further and focus its attention on the man. The *faena* with the *muleta* is the point of the show, the matador's chance to shine. But it, too, serves a purpose, preparing the bull for the sword by wearing it down to the point where it is slow and sluggish and can be killed in the prescribed fashion. The sword ends the spectacle and can be a spectacle in itself. Each stage of the bullfight prepares the bull for the next stage, and the art of bullfighting consists of this preparation.

If bullfighting is an art, then what does it do for the viewer? No writer can sum up the effect of an artwork on an average person, but this much can be stated: the movements that a talented matador makes with his cape are beautiful to watch even when he is standing alone in his bedroom, dressed in sweatpants and a T-shirt. Without a bull, the cape passes of bullfighting are like the steps of a lovely folk dance, but when the charged atmosphere of the ring and the menacing beauty of the bull are added to the dance of the cape, and when the dancer is made to perform under the threat of bodily harm and with the dual aims of controlling a wild animal and then working with it to create something pleasing to the eye, then that is a performance that can inspire a depth of emotion.

Aficionados say there is a special feeling that comes when a great matador passes a bull low and slow around his body and the bull responds, charging hard at the cape and lending solemnity and danger to the matador's movements. Hemingway described it as a lump in the throat. García Lorca called it "man's finest anger, his finest melancholy and his finest grief." It is an electric mixture of fear, pleasure in beauty, sadness, anger, horror, joy, tension, the feeling of victory over death, and the viewer's relief that he or she is safe and not facing the bull. According to García Lorca, this dark yet sweet emotion can be inspired by any art form, but especially by the two Spanish arts of bullfighting and flamenco music. When a torero or a flamenco artist loses himself and begins creating on the very edge of reason and capacity he may, García Lorca said, summon up a demon called the *duende,* who can make the powerful emotion run. This *duende* is not brought into being by talent or skill but rather by the artist's ability to give himself over to the moment and by his ties of blood and history to the essential culture of Spain, which for García Lorca is found always in the bullfight.

"Spain is the only country where death is a national spectacle," he wrote, "the only one where death sounds long trumpet blasts at the coming of spring, and Spanish art is always ruled by a shrewd *duende* who makes it different and inventive."

The only trouble is, this special emotion is rarely evoked in the ring, because the art of bullfighting is made from an adversarial collaboration between a human and an unwilling animal. It is this emotion that Fran would be seeking to create in his corrida in Valencia.

4

·◦·─◄●◦◉◦●►─·◦·

The Challenge Accepted

On the road, March 13. Along with its small neighbor Portugal, Spain occupies the Iberian Peninsula, which juts out from southern France at the western edge of Europe. This vaguely square piece of land, described by the ancient geographer Strabo as looking like a bull's hide stretched on a wooden frame, is girded by the Bay of Biscay to the north, the Atlantic Ocean to the west, and the Mediterranean Sea to the south and to some extent the east. Most of Spain is mountainous. The average height of the land there is greater than in any European nation save Switzerland. At Spain's center, taking up as much as half of its five hundred thousand square miles, is the arid and sparsely populated tableland called the *meseta*. A range of snowcapped mountains splits the *meseta*, and thus Spain, into north and south. There are also formidable mountain ranges along the northern and southern coasts, in the northeast, and along the border with France, which is protected by the Pyrenees Mountains.

Few European nations contain such a variety of people and landscape within their borders. The north coast, comprising the regions of Galicia, Cantabria, Asturias, and the País Vasco (Basque Country), with landlocked La Rioja and Navarra just below it, is damp and green, and its people are serious and industrious and are closer to northern Europeans in culture and attitudes than any other Spaniards. The center, comprising the regions of Castilla-León, Madrid, Castilla–La Mancha, Aragón, and Extremadura, is a place of empty plains, castles, poor farmland, and windmills. It is the land of Don Quixote and of the capital city, Madrid, and the classic resident is dour and hardworking and has an outlook on life not far removed from his peasant forebears. The eastern coast of Spain — the regions of Cataluña, Valencia, and Murcia — is like the rest of the Mediterranean, and the people there are of the same agrarian-cosmopolitan-mercantile type found along the Italian and French coasts. Meanwhile, southern Spain, the vast region of Andalucía, is the Spain of Romantic tradition, the Spain of Gypsies and flamenco music, of Arab palaces and whitewashed houses, of gazpacho and sherry, and of bulls and bullfighters.

Fran was driving from Sevilla, the capital of Andalucía, to the city of Valencia, on the middle Mediterranean coast. It was eight P.M., and his driver, Juani, planned to kill the four-hundred-mile journey in less than six hours, with a break for dinner at a roadside restaurant. Juani started out from Sevilla under a clear night sky and made good time up to Córdoba. From there he planned to head farther north, past the town of Linares — where a bull from the ranch of Miura killed the legendary matador Manolete — and into the wine-producing region of Valdepeñas, in La Mancha, then east to the shore and straight into Valencia, where Fran had bulls the following day.

Bullfighters in Spain travel by automobile, as they have done since the early decades of the twentieth century, when they gave up on the train. During the season to come, Fran would crisscross Spain in a late-model burgundy-red Chevrolet van. The two rows of passenger seats in back flipped down to create a level surface, and Fran made himself a comfortable bed there with the freshly laundered bolsters, pillows, and blankets kept for him. Like most successful matadors, Fran traveled alone with a private driver, sending his cuadrilla of assistant bullfighters on ahead in a minibus, which could accommodate nine men and all of the bullfighting gear.

The atmosphere in Fran's car that night was relaxed; there was no sense of personal or professional crisis, nor any urgency over what Fran would be up to the following day. Fran sat in the back seat and made a few calls on his mobile phone and listened to flamenco on the Chevy's CD changer. Seated next to Juani was a friend of Fran's who had been putting Fran up in his house during the weeks following his separation from Eugenia. After an hour of driving the night grew cloudy. The highway narrowed to one lane in either direction and Juani began a nerve-racking game of tag with the broken line of eighteen-wheelers that were clogging the road. Fran's face fell into shadow.

"It has been hard, very, very hard," Fran said in English, the language he used for almost all of the interviews in this book. "I was thinking about ending the bullfighting season. After what happened to me, I thought, 'I can't take it. I can't take any more.' But this is something . . . well . . . it is my job, it is my life, it is something that I have to do."

It was only later that a rough picture emerged of what Fran had gone through during the first months of the year. It seems that when he and Eugenia split in February, Fran fell into a deep depression and talked about quitting the ring. During this time he continued to appear in a few warm-up corridas in smaller bullrings, and each afternoon when he put on his matador's costume he broke into tears. On March 3, the day Eugenia announced the separation to the press, Fran was performing in a town named Calahorra. Minutes before the opening parade of toreros, in the tunnel that led out to the sand, Fran made a request of his assistant bullfighters. "Watch out for me," he said. "I really don't know where my head is at right now."

The person who seems to have turned Fran around was his *apoderado*, José Luis Segura. In bullfighting, the *apoderado* is like a manager, coach, and agent rolled into one. He travels with the matador, makes bookings, handles the cash, helps with training, and offers encouragement and artistic advice, all for ten to fifteen percent of the matador's earnings. One day shortly after Fran and Eugenia's separation, Pepe Luis — Pepe is a nickname for José — took Fran aside for an all-out pep talk. The *apoderado* reminded Fran that he was still a star in the bull world, and that if he quit the ring in the face of marital troubles, he would lose something as a man and as a bullfighter, something he might never get back again.

Fran responded that his wife and child were his world. He went on to say that unlike most bullfighters' wives, his wife had traveled with him on the road and advised him on his bullfighting. Pepe Luis countered that even though Fran was going through a rough patch personally, he had a career that he'd worked hard to create, and this career was important enough to fight for. In the end, Fran agreed and decided to continue with the season. Pepe Luis assured him that he was doing the right thing. Following this, Pepe Luis placed a call to his cardiologist and begged for some anti-anxiety pills. The *apoderado*, who had a heart condition, had just convinced a sad and distracted young man to go back to the bullring, a place where there is no room for distraction.

It was a frustrating state of affairs for all concerned, particularly since Fran had seemed to be on the verge of a comeback. The season before had been his best in years, and he had finished up with a corrida in Madrid, where he'd cut an ear in the greatest bullring in the world. During the off-season, Fran had made a number of changes he'd hoped would get him back on track. He'd replaced three of the five men in his cuadrilla of assistant bullfighters, parted ways with his old *apoderado,* and signed with Pepe Luis. Then, over the Christmas holiday, the hopeful matador and his new *apoderado* had begun intensive strategy sessions and agreed that this was going to be the year Francisco Rivera Ordóñez would climb back on top.

They talked about a number of ways Fran could achieve this goal, but the essence of their conversations was that Fran had to be true to himself as an artist. What that meant exactly is hard to explain, but it was a question of style. In many ways matadors are like opera singers. Opera singers the world over perform the same limited repertory, everyone working the same material. But even though the operas of Mozart, Verdi, and Puccini don't change, each singer brings his or her own voice and style to the words, movements, and music. Different singers specialize in different facets of opera performance: some singers are suited for romantic leads, others play villains; some devote themselves to a certain type of opera, such as the works of Wagner; some are known as great actors with average voices, others are pure singers devoid of acting talent.

Similarly, each successful matador has his own style and his own niche in the profession. One corrida is almost identical to another, and what any one matador does is pretty much the same as what every other matador does. All matadors perform the same basic passes, but each matador does these passes his own way, putting his own physical stamp on the material. Also, matadors have different personalities: some are artistic types concerned with the aesthetics of their craft, others are daredevils who specialize in taking on the biggest, meanest bulls that can be found; some are known for their *capote* work, some for placing the banderillas, some as great killers.

Fran possessed talent in abundance and was a naturally gifted athlete who could perform in a number of different styles. This had been a blessing in the early years, when he needed physical prowess and innate skill to make up for his inexperience and, worse, his lack of training. But as his career progressed, his talent had hurt him somewhat, because he had never really been forced to answer the fundamental question of who he was as a matador. Fran was like a singer who could play basso villain roles and heroic tenor roles but had never found a voice of his own. This was part of the reason why bullfighting fans could not decide what they thought about Fran, and why his most recognizable traits continued to be his good looks and his lineage.

In the beginning of his career Fran adopted a rough, straightforward style that made sense given his lack of training. He wasn't elegant in what he did in the ring, but he took chances and passed the bull in a blunt, old-fashioned way, facing it head-on, reaching out and bringing the bull to his body with the cape. In time he moved from his early roughness and found his way toward a more classic and aesthetic style, which on good days reached for something the Spanish call *toreo puro* (pure bullfighting). This is a kind of austere yet aesthetic approach based on the exquisite performance of a few fundamental passes, made without trickery or theatrics.

The trouble was that Fran never quite grew out of his original style and never quite became comfortable with his new one. On days when he was having problems, it seemed as though he couldn't decide what he wanted to do with the bull, trying this and that without being able to put it together in a satisfying whole. He was stuck in a limbo between styles, of two minds as to what he should do. His work deteriorated, and so did his confidence. He was always strong with the *capote,* but his performances with the *muleta* were increasingly spotty, especially the dangerous left-handed *natural* passes, the very basis of the matador's art. He also began to have problems with the kill, which is — pardon the choice of words — a fatal flaw in a matador, because in most bullrings if the matador cannot sink the sword on the first try, he will lose any chance at an ear.

Sitting in the minivan that night on the road to Valencia, Fran analyzed why he'd struggled in his bullfighting. He said he had done too well too quickly, had become conceited, hadn't worked hard enough to improve. Then the hard times had come, and he'd lost his confidence and that sense of composure and focus that he'd possessed in the early years, and the whole thing had fallen apart. "You need to go to the ring with a clear mind," he said. "And one moment I thought I was God, maybe the top, the second coming of Christ, then came the problems with my grandfather, and I lost the feeling. I lost concentration and one day I lost the touch in front of the bull."

We talked a little about what he meant by losing touch.

"When you go into the ring," Fran said, "you can't think, 'Now I will do this pass, then this pass, then this other pass.' No. You must do the performance the bull needs and deserves, and this is different every time."

"If you are thinking about yourself, you can't be thinking about the bull?" I asked.

"Exactly."

Then Fran's focus shifted to the future.

"I am very nervous for tomorrow," he said. "This season is very important for me. I think it is time. I can take my place in *la historia*. We bullfighters, when we talk among ourselves about other bullfighters, we say, 'For that guy, the train has already left the station.' The train left, and he didn't get on it. He lost his chance. I think I can get on the train and take my position. I think I still have many things to say."

Fran said this with such casual conviction that it seemed quite natural, but in retrospect it was startling. That night Fran had spoken, with rare humility for a matador, about how things had not been going well for him and why, and then he had made a complete turnabout, showing a titanic sense of pride and ambition. That night on the road to Valencia, Fran had challenged himself. He might have hedged. He might have said that, given his marital troubles, this was a year to mark time, solve his personal problems, and live to fight again. Instead he had declared his intention to make it back to the top that very season and do it on his own terms, being true to his idea of what a great bullfighter should be.

To achieve his goal, Fran was going to have to find a way to forge a style of bullfighting that would make his public and himself happy. He was going to have to triumph in big cities and small villages all over Spain. He'd have to please the critics and the elite core of knowledgeable fans, most of whom were against him, as well as the masses who just wanted a good show. He would have to succeed with the solid burghers of Spain's northern regions and charm the fun-loving denizens of the Spanish southland. Most of all, he was going to have to come to terms with the crushing legacy of his forefathers — El Niño de la Palma, Antonio Ordóñez, and Paquirri — shake off the mental, physical, and moral fatigue of his own eventful life, and try to regain the touch he had possessed in those early years, when bullfighting was like singing a tune and he knew just how to give each bull what it needed to make a great performance.

"I want to feel happy in front of the bull again," Fran said. "That is the most important thing to me."

Fran fell silent and after a while he slept. When he woke up, Juani was parked beside the curb of a wide and empty boulevard. A young couple was leaning into the window and Juani was asking them for directions to the hotel. Fran's minivan was in the middle of a city, which turned out to be Valencia. It was two o'clock in the morning and the wet air glowed pink under the streetlights. As soon as Juani got his directions and was driving again, Fran lashed into him in rapid-fire Spanish. The following is an approximation of what was said.

"Juani, I've told you time and time again," Fran said, his voice loud after the long silence of the ride. "Find the hotel on a map before we arrive somewhere."

"But Matador, Matador," Juani said, "this is a new hotel. I've never been there."

"All the more reason to figure out where it is *before* you start driving," said Fran. "Anyway, what's the hotel called?"

"It's something like the Vin . . . the Vinki . . . like the Vinki Lass."

At this Fran turned to me, switched to English, and said, "He never knows the way to the hotel. I find this so . . . how you say? Depressing."

Juani circled around downtown Valencia for a while and presently found his way to a new hotel on a pedestrian alley a few blocks from the bullring. The hotel was named the Vincci Lys, which, in Juani's defense, was an odd name in Spanish or English. The lobby was empty apart from the night manager and a tired-looking girl behind a desk. The girl stared at Fran the way people stare when they see a celebrity; the manager asked Fran to autograph a menu that was hanging on the wall. The hotel was trying to attract bullfighters and aficionados, and offered a "bullfighting menu," which consisted of the same Spanish food on offer in every hotel restaurant from Barcelona to Badajoz. Fran checked in, grabbed his suitcase, and headed for the elevator. He wouldn't be seen again until just before the bullfight.

When I got up to my room and turned on the television, whom should I see on the screen but Fran's mother. Carmen was appearing on a program called *Tómbola*, which was like a demented version of an American Sunday-morning chat show. But instead of a governor or senator facing political journalists, there was Carmen in a sequined blouse, squaring off against a group of tabloid reporters. They peppered her with personal questions and impertinent comments before a studio audience that shrieked, groaned, and howled, enjoying the spectacle of a rich and famous person being humiliated.

"Where is your son?" asked one of the reporters. "Is he living at your house?"

"No," Carmen answered. "He is bullfighting tomorrow. He is risking his life tomorrow."

"Do you feel terrible about your son's situation?"

"Absolutely."

Then a reporter turned to Carmen and said, "When you sell your life stories to the press, you hurt your children, don't you?"

I couldn't hear Carmen's response. The cries of the audience drowned her out.

I don't know whether or not Fran saw his mother on television that night.

5

The Season Begins

Valencia, March 14. Valencia turned out to be a pleasant, muggy, and prosperous town with some attractive nineteenth-century neighborhoods surrounding a seedy central district whose jumbled street plan is all that remains of its medieval origins. Valencia is not on Spain's main tourist route. It has no must-see sights, museums, or other attractions. But in mid-March Valencia puts on the Feria de las Fallas, which is one of the nicest *ferias* in Spain, especially for the tourist, because most of the excitement takes place in the streets and is open to all. The Fallas of Valencia is the first crucial *feria* of the bullfighting calendar, and thus the effective start of the season, because during the early part of the twentieth century it became established that most bullfights and almost all the important bullfights would take place during *ferias,* and the season follows the *ferias* around Spain.

Valencia's *feria* is dedicated to San José — Saint Joseph — the father of Jesus and a patron saint of the city. It lasts for about a week, and there are daily fireworks displays, processions of marching bands, and women dressed in traditional Valencian costumes. The *fallas* themselves are statues, two stories tall, made of wood and wax and painted papier-mâché. They are built throughout the year by local artisans who represent each of Valencia's neighborhoods, and are displayed in the streets. On March 19, the saint's day and the climax of the festival, the *fallas* are burned to the ground. During the *feria* that year, the city planned to present eleven bull-related events in its 150-year-old ring, which is in the center of town near the train station. On the card were eight corridas (bullfights of full-grown animals and matadors), two *novilladas* (bull-fights of aspiring matadors and young bulls), and one *corrida de rejones* (Portuguese-style bullfighting in which a torero confronts the bull on horseback).

Fran was to appear in the fifth spectacle of the cycle. By the day of his bullfight the *feria* was in full swing, and the brass bands marched along the wide avenue beside the bullring in a thunder of music, accompanying the swaying processions of women in their peasant skirts, their hair rolled up like cinnamon buns on both sides of their head. The sound of small firecrackers was constant, and at noon each day the city sponsored a thunderous fusillade of fireworks designed purely to generate as much noise as possible. The streets were filled day and night. There were many tourists in evidence, but most of the crowd was composed of well-dressed Valenciano families out for a drink, a bite to eat, or just to show themselves off. Here and there, in back streets and alleys, people built wood fires and cooked massive flat black pans of saffron-colored paella, the rice dish that was perfected in Valencia.

The scene outside Fran's hotel was a mess at bullfight time. The paparazzi and television crews were out, hoping to glean a few new tidbits from the ongoing Fran-and-Eugenia saga and get his reaction to his mother's latest comments. There was also a mob of little old ladies and adolescent girls angling for a pre-corrida kiss from the best-looking matador in the country. Fran walked out of the hotel with less than twenty minutes to go before the corrida was set to begin. He was dressed in a light blue and gold matador's costume and had his game face on as his associates led him through the crowd and piled him into the minibus and rolled down the street to the bullring.

The ring was damp and the sky gray when the toreros crossed the sand to start the corrida. Fran was the matador with the least seniority that afternoon, and so was appearing with the third and sixth bulls of the lineup. The other two matadors were stars, but not superstars. Without a major draw on the card, like the number-one matador of the moment, Julián López, El Juli, the bullring was half empty, the gaps especially evident in the cheap seats. The bulls were from the Jandilla ranch, bred in southernmost Andalucía, and the program said each bull weighed around twelve hundred pounds. The newspapers the following day would agree that the bulls had been good—charging with passion and offering opportunities for the matadors to create emotional passes with them. But the first two matadors couldn't seem to do anything special with their animals. Perhaps it was the lack of a crowd, or the cloud-bursts that poured over the ring at intervals throughout the afternoon.

A ring attendant opened the heavy door to the bullpens and Fran's first animal came out, shiny black, rippled with muscle, built along the lines of a small pickup truck. The bull was terrifying and freakish. It belonged in the forests of an earlier age or in someone's bad dream, not in the middle of a city at the beginning of the twenty-first century. The bull stopped for a moment, raised its head, looked around and sniffed the air, and the great pot roast of muscle on its neck rose and twitched with fear. Without warning, the bull galloped stiff-legged across the sand, a rope of drool spilling from its black mouth. As it approached the wooden barrier, it lowered its head and chopped hard with its right horn, flicking the horn up and taking out a hefty chunk of wood, leaving a white scar in the red paint. Then the bull sauntered back to the center of the ring and waited to be challenged.

Fran slipped through a small opening in the wooden fence. He spread his purple and yellow *capote* out with both hands, letting it fall in front of him like the skirts of an elegant ball gown. Then he raised the cape, shook it, and shouted. The bull wheeled and headed straight for Fran. His hat pushed down over his eyes, Fran flared his nostrils and scrunched his lips into his face, grimacing with the effort of staying still. The bull came. Fran didn't move. The bull lowered its head, arching its neck forward. The left horn—a white curve with a black tip—sliced at Fran's left leg. But just before the horn reached flesh, Fran dropped his right hand, spreading out the cape—and the bull followed the motion of the cloth a few inches to the right, just enough for the horn to whiff by Fran's leg as he moved the cape, turning it first with his shoulder, then his waist, then his arms, capturing the bull in the gentle slipstream of the cloth, slowing the bull and moving it across his body and on out the other side.

"*Olé!*"

Whatever else Fran's critics said about him, no one could deny that he was an artist with the *capote*. It was always the cornerstone of his performances, and his skill with the big cape didn't leave him all season. This was a *verónica* pass, named for Saint Veronica, who used a cloth to wipe Jesus's bloody brow on his way to Calvary. The *verónica* is the basic pass made with the *capote,* the man positioning his feet much as he would for a *muleta* pass — lead foot away from the bull's line of attack, back foot into the line of the charge — gripping the big circle of the *capote* with his hands on both sides of the wedge that's cut out of it and swinging it in a semicircle around his body. The pass was done about as well as you can do one.

Fran passed the bull a few more times, each time stepping toward the center of the ring — as the Spanish say, "gaining ground on the bull" — teaching it who was boss, teaching it to follow the cloth. The passes were slow and clean. The horns were always close but never touched the cape, and Fran followed through on each pass, leaning out over the bull, forcing it to move past his body. The emotion of bullfighting was there and the Valencianos shouted *"Olé!"* and *"Olé!"* and *"Olé!"* as the series unfolded. Then Fran shut off the flow with a half-*verónica* — like a regular *verónica,* but the matador gathers the cloth at his back hip at the very last moment, suddenly removing the bull's target, whipping the bull's head around and taking away its desire to charge again.

A trumpet blast, and Fran's picadors trotted into view. The bull charged the horses twice, taking two stabs of the lance. Another trumpet, and Fran's banderilleros put in three sets of sticks. Fran took off his hat and laid it on the sand. It was time for the *faena* with the *muleta.* Fran and the bull were alone in the ring. The audience was all around them, and the ugly office buildings loomed over the roof of the red brick bullring. The sky was dry for the moment, and the air was filled with the guerrilla-warfare sounds of firecrackers exploding and the brassy, percussive music of the bands marching and the people out on the streets. Fran started with the *muleta* in his right hand, reeling off several uneven series of *derechazos* that were marred by the bull's growing tendency to become distracted and slide away at the end of each pass. So Fran got down on one knee and executed a set of low, pretty, punishing passes, using the semaphore of the cape to command the bull to lower its neck, bringing the head down and giving Fran greater control. Then he stood tall again and twisted the bull around his body in three rhythmic progressions of passes with the right hand that squeezed taut *olés* from the crowd.

The bull stood its ground, waiting for Fran to act, its flanks heaving, a saddle of blood spreading down its back from where the picador had injured it. Fran gave the animal a few seconds to catch its breath. Then he offered the cape and shouted. The bull struck. But this time it didn't charge in a straight line. Instead it took its eye off the cape for a moment and made straight for Fran. Without hesitation Fran spun, twirling in a circle, wrapping the *muleta* around his leg, bringing the bull's head around with a snap, forcing the bull to wrench itself after the cloth, stopping it cold. Fran had solved the problem presented by the bull with courage and artistry, and Valencia loved it.

"O—LÉ!"

Someone in the crowd yelled *"Maestro, musica!"* and the band began to play. The audience quickened, focusing its will on the sand. Fran moved the *muleta* to his left hand and began to work *naturales*, luring the bull with the small square of cloth hanging lifelessly from the stick. The series worked, as did the next, and the next, building up and up in emotion, and then Fran made his way to the fence and traded the light sword for the steel death sword. Fran lined up in front of the bull, in profile, and ran forward, leaning over the horns and sinking the sword into the bull's back. The hilt was a little below where it should have been, according to the textbooks, but it was good enough. The bull staggered around for a few seconds, mouth gaping, tongue hanging out. Then it walked over to the wooden fence and folded its legs underneath its body. Dead.

The audience waved white handkerchiefs and the president of the corrida awarded Fran an ear, the only ear awarded that day. Yet the reviews in the papers were unenthusiastic. Fran had done a passable job, the critics agreed, but it had been a bull that was willing to cooperate. "Rivera Ordóñez was good with his first bull," wrote Javier Villan, of the newspaper *El Mundo*, in a review that was typical of the rest, "although he could have been, and should have been, better."

It was night by the time Fran stabbed the final bull of the corrida and killed it. Then he and the other two matadors and their assistants walked out of the ring to their vans. Fran got back to the hotel in less than ten minutes, went up to his room, stripped, and took a quick hot shower. Then he wrapped a white hotel towel around his slender waist and settled into the couch in the sitting room of his suite to entertain the stream of guests that always come to visit a matador after a bullfight.

Fran seemed to be pleased. He hadn't taken Valencia by storm, but he had done well, especially considering what had been going on in his life. The season had begun and the first result had been positive. Maybe this was what he needed to get his head in shape for the all-important weeks to come. The next two months would bring with them the two most prestigious *ferias* of the year: Sevilla in April and Madrid in May. If he was going to get back on top, he'd like to start with triumphs in those places.

The first person to show up at Fran's door was a bull breeder from the province of Salamanca. Then came the president of the Rivera Ordóñez fan club, up from Granada with her boyfriend. Next came a bullfighting photographer who had shot Fran many times over the years. After the group had chatted for a few minutes, there was a knock at the door and the most popular matador in Spain walked in. Julián López, El Juli, was a small, slender twenty-year-old boy with a half-moon horn scar running out from the side of his mouth. El Juli had just arrived from his ranch outside Madrid. He was performing in Valencia the following afternoon. The air in the room shifted a bit, as it always does in the presence of white-hot fame.

The breeder from Salamanca turned to face him.

"Ah, Maestro," said the breeder. "Good evening."

Then the breeder looked around. He had just called one matador a maestro while in the hotel room of another matador. That was like calling a young woman beautiful when in the presence of one's wife. The breeder turned to Fran, who sat impassively on the couch.

"Of course you are a maestro as well," the breeder told Fran.

"Don't worry," said Fran, in prince mode. "Julián is also my maestro."

Everyone was still smiling at this bit of diplomacy when there came another knock on the door. Fran's manservant, Nacho, answered it. When Nacho saw who it was, he gave the visitor a quick hug and let him into the room.

"Fran," said the visitor in a public school British accent.

"Noël," Fran said, and then in English, "How are you doing?"

The two men shared a warm embrace. Noël Chandler, a Welshman, was a retired computer executive who lived in Spain and was Fran's biggest fan. This was Noël's traditional beginning-of-season visit. The two men chatted about the upcoming year — where Fran would be performing, how he was feeling about the season. As the conversation wound down and Noël got ready to leave, he asked the sort of serious bullfighting question any aficionado might ask of a matador at the start of a new campaign. He wanted to know if Fran would be favoring bulls from any particular breeders during the coming season.

"What kinds of bulls are you interested in fighting this year, Fran?" Noël asked.

"Dead ones," Fran said. "Dead ones."

SECOND THIRD

The Struggle

APRIL–AUGUST

Journalist: Maestro, what does it take to be a
  great matador?
Antonio Ordóñez: The ability to sleep in cars.

— a legendary remark of Fran's grandfather

6

Melons, Bitter and Sweet

Ruta del Toro, late March. One morning during the lull between the *ferias* of Valencia and Sevilla, I drove about sixty miles south of Sevilla to the town of Jerez de la Frontera, where sherry wine is made. Jerez sits at the head of a web of roads and highways known as the Ruta del Toro (Route of the Bull), which runs through country rich in the ranches where bullfighting bulls are bred and raised. The day grew hot and sunny and the highway swung in and out of fields of green grass that were spotted with twisted olive trees and rocky hills. Herds of cattle wandered in the distance, but none resembled the fierce bulls I had seen in the ring.

I turned off the highway and passed beside a hillside town named Vejer de la Frontera (the word *frontera* [border] in a town's name indicates that it stood on land contested by the Moors and Christians in the Middle Ages). At Vejer I turned onto a country road and drove past a rising tract of land with a whitewashed house atop it. This was La Cantora, the ranch that had belonged to Paquirri and still belonged to his widow, Isabel Pantoja. Soon the road narrowed and I saw stands of cactus, imported from the New World, and ahead a small, arrow-shaped sign that read *Jandilla.* I followed that arrow and began seeing other signs that said, in Spanish, *Danger, Bullfighting Cattle.*

Eventually I passed the ranch's gate and drove along a bumpy dirt track that trailed through fields alive with pheasants, rabbits, and other small game animals, and grazing black cows. The big villa where the ranch's owner lived rose out of a hill on the horizon, and soon I came to a concrete building with antennas on the roof and chickens in the yard. This was the home of the chief herdsman of Jandilla, Juan Reyes, a broad-shouldered thirty-five-year-old man with a sun-reddened face dominated by a bulbous nose. Reyes had agreed to show me some bulls, and he led me to his ancient white Land Rover, which would take us into their pastures. The door to the passenger seat was dented in two places, and in the center of each dent was a hole that looked as if it had been made by a small cannon.

"Horns," Reyes explained.

There are approximately three hundred breeders who raise the bulls used in top-shelf professional bullfights in Spain, and each breeder is known by its brand — which is both the name the bulls appear under and the symbol (Jandilla's is a star) that is seared into their hide with a branding iron. The proprietor of the Jandilla brand was Francisco de Borja Domecq y Solís, a member of an old and powerful Jerezano family that had become a major force in the breeding of bullfighting bulls. Don Borja, as he was called in bullfighting circles — the "Don" indicating the respect accorded to bull breeders — raised his bulls on two ranches: Jandilla in Andalucía and Los Quintos in Extremadura. The Jandilla ranch comprised four square miles, much of it devoted to corn and rice, its two cash crops. Bull breeders claim that raising bulls is so consuming of time and resources that they don't make money at it, a claim many aficionados dismiss.

The breeding stock of the Jandilla brand was spread out over both of Don Borja's ranches and consisted of around 500 cows and 30 seed bulls, which were mated each year to produce about 350 offspring that would eventually yield up to 90 mature bulls — enough to supply fifteen full corridas. Like all bullfighting bulls, Don Borja's animals lived a mostly wild existence, interacting with humans rarely apart from a few special days. These included the days when they were vaccinated, separated from their mothers, and branded with the year of their birth, a serial number, and the Jandilla star. (On the day of branding, each animal was also given a name, which was written into the ranch's ledger. There is no apparent rhyme or reason to these names, but at Jandilla, as on some other ranches, the names related to the bulls' parents.)

At two years of age the calves were tested for bravery, but the males and females were tested in different ways. The female calves were tested in a manner similar to the testing Fran had participated in before his corrida in Valencia. The cows were made to charge a picador in a bull-ring, and those animals that charged the picador repeatedly after being hurt by the lance, and charged the *muleta,* were set aside for breeding. Male calves, on the other hand, were tested in open fields by horsemen who knocked them down with wooden poles, and those male calves that got up and challenged the horsemen after being thrown down were reserved for the ring. Males and females that failed their trials were slaughtered for meat.

The cows and bulls were tested differently because the bulls were destined for corridas, and the Spanish corrida is grounded on the fact that the bull has never faced bullfight conditions before. Bulls are intelligent creatures with long memories. A bull that's been caped or pic'd will learn from that experience, and if that bull is confronted by those same circumstances later in life, it will be more likely to ignore the cape or the horse and try to kill the man, and no matador could create artistic passes with such a bull. But even so-called virgin bulls that have never been caped or pic'd learn quickly during the twenty minutes they spend in the ring, becoming more likely, as the bullfight progresses, to ignore the cape and strike the man. This ability to learn is part of the reason bulls are killed in bullfights. You cannot perform with the same bull twice.

Bulls learn to use their horns by fighting with their cousins in the field, and they become more dangerous as they age. By Spanish law, bulls used in formal corridas must be between four and six years old, but in modern times most bulls are sent to the ring before they turn five. When Jandilla bulls mature they are divided into lots of six animals that will be sent to the same corrida, the breeder selecting each lot to make it consistent in size, beauty, and bravery. The best lots are sold to the most prestigious rings; lesser groups go to lesser rings. A top corrida of Jandillas, of the type appropriate for a bullfight in Madrid or Sevilla, would have cost about ten thousand dollars an animal during the year in question. This is a reflection of the time and energy it takes to raise such a bull, and the fact that the breeder may reject as many as half the male animals born during a season because of physical defects or lack of ferocity.

Juan Reyes drove his white Land Rover over a wooded ridge and down into a forested valley that had been divided by barbed-wire fencing. He came to a gate and asked if I would open it for him. I got out of the car.

The air was quiet, but there was a musky animal smell on the wind and the hairs on the back of my neck tingled. I opened the gate. After Reyes drove through I shut it and scrambled back into the car. We rumbled up a hill. The day was bright and the sun made it hard to look through the windshield. Then Reyes pointed into the middle distance and I saw them for the first time.

Their coats were sleek and shining. Four of them were black and two were a dark chestnut color. Their faces were short, with short noses and wet muzzles. The horns were as thick as a man's fist at the base, and spread out a few inches, then turned forward and rose to sharp black tips. Their necks were long, and at the top of each neck was the bulge of tossing muscle that crests and shivers when the bull feels danger. Their backs would have reached above the waist of a tall man. Their bodies were thick and covered in sturdy knots of muscle. By comparison, their legs and hooves were delicate and thin. Their tails were long with a tassel of silky hair at the end. Each weighed more than a thousand pounds.

"These are the bulls for Sevilla," Reyes said. The bulls we were looking at had been earmarked for a corrida on April 14, with Fran on the card. Reyes stared at the bulls for a minute in silence. "The bull in the country is a magnificent sight, isn't he?" he said.

Reyes was right. When a bull entered the stone enclosure of the bullring, surrounded by the atmosphere of the city, it was an exotic and theatrical presence, a menacing emissary from nature, a circus performer sent into the modern world to excite a jaded public. But in the fields of a great ranch like Jandilla, the bulls displayed a different side of their character. They were frightening, yes, but not horrifying, because they were suited to their setting.

As I watched them, I became aware that my window was down and there was nothing between those horns and me, and I panicked. Without thinking, I grabbed at the knob and tried to roll up my window as fast as I could. I was pumping away when Reyes grabbed my arm, stopping me short. I had made a sudden motion, and a chestnut bull with a splotch of white hair on its forehead swung its head in my direction. I froze. My face reddened and sweat beaded. The bull looked at me for a few seconds. Then it dropped its head and shook off some flies. The moment had passed, but the fear of it stayed with me. Later I realized it wasn't the horns or the bull's size or its power that had struck me. It was the eyes. They were cold, shark eyes.

Before we said goodbye I asked Reyes if his years of raising bulls had given him any insight into whether the chestnut animal I had met was going to perform well in Sevilla on April 14.

Reyes smiled. "A bull is like a melon," he said. "You can't tell if he is going to be sweet or bitter until you open him up."

Like all bullfighting bulls, the bulls of Jandilla were wild animals, in the sense that they lived in the open, took care of themselves more or less, and were too ferocious to coexist with humans in close quarters. Certainly they were as wild as any other animal in this world, where wilderness has dwindled and even the most feral creatures live constrained lives in national parks. Yet wild as they were, Spanish bullfighting bulls were also the highly refined products of human tinkering, the result of three hundred years of selective breeding designed to produce specific characteristics — although those characteristics have changed over time as bullfighting has changed.

The people of Iberia have always killed the wild bulls that are indigenous to their land. Early humans hunted bulls for meat. But from the beginning of recorded history, the societies founded by each of the successive conquerors of Spain have also killed bulls for entertainment. The ancient Romans staged bull killings by gladiators in their arenas, and some of these spectacles may have included the use of red capes. During the Middle Ages, Arab and Christian nobles hunted bulls on horseback with the assistance of peasants on foot, and there were also occasions — most often the birth, wedding, or coronation of an important lord — when bulls were rounded up alive and killed by the nobles themselves before an audience of their peers in what we might recognize today as an early version of the corrida, though an aristocratic version that was always on horseback.

The modern bullfight on foot arose during the eighteenth century, a time when Spain was in decline as a military and economic power and its once proud aristocracy was falling into decay. The king at the beginning of the century, the French-born Felipe V, discouraged aristocratic equestrian bullfights at his court, which caused the nobility to lose interest in performing in them. This void was filled by a new breed of bullfighters, men of humble birth who acted as paid entertainers, killing bulls on foot, with cape and sword, before large audiences drawn from all strata of society. This switch from the aristocratic to the plebeian was a symptom of a fundamental trend in Spain. At a time when western Europe looked to its aristocracies for cultural leadership, at a time of the advances in rational science and philosophy known as the Enlightenment, Spain became obsessed with bullfights, flamenco, and popular theater.

These three newly constituted art forms had roots in antiquity. Far from being rational, scientific, or aristocratic, they were coarse, energetic, irrational, intoxicating, pagan, style-obsessed, and low class. The bullring, flamenco party, and dance hall performance gave rise to a modern Spain that developed on its own, separated from the rest of Europe by its growing tendency to look inward, by its irrelevance in world affairs, and by the physical barrier of the Pyrenees. Bullfighting was so central to this idiosyncratic development that in 1948 the noted Spanish philosopher José Ortega y Gasset made this oft-quoted observation: "One cannot write the history of Spain from 1650 to our own time without keeping the bullfight clearly in mind."

Like many before and after him, Ortega y Gasset viewed bullfighting as emblematic of Spain's singular and backward nature. There is, however, another way to look at it. As one of the first forms of mass entertainment, as an early commercial spectacle, as a triumph of popular culture, and as an art form that created national celebrities, bullfighting was one of the most advanced aspects of eighteenth-century European society, a signpost to the culture of today. The first star matador emerged in the mid-1700s. A former carpenter, Francisco Romero, along with his matador sons and grandsons, came from a hilltop town in eastern Andalucía by the name of Ronda, a town that would produce a twentieth-century torero dynasty, the Ordóñez clan.

Traditionally, the bulls meant for bull spectacles were provided in haphazard fashion, but by the time the Romeros were getting the modern bullfight going, Spaniards were breeding wild bulls. These early breeders were among the first people in the world to practice selective breeding, keeping records of the characteristics of their animals and attempting to mate certain individuals to produce desired traits in the offspring. By the middle of the eighteenth century things had become advanced enough that one can speak of original strains or castes of bullfighting bulls. There is some controversy about how many original castes there were, five or six. But it is generally agreed that most of the bullfighting stock in Spain comes from the Vázquez, Vistahermosa, and Cabrera lines, which were founded in the eighteenth century by three gentleman breeders in the town of Utrera, just south of Sevilla.

Don Borja's Jandilla brand can trace its lineage back to one of those herds, the one formed by Vicente José Vázquez in the 1770s. After Don Vicente's death, his herd passed to his children, who sold it to the bull-crazy king Fernando VII in 1830. Some twenty years later, Cristóbal Colón de la Cerda, the duke of Veragua, bought most of the late king's herd. The duke's name is the Spanish form of Christopher Columbus, and Colón was indeed a direct descendant of the famous explorer. The duke was equally famous for his bulls, which acquired great renown in the nineteenth century. History records a number of notable specimens, including the bull Aborrecido, who took five pics and killed two horses in San Sebastián on August 30, 1886; Regalón, who withstood six pics, killed two horses, and died fighting in Madrid on May 12, 1890; and Confitero, who took an astounding twenty-four pics in the Valencia ring on July 24, 1877.

These old accounts stress two statistics—pics received and horses killed—that are of no importance today, because of the profound ways in which bullfighting has changed as a spectacle. In the eighteenth and nineteenth centuries, the points of the picadors' lances were rather small and their horses unprotected. This meant the first act of the bull-fight was a prolonged affair, and it took many pics and often the deaths of a few horses to wear down a single bull. During this era, the mata-dor's *muleta* was seen as a functional tool used to give a few choppy passes to get the bull into position for killing. But in the 1920s the horses were given padding, and over the ensuing decades the standard pic was made bigger and more destructive, thus shortening the first act of the corrida to a small number of pics. At the same time, matadors improved and embellished their *muleta* technique, to the point that the cape work with the *muleta* replaced the act of the horses as the focal point of the spectacle.

As the bullfight changed, so did the kind of bull desired by audiences and bullfighters. Old bullfighting required a big, tough animal that was hard to dominate and could endure the pain of repeated pics, whereas modern bullfighting called for a bull with speed, good eyesight (to see the cape), a taste for charging repeatedly, the stamina to keep charging, and the type of personality that would bend to the dominating will of the matador.

In 1910, the heir of the old duke of Veragua sold his cattle, which ended up in the hands of Juan Pedro Domecq y Núñez de Villavicencio, the founder of the Domecq bull-breeding dynasty. Juan Pedro Domecq moved his new cattle to his ranch, Jandilla, and died in 1937, leaving his land and bulls to his son, Juan Pedro Domecq y Díez. It was this Juan Pedro who developed the Domecq strain of bull, which has taken over contemporary bullfighting. After Juan Pedro Domecq y Díez died, his herd was distributed among many heirs, and today there are Domecqs sending bulls to top bullrings under various brands: El Torero, Torrestrella, Marques de Domecq, Santiago Domecq, Juan Pedro Domecq, Zalduendo, Martelilla, and Jandilla. The owners of Domecq bulls have also been more than willing to sell their animals to other breeders, so that today just about forty percent of all bulls sent to the ring are related somehow to Juan Pedro's original herd.

Domecq bulls are popular for a simple reason: they make it easy on matadors. Since the early days there have been two basic philosophies of bull breeding. Some breeders create bulls to help bullfighters, while other breeders produce bulls to make life harder for them. The so-called hard bulls are bred large and tall with wide horns, to make it difficult for toreros to work near them. These animals are less likely to follow the cape, less likely to charge straight, more likely to go on the defensive, and more likely to learn that the cape is a trick and to go gunning for the man. The so-called easy bulls are bred lower to the ground, smaller, with smaller horns. They are more likely to concentrate on the cape, charging it straight and true and never catching on that there is a man manipulating that cape.

There are different types of Domecq bulls, and the Jandilla ranch is known for producing the fiercest animals among the various Domecq herds. Still, according to Julio Fernandez, the bull geneticist for the Unión de Criadores de Toros de Lidia, which is the top association of breeders, the Domecq bull on the whole is the ideal matador-friendly bull. Domecq animals are short of stature and long-necked, which means that when they drop their heads following the punishment of the pics, they carry their horns low to the ground and away from the matador's vital organs. More important, Domecq bulls are said to "grow" as the bullfight progresses, attacking the cape with vigor and stamina, charging and charging again, allowing matadors to shine. "These bulls have been adapted well to the modern bullfight," Fernandez said. "They give the toreros the type of bullfight that toreros want."

Like most modern matadors, Fran dreamed of facing the ideal modern bull, a creature that charged repeatedly, straight and true, with enough personality to evoke a sense of fear in the audience. Sadly, however, such bulls rarely appeared. Despite the efforts of Spain's best breeders, the average bullfighting bull fell short of ideal. Some bulls were ugly, skinny, small, or had twisted and malformed horns. Some were too myopic to see the cape. Some bulls fell down from having weak legs. Some bulls charged but hooked at the matador, while others stopped in the middle of each pass. Some refused to charge, backing up against the fence and defending themselves. Others sat down in the sand and mooed. There was also a measure of cheating when it came to bulls. Undersized bulls were stuffed with grain at the last minute to bring them up to the legal weight minimum for appearing in proper corridas, and this produced sluggish animals that tended to fall. A picador could ruin a good bull by punishing it too severely, leaning too hard on the pic or shooting it back on the bull's spine.

Another deception was horn-shaving. A few days before the corrida, the bull would be immobilized, often in the crate used to truck it to the arena. Then someone would saw a few inches off the end of its horns, filing what was left to give them points again and dyeing them black so they looked like normal horns. Many aficionados believe that a bull with shaved horns is handicapped, because its sense of the distance it needs to strike a target is thrown off by a few inches, and because the shaved horn will be tender the way a human nail is when it has been trimmed too close. The bull world had suffered through a few horn-shaving scandals, notably in the 1950s, when the practice was revealed to be widespread. But even more recently horn-shaving was indifferently policed, and it was generally thought that some bulls used in provincial rings had doctored horns. Nevertheless, if bulls were being shaved, it did not seem to be making bullfighting any less dangerous. The rate of injury to bullfighters had not fallen over many years.

In the end, the biggest frustration for a matador was coming to a bullfight hoping to give a great performance, only to be confronted with animals that rendered such a performance impossible. It was a constant problem, one that was magnified many times over when the bullfight was an important one, like Fran's upcoming corrida in Sevilla, Fran's hometown and the capital of the bull world. "You have many days and nights thinking about what is going to happen in Sevilla," Fran said, "looking forward to Sevilla, working hard, waking up early in the morning to practice. Then you go to Sevilla and the bull comes out and says, 'No!' Among bullfighters, we say many times, 'Man proposes, God disposes, and the bull discomposes.' "

7

Afternoons of Responsibility

By mid-April the bullfighting season was six weeks old and Fran had appeared in eight corridas, which put him fourth on the *escalafón* (leader board) of active matadors. The *escalafón* comes out weekly in the two national bullfighting magazines, *6 Toros 6*, published in Madrid, and *Aplausos*, published in Valencia. But the *escalafón* isn't a league standing or world ranking in the sports sense of those terms, because there is no National Bullfighting League or Professional Bullfighters' Tour to oversee or regulate an official ranking. Instead the *escalafón* is more like a bestseller list. It ranks matadors solely by how many bullfights they've performed in during the current season, the theory being that the best matador is the one who gets the most offers of work.

The idea that the best matador is the one who works the most comes from the fact that work has always been scarce for matadors, something the *escalafón* illustrates with eloquence. The final *escalafón* of the season in question showed that about two hundred matadors had appeared at least once during the preceding eight months. But approximately half of those matadors had performed fewer than five times, and only twenty — the group at the very top — had performed more than forty or fifty times. The reality was that no more than forty matadors in Spain worked with any regularity. The rest of them spent their days practicing and waiting, or working at other jobs. One fairly successful matador named Pepín Jiménez — he performed thirty times that season — was also a middle school math teacher.

It is generally true that the best matadors in Spain at any given time are the top forty on the *escalafón,* but not exactly true. Some matadors worked a lot because fans loved them, while the elite aficionados and critics despised them. Some matadors who weren't fan favorites worked because their *apoderados* were well connected, or they sold their services cheaply, or they weren't picky about performing in low-end bullrings. There were matadors who could work as much as they wanted but kept their number of performances small because of a nagging injury, or fear, or the simple choice to shoot for quality of performance over quantity. As in most art forms, in bullfighting there was no direct correlation between popularity and quality.

In addition to number of corridas performed, the *escalafón* also lists the number of ears and tails cut by each matador — another misleading statistic. Cutting ears and tails is a tangible way for a matador to prove he can impress audiences, but the value of those ears depends on where they were won, since ears cut in small-town bullrings are worth much less than those cut in the big arenas. In any event, Fran, who'd cut eleven ears and a tail in his eight performances that season, was happy to be among the top five matadors on the *escalafón* so early in the year — and his good showing reinforced the growing impression that he was on his way back to glory.

It was all very encouraging, but Fran knew that *escalafón* rankings, ears, and tails, were not what he needed to reestablish his reputation. Those things would all take care of themselves if only he could rack up a few triumphs in the very top *ferias.* Just as the leading professional golfers and tennis players are judged by their performances in the handful of so-called major or grand-slam tournaments, so matadors are judged by what they do in the small number of prestigious *ferias.* These blue-chip corridas are known among bullfighters as "afternoons of responsibility," because in order to succeed in them a matador takes on the heavy burden of performing without cutting corners, facing every danger head-on. Or as Fran's grandfather put it: "A bullfighter who really wants to be great has to not worry about his life four or five days a year." Those days are the afternoons of responsibility.

These charged afternoons came during the top *ferias,* which comprised less than a tenth of the 850 corridas that would be mounted that season, and which were spread over the eight-month bullfighting calendar. From a matador's perspective, the bullfighting season was divided into three parts. During part one — March, April, and May —

there were few corridas, but the most important *ferias* took place then. During part two — June and July — the frequency of corridas increased, but aside from Pamplona and Valencia, there were few prestige *ferias*. Part three — August and September — was the high season, when there were so many *ferias* of all degrees of prestige that the bullfighters lived in their vans, driving night after night from corrida to corrida until October, when the season would end with a diminishing trickle of dates.

The crucial *ferias* were those of Valencia in March, Sevilla in April, Madrid in May, Pamplona and Valencia in July, Bilbao in August, and Zaragoza in October. But head and shoulders above the rest were Madrid, first, and then Sevilla. Why were some *ferias* more important than others? There is no logical explanation. It was more or less a matter of tradition. In many ways, though not in all, bullfighting was as tradition-bound as anything that has survived into the modern world. Why did the two top *ferias* occur at the beginning of the season rather than as a climax at season's end? Tradition. Why were toreros always clean-shaven? Tradition. Why did matadors employ two picadors when one was enough? Tradition. Why did matadors take their hats off when performing with the *muleta* at the end of the bullfight? Well, you get the picture.

As soon as Fran plunged his sword into the back of his second bull in Valencia, washed the bull's blood off his hands, and walked out of the arena, he began to dream about the two corridas he was contracted for in Sevilla. More than anywhere else, Sevilla was Fran's home. He had lived there much of his life, married there, raised his daughter there, and lived his greatest bullfighting triumphs in the city's ring. Sevilla was where Fran's father was buried. His grandfather had lived in a flat in a small building on a short alley — the famed Calle Iris — that ends at the wall of the bullring. The very stones of Sevilla reminded Fran of who he was.

But it wasn't just bullfighting history or family tradition that made Fran love bullfighting in Sevilla so much. It was the atmosphere of the city's magnificent and ancient bullring during the April *feria*. Sevilla is at the center of the greatest section of bull-breeding country in Spain, and so it is home to more toreros, breeders, and other bullfighting professionals than any other city in Spain, and most of the people who attend the April bullfights there have some connection by trade, blood, or friendship to the bull business. For this reason, the crowd in the Sevilla ring demands good bullfighting and knows good bullfighting and treats events in the ring with a kind of reverence that is unusual, if not singular, among bullfighting audiences.

During the Sevilla fair, people come to the corridas dressed up: men in suits, women in their best ensembles. In Sevilla they sit in rapt silence, watching events unfold with the intensity of an opera audience on opening night — until something good happens, and then the Sevillanos erupt into cascades of applause and *olés,* and the bullring band plays, and the ring is awash in *alegría,* that special kind of wild joy that is native to southern Spain. Above all, it was this mixture of refinement and *alegría* that made Fran love Sevilla so. "The way the people in Sevilla feel the bullfight is different than in any other place," he said. "In Sevilla you have to do things better, because all the bullfighting world is here."

Sevilla is the largest and most important city in southern Spain and the capital of Andalucía. Its skyline is dominated by an expanse of small whitewashed buildings that honeycomb out from the colossal Gothic cathedral — carved from a medieval mosque — and by the Giralda, the cathedral's bell tower, which in the Middle Ages was used by muezzins to call the Muslim faithful to prayer. On the cathedral's eastern flank is a labyrinth of whitewashed houses, ramshackle palaces, broken-down churches, and tiny squares. This was the Jewish quarter until 1492, when Columbus sailed for the Americas and the heroic "Catholic king and queen," Ferdinand and Isabella, expelled the Jews from Spain. Today this area is called Barrio de Santa Cruz, the Neighborhood of the Holy Cross, as if the Jews had never existed.

To the west of the cathedral is the Arenal, a district of restaurants and inns. The Arenal is bound by the curving sweep of the Guadalquivir River and the avenue named Paseo Cristóbal Colón, which runs along the water. Across the river is Triana, the old Gypsy quarter, which has been the birthplace of more famous matadors than any neighborhood in the world. Bullfighting, like its sister art flamenco music, has always been associated with Gypsies and Gypsy culture. Some of the most famous matadors, including Joselito, were Gypsies; Fran himself had Gypsy blood. From the bridge that joins Triana to the Arenal, the Guadalquivír washes south and west through a fertile plain — past Utrera, where the first bullfighting bulls were raised — some seventy miles before it spills into the Atlantic Ocean at Sanlúcar de Barrameda.

Just down from the Triana Bridge, on the cathedral side of the river, is an elegant wedding cake of a building—whitewashed with ocher trim and an austere yet beautiful main gate decorated in marble. At first sight, this building looks as if it might be a Baroque church or the palace of a cardinal or prince. In fact, it is the most storied bullring in the world, the Real Maestranza de Caballería de Sevilla. The Maestranza, as it is known, is owned by the Maestranza, an order of nobility dedicated to horsemanship. These aristocrats built the ring in 1761 and have refurbished it several times over the centuries. The Maestranza may not be the most important ring in Spain—that title would surely go to the monumental ring in Madrid—but in many ways it is closest to the hearts of bullfighters, for its age, its beauty, its location, and the fact that every great matador in history has performed there.

No two bullrings are alike, but the Maestranza has a number of striking peculiarities. It is one of the oldest rings in Spain, and it isn't a true circle: it bulges out at one point, perhaps because of an eighteenth-century engineering glitch. The sand used on the arena floor comes from a special quarry and is the rich golden shade found so often in bullfight paintings and so rarely in life. The rows of seats end in a section that's covered by a roof of antique white, black, and blue tiles and supported by a colonnade of mismatched marble columns. A domed chapel belonging to the Maestranza club sits alongside the ring, and the ring's back façade is encrusted with houses that have been there for ages. The overall effect of the ring and its setting by the river, with the Giralda bell tower peeking over it in the distance, is stunning day or night.

Eleven months a year Sevilla is a lazy and quiet place, more like a country town than a city of eight hundred thousand people. But each spring the regular life of Sevilla stops in its tracks while its citizens pitch themselves into six weeks of celebrations, sacred and profane. First comes the observance of Semana Santa (Holy Week), the week that leads up to Easter. During this time the streets fill to bursting with tourists and locals, who come out to watch religious brotherhoods and clubs on parade, carrying on their shoulders heavy platforms topped with statues of saints and scenes from the Bible. The atmosphere is laden with religiosity and repentance, and it is difficult to get around or find a hotel room.

Then, after about a fortnight's break, the two-week Feria de Abril begins. This is the fanciest, most insular and elitist *feria* in Spain. Like many fairs in Andalucía, the action is not in town but on the outskirts, at a fairground. Here locals set up large pavilions called *casetas,* which are constructed on the same patch of ground each year, along streets named after famous bullfighters. The *casetas* range in size from single-family affairs, large enough to accommodate a dinner party, to gigantic structures erected by businesses, clubs, political parties, and unions. No matter what the size, the standard *caseta* consists of an eating area, a bar, a kitchen, and a stage of some sort with a speaker system. Twenty-four hours a day, the *casetas* are full of dancing, chatting, smoking, and laughter. But the parties are by invitation only, and can be rather off-putting for tourists and other outsiders.

The month of April was a wet one that year, but Sevilla was at its prettiest in time for the fair. The streets had been washed clean by the rains, and the cobblestones were black and slick. The orange trees that line many of the city's sidewalks were in bloom, and the sweet citrus smell mingled in the evening air with the scents of good cigars, fruity red wine, horse manure, and food frying in a thousand kitchens. Spaniards had come from around the country, and there was a strong foreign contingent: mostly French, with some Germans, Italians, British, and Americans, South and North. Those who knew how to behave as the locals do dressed formally or in traditional *feria* outfits: Spanish cowboy suits for men and frilly polka-dot flamenco dresses for women, their hair pinned up with tortoiseshell combs, silk shawls covering their bare shoulders, red carnations behind their ears.

The city woke up late during *feria* and took its time getting started. Nothing happened before noon. Lunch was taken after two. Tourists ate in restaurants or their hotels. Sevillanos and their guests dined at home or in the *casetas.* In the afternoons it was nice to walk down to the fairgrounds and watch the Andalucían gentlemen — can there be any finer-looking men anywhere? — riding their Arabian chargers. Dressed in tight-fitting cowboy suits, their flat-topped hats tilted at a rakish angle, young ladies riding sidesaddle behind them, these caballeros cantered about, showing themselves off, stopping at this *caseta* or that to lean over their saddles and accept a cool cup of sherry from an equestrian bar. Mixed in with the caballeros were the gleaming carriages of the local nobility, many of the carriages centuries old, attended by footmen in livery and drawn by teams of horses.

At half past five, the focus of the city turned away from the fair for a few hours and shifted to the area of the bullring. About this time the bars near the ring began to do a brisk trade in cold beer, gin and tonic, and whiskey on ice. Plates of boiled shrimp and plates of sliced ham and nibbles of cheese and olives made their merry way around. By six the crush was tremendous. People hugged and kissed and smoked and jostled. There was a lot of talk about the separation of Fran and Eugenia. (*Semana* declared the estranged couple to be the "stars of the *feria*.") Sellers of nuts, candy, cigars, and water bottles hawked their wares alongside vendors of bullfighters' pictures, posters, books, videos, and other bric-a-brac. Big television trucks rumbled and coughed, generating power and gearing up to broadcast the corrida across the country. It was the best moment of the day, the time of anticipation before the start of an afternoon of responsibility.

8

The Melons Opened

Sevilla, April 14. Fran leaned against the dusty brick wall of the tunnel leading to the bullring. He looked ill. His face was washed out. His lips clenched in a bloodless scowl. His eyes were clouded and unfocused. Just above him, the Maestranza was filling with the best people of Sevilla and elite aficionados worldwide. It was six-thirty on a Sunday evening and the eleventh corrida of the *feria* was about to begin. The people in the stands were festive, as they should be in Sevilla at fair time. But it had rained all day and the air was still damp, and the ring servants used wooden rakes to push pools of water into drains along the margins of the sand and dumped dry sand over the wettest patches.

Down in the tunnel, the bullfighters stood around smoking cigarettes and adjusting the heavy, embroidered capes they wore for the opening parade. Federico Arnás, the roving reporter for Via Digital, the cable network that was broadcasting the bullfight to its subscribers, pushed his way through to where Fran was standing. "Today we have bulls from the ranch of Jandilla," Arnás said into the camera in front of him. Then he turned to Fran and stuck a microphone in his face. "At the very least, it has to give you some comfort to think you will be performing with the same bulls that you did so well with last month in Valencia."

"Jandilla is a ranch that I like very much," Fran replied in a dry whisper. "It produces bulls that are very good for my style. But, well, Sevilla is very hard. It is a hard place. But you have to hold your head up and move forward."

Arnás stepped away from Fran and looked into the camera, waiting for a comment from his colleague in a booth in the stands. "It's a pretty tense atmosphere down there," said the disembodied voice.

"Oh, yes," Arnás said. "You can almost feel the nerves of the bullfighters. But look, this is a *feria* of high responsibility, and you always feel this kind of tension before a corrida in a Sevilla, or a Madrid, or a Pamplona, or a Bilbao."

"What a hard job we have," said the voice. "Going down and asking these bullfighters questions at moments when they are so nervous they can barely speak."

Just then, a splendidly turned out Andalucían gentleman in a crisp blue suit, white shirt, and pink necktie made his way down to a good seat near the sand. This was Don Borja Domecq, the proprietor of Jandilla. Don Borja seemed calm and cool as he shook hands here and there with friends and admirers. But inside he was almost as agitated as the matadors beneath him. Each time a breeder's bulls appear in a bullfight, especially in a ring like Sevilla's, that breeder's reputation is on the line. After each bull is killed the audience has a chance to whistle and jeer or applaud it, and the breeder, who is usually in the ring at the time, will get the message.

"I am as nervous as can be before a corrida," Don Borja said. "The bulls are a vehicle for the matador to triumph with, and the public have paid their money to see this and enjoy themselves. If the bulls are not up to the mark, it's a disaster for all concerned."

The first bull was named Recitador. The program said it was four years and two months old, was dark chestnut in color, and weighed about 1,260 pounds. Recitador dashed out of the bullpen and attacked the *capote* of the veteran matador José Ortega Cano. The bull took two pics, pushing hard against the horse on the first encounter but jumped away from the pain of the spear on the second encounter. The bull behaved well during the act of the banderillas, running at the toreros and lowering its head. But it arrived at the final act of the bullfight a bit winded, becoming more and more lethargic under Ortega Cano's cape work. When Recitador began pulling up and stopping in the middle of each pass, Ortega Cano lined up and killed it.

When the attendants hitched the bull to the mule team and dragged it from the ring, the audience offered up some polite applause — faint praise for Don Borja, who sat in his seat studying a piece of paper in his lap. He'd been taking notes during the performance, and now he summed up the bull for the records of his ranch. On the plus side, Recitador had charged the *capote* well and had been strong during the first pic. On the minus side, the bull had broken away from the second pic and lacked the energy to charge well during the final act of the *muleta*. On a scale of one to ten, Don Borja gave Recitador a seven for *bravura*, which meant ferocity and willingness to charge. He gave the bull another seven for what he called *toreabilidad*, "bullfightability," meaning the bull's capacity to help the matador by lowering its head and following the cape without hooking left or right. In Don Borja's mind, Recitador had been a good bull overall. Not great, but good.

The chestnut bull with the splotch of lighter fur on its forehead, the one that had scared me in the fields of Jandilla, was Fran's first. The bull's name was Radiante, four years and three months old, weighing some 1,240 pounds. Radiante came out in sluggish fashion and meandered along the fence surrounding the ring, only to perk up when Fran offered it the cape. Radiante did charge well in the horses and the banderillas, but deteriorated in the third of the *muleta*, refusing to lower its head and cutting many of its passes short. This bad characteristic seemed to grow worse during the three series of right-handed *muleta* passes Fran managed to coax out of the bull, and by the time he tried a few left-handed passes, Radiante was all but immobile and therefore useless. Fran killed with a forceful sword thrust and received some applause.

Don Borja added up his impressions. The bull had run well until the end, when its charge had fallen off. He gave Radiante a six for bravery and a four for bullfightability. Not a good bull.

The third bull was Vicioso: black, 1,230 pounds, four years and three months old. It was the first bull of the third matador, a young Madrileño named Eugenio de Mora. Vicioso was a great bull. It charged the *capote* with energy and class, lowered its head and pushed under the pics, and was everything a matador could ask for in the *muleta*. It attacked long and hard and charged with rhythm, allowing de Mora to unfurl a full repertoire of linked passes. The audience got aroused. The band played. But just when everything seemed to be going de Mora's way, Vicioso displayed a touch of the bad humor of its two cousins who'd died before it, and hooked into de Mora's leg.

The matador jerked skyward and thudded to the ground. The bull hit him again, knocking him for a somersault, then sliced its horn into his right buttock. When de Mora finally got to his feet, blood was welling through the fabric of his costume. His banderilleros begged him to go to the infirmary, where the doctors were already preparing to deal with the wounds, but de Mora shook them off, gave the bull a few more passes, and killed it with a single sword, winning a hard-earned ear. Don Borja gave the bull a six for bravery and a nine for bullfightability. When all was said and done, Vicioso was the best bull of the corrida. That was of little comfort to de Mora, however, who went off to the infirmary, not to return that day.

Ortega Cano's second bull of the afternoon, the fourth of the bullfight, was named Pomelo. It was black, four years and three months old, and weighed in at around 1,240 pounds. Pomelo took a good initial rush at the *capote*, but showed an unfortunate desire to wander off at the end of each pass rather than wheel around and come back for more. The bull pressed on under the pain of the horseman's lance, but reverted to its escapist ways in banderillas. Like Recitador before him, Pomelo began cutting his charges short during the final act, making it hard for Ortega Cano to link his passes. The matador seemed unnerved by the bull, and killed it.

Don Borja noted that Pomelo was *noble,* meaning it had been willing to charge the cape without trying to gore the man. But the bull also had had the tendency to be *manso* (tame, or uninterested in fighting). The breeder noted the bull's fine performance in the act of the horses and its disappointing thirst for retreat during banderillas. He judged Pomelo to be straight-charging with the *muleta.* He gave it a seven for bravery and an eight for bullfightability — in his mind a good bull.

Fran's second bull, the fifth of the afternoon, was named Tirador. In a pre-bullfight television interview, Don Borja had predicted it would be the best of the lot, and it was easy to see why. The bull looked great. It was a thickly muscled animal with a powerful hump on its back and horns that spread with the sweep of eagle's wings. Tirador was four years old. It was black and a hefty 1,273 pounds. But when it entered the ring, Tirador had no fight. Rather than charge nobly, the bull preferred to back up against the wall and dare anyone to come in and get it. By the time Fran marched out with his *muleta,* the bull was in such a defensive posture that it didn't charge at all. Fran killed it.

Tirador had attacked the *capote,* Don Borja noted, but without making the kind of long, deep sallies that are most desirable. The bull had turned the banderillas into a dangerous exercise by being on the defensive. "He did not give himself over to the *muleta*," Don Borja wrote. He assigned Tirador a six for bravery and a three for bullfightability. This was the worst bull of the day.

After the corrida Fran was disgusted. "Giving me those bulls was like giving a Formula One racer a truck," he said. "They didn't charge. They didn't say anything. The first one was dangerous, but it wasn't the kind of danger that spoke to the crowd. The second was *manso, manso, manso.* I had bad luck."

The sixth and final bull was Flagelado, black, 1,230 pounds, four years and a month old. Since de Mora was out of action, Flagelado became the responsibility of the senior matador of the day, Ortega Cano. It was a good bull and got better as the bullfight progressed, striking at the *muleta* and allowing the matador to put together two or three series of nice passes. Unfortunately, Ortega Cano became overexcited and engaged in certain theatrical flourishes between passes—gesturing up at the fans, shouting in triumph, and flouncing around as though this were one of the greatest performances in the history of the Maestranza—which turned the crowd against him. By the time he lined up the bull for the kill, the fans were laughing, whistling, and jeering, and Ortega lost his shot at an ear.

The next day, the Sevilla papers would blame the crowd's rude treatment of Ortega Cano on the presence of an excessive number of Madrileños who had come down from the capital for the *feria*. There was no way, the local critics reasoned, that a well-behaved Sevilla audience would whistle at a matador in that fashion unless it was larded with uncouth savages from the north.

Don Borja gave Flagelado a six and an eight, and marked it down as the second-best animal of the bullfight. It started to rain. Ortega Cano stalked out of the ring and told reporters he was furious with the crowd for turning against him on the final bull. Privately, he probably believed he should have cut an ear. Eugenio de Mora cut the only ear of the day on the best bull of the day, but he was laid up in a hospital room and missed the fine sixth bull, which might have helped him win a rare and historic two-ear afternoon in Sevilla. Fran was depressed. He had drawn the two worst bulls of the corrida. Now all he could do was wait for his second Sevilla performance.

Sevilla, April 18. Fran's second bullfight took place on a bright, hot Thursday afternoon with little breeze. It was a perfect day for a bullfight, and the Maestranza was full, in part because El Juli was on the card. All of the omens were good except one: the bulls. They were from the ranch of Don José Luis Marca, a breeder from Badajoz, in Extremadura, a herd founded on Domecq blood. Don José Luis had brought thirteen animals to Sevilla, only to see the bullring veterinarians reject seven of them for lacking *trapío,* an almost untranslatable word that means something like "the look of a proper fighting bull." The six bulls that were eventually killed in the ring did not exhibit much *trapío,* or anything else for that matter. They were the worst kind of bull from a matador's perspective. They gave the appearance of weakness — falling down a lot on shaky legs — but were deadly to work with because of their marked tendency to cut in on the matador.

Fran was the first performer of the day, and right from the start he made it clear to the audience that he was ready to cut a few ears. While the bullring servants were still smoothing the sand in preparation for the first bull, Fran entered the ring and walked across the sanded circle alone. He stopped about ten feet from the gate to the corrals, and seeing this, the audience began to murmur, and then to applaud. The trumpet sounded and the band stopped playing. There was dead silence in the ring, apart from the cries of swallows as they hunted bugs in the Mediterranean sky. An attendant appeared and swung open the heavy, squeaky wooden gate. Fran dropped to his knees.

Fran was almost in the doorway from which the bull would burst out. He was positioned to perform a *larga cambiada de rodillas a porta gayola,* one of the more dangerous passes a matador can attempt. The moment the bull showed itself, Fran was going to flip his cape over his right shoulder and pray the animal would follow the motion of the cape safely over that shoulder. This was Fran's only hope. On his knees he would be unable to move out of the way, and there was nowhere for the bull to go but over or through him. The wound, if it came, would be a bad one, in the face or the chest. The bull, rushing from its dark stall, would not have time to adjust its eyes to the sunny ring and might not be able to see the cape.

Fran gave a quick nod. The attendant signaled back, then opened an inner door. A heartbeat passed. Then another. Then another. From deep inside the tunnel that led to the corrals came banging and clashing sounds and a human voice calling out — and out trotted the bull, looking a bit disoriented. It loomed in front of Fran. Its head was up and it seemed unaware that Fran was kneeling just underneath its great dewlaps. Fran shouted, *"Hey, toro, hey!"* The bull looked down and surged forward. The bull was in Fran's face. Fran swung the cape. The cape spread out into the air, a purple-yellow flash. The bull lurched right with the motion of the cloth. The bull's horn swooshed past Fran's cheek. The bull was past Fran. *"OLÉ!"*

Fran rose to his feet, cited the bull, and gave one (*"Olé!"*), two (*"Olé!"*), three (*"Olé!"*), four (*"Olé!"*) *verónicas*—each pass slow and measured, Fran's body the picture of relaxation, the bull coming within centimeters of Fran's legs. He finished the series with two half-*verónicas* and a pretty *revolera* pass in which he flicked the cape around his waist in a full circle, the cloth swelling out around his torso like a flower opening in the sun. And Fran walked away with the bull staring in total incomprehension while the crowd got to its feet and poured out its ovation. But that was the best Fran could do with the bull, which lost its will to charge in the act of the *muleta* and had to be killed.

Fran's second bull was a living deathtrap, a hysterical creature that charged without rhythm or reason. It would charge one time, stop the next time, start up again, cut in, cut out, run away, then wheel around asking for more. If Fran had been in a small town, he might have killed the bull and forgotten about it. But this was Sevilla, an afternoon of responsibility, so Fran felt honor bound to do the best he could under the circumstances. The result was an ugly, stuttering exhibition. The only way to squeeze a decent pass out of this bull was to walk right up to it, get in its face, begin the pass, and brace for whatever the bull could do in response. Most times, Fran got through a pass by dodging or blocking the horn, getting spanked by the dangerous flat side of the horn, which can produce a nasty wound that in some cases causes terrible internal bleeding.

Fran got in there and rode out six series of bumpy, choppy, ugly passes, skipping around the bull, getting hit by the horns, bouncing here and there around the ring, chasing after the animal at the beginning of each pass and evading it at the end. While Fran did this, the crowd was silent. Those who didn't understand what they were seeing were bored. Those who did understand were choked with fear. By the time Fran killed, he'd been beaten half silly by the horns and his costume was raked with bull's blood.

"The bull was difficult," Fran said after the corrida. "One pass he was good. One pass he stopped. One pass he came at me. Every pass, the bull would go by me, then turn around on me, then look at the cape, then look at me. The danger of this bull was that if I didn't do what I did, if I didn't stay with him, if I didn't stay with this bull, he would eat me." I asked Fran why he had attempted so many passes with such an animal. "I am hungry," he replied. "I am still hungry. What I said with that bull was: I am going to do something and you will have to deal with me, because I am back."

The following day, the newspapers treated Fran's work with uncharacteristic respect. "It's been quite a while since we've seen a performance as classic and brave as the one turned in by Rivera Ordóñez with the dangerous fourth bull," wrote Juan Posada of *La Razón,* a critic who was no friend of Fran's. "He showed that beautiful passes, which are so often discussed by bullfighting fans, take a back seat when danger rules in the ring. Rivera, bullfighting his guts out, lived up to his family heritage and applied it in the best bit of bullfighting that has been achieved in this *feria.*"

What did Fran get in return for risking his life? Well, he got a nice round of applause and the satisfaction of having lived up to his responsibility. It had been a worthy performance, but worthy doesn't cut ears in Sevilla. You cut ears for something special, something that moves people. Man had proposed. God had disposed. The bulls had discomposed. Another year had passed and Fran had failed to cut an ear in his beloved Sevilla. The toreros had come to town praying for good bulls. The breeders had arrived with what they hoped were their best animals. The aficionados were ready to wave their white handkerchiefs and award ears. But as so often happened in the bull world, the melons, once opened, were more bitter than sweet.

"I had four bulls in Sevilla, and nothing," Fran said. "Madrid is now the second chance for me to say something big. Now I have to put all my hopes into Madrid. I really want it to be good."

El Rocío, April 21. Without a home since the separation from his wife, Fran was living on a tiny horse farm on the edge of El Rocío, a village about an hour south of Sevilla. It was a rustic place, a small thatch-roofed cottage surrounded by uncultivated fields, and it belonged to Juan, the thirty-eight-year-old heir to a modest fortune from his father's shoe factory. Fran loved it there. The paparazzi hadn't discovered it yet — they would in short order — and Fran had everything he needed to stay in shape. Mornings he rode horses, then did some practice cape work, then had a light lunch, a nap, and another exercise session in the afternoon. But the best thing about the place for Fran was the presence of the owner's family. Juan's father and mother made daily visits and treated Fran like a son. It was the kind of steady, low-key parenting Fran never got from his own family.

That afternoon, after the midday nap, Fran showered and put on an immaculate blue suit and a crisp red and blue Hermès tie. He was going to drive into Sevilla and attend the corrida, the final one of the *feria*, which always featured the dreaded Miura bulls. Fran's daughter, Cayetana, and her nanny were staying with him that day, and he had arranged to drop them off with her mother in town before the corrida. Fran, Cayetana, and the nanny got into a green Toyota SUV and took off for Sevilla. Once inside the city, they made their way over the Triana Bridge to a spot across the river from the bullring where Eugenia was waiting, a slender, pretty blonde dressed in a white T-shirt, blue jeans, and tan cowboy boots.

Just then Fran spotted a press photographer standing about fifty feet away from them, snapping pictures. Fran took off after him, but the man hopped on a moped and sped away. Then Fran handed his daughter off to his wife and leaned over to kiss her on the lips, and Eugenia turned her face, leaving him nothing but her cheek, and they parted company, tense and sad.

Outside the bullring was the usual crush. It was time for Fran to be a star. Everywhere there were hands to shake and autographs to sign and women to kiss. During the corrida Fran used the season tickets he'd inherited from his grandfather and sat with the man who managed his business office. It turned out to be a boring corrida, and when it was over Fran disappeared into the crowd.

9

The Outsider

Madrid, May 15. Noël Chandler sat in the kitchen of his elegant two-bedroom flat, sipping strong tea, catching up on the rugby news in the London *Daily Telegraph,* getting ready to begin his day. The odd thing about this very British domestic scene was that it was taking place in Spain's capital city, and Noël was off to meet a ticket scalper in a tapas bar and then attend a bullfight. Although a Welshman by birth, Noël was one of the most maniacal bullfighting aficionados on the planet, a man who had attended more than 940 bullfights over the preceding seven years, an average of around 135 corridas a year, sometimes camping out at *feria* after *feria,* other times driving through the night to follow the exploits of a single matador who'd caught his eye.

Like most bull-obsessed people born in nonbullfighting countries, Noël attended his first corrida on a whim during a vacation and underwent a life-changing, semireligious conversion on the spot. "Looking back, I almost immediately became entranced," said Noël of that corrida, which he saw in 1959 when he was twenty-five. "At first I was captivated by the bulls. But then my interest in the whole thing deepened and I came to regard bullfighting as a world I wanted to inhabit." Noël would go on to organize his entire adult life around bullfighting. He chose a career in computers to earn enough money to feed his habit, took postings in remote foreign offices where his protracted disappearances to Spain wouldn't be noticed, divorced his wife when the relationship got in the way of his obsession, and retired to Madrid at the earliest possible moment to follow the bulls and matadors around Spain.

Noël referred to bullfighting as his "work," and he treated it seriously, reading all he could on the subject and spending his time, money, and energy traveling to see the best corridas. After decades of such devotion he had transformed himself into a consummate expert, not unlike a world-class connoisseur of art, music, or wine. Although he wore his knowledge lightly and almost never bragged about it or showed it off, Noël was an excellent judge of bulls and had wide-ranging taste in matadors. Unlike most English-speaking aficionados, Noël lived in Spain, was fluent in Spanish, had many Spanish friends, and owned flats in Madrid and Pamplona, where he'd been a great bull runner in his day and had lately become something of an elder statesman among the non-Spanish regulars of that city's *feria*.

Ray Mouton summed up Noël this way in *Pamplona,* his book about the running-of-the-bulls festival. "Though he does not talk a lot about *toreo,*" Mouton wrote, "there is no question among critics and aficionados that Chandler knows as much about bullfighting and running the bulls as anyone . . . He is the exception, the foreigner who does know and understand these things the way the Spanish do."

Mouton was right. Noël saw the bullfight as a Spaniard would, not as a picturesque escape from everyday life, but as a part of everyday life. In fact, bullfighting had become more a part of Noël's life than it was for all but a handful of Spanish fans. Yet while Noël could sometimes seem like a Spaniard with a British accent, he remained something of an outsider wherever he went. He was an Englishman in Wales, a Welshman in England, a Spaniard in the British Isles, a Brit in Spain, and a non-torero inside the bull world. As much as he understood the Spanish way of being an aficionado, Noël was an aficionado in his own way. Few Spanish fans traveled beyond their native city to see a bullfight, the way Noël did. In Spanish culture the bullfight is something meant to be enjoyed as part of the hometown *feria*. A fiercely parochial people, the Spanish give their allegiance to family and friends first, then to city and province, and only then to Spain. For that reason, the average Bilbaino bullfighting fan has as little urge to see a bullfight in Málaga as the average Malagueño does to see a bullfight in Bilbao.

Noël also betrayed his non-Spanish roots in the way he'd become friendly with bullfighters, something most Spaniards would never dream of doing. Toreros are celebrities in Spain, but in a much quieter way than movie stars or pop singers or soccer heroes are. The torero plays a special role in Spanish culture, one that requires the maintenance of a certain level of dignity. For the most part, bullfighters do not appear in ads or commercials, nor are they regular guests on chat shows. Aficionados idolize bullfighters, but they do not usually stalk them or dream of being their friend. It is okay for women and children to loiter in hotel lobbies hoping for a kiss or a free publicity photo from their favorite matador, but that is about as far as the adulation goes.

Possessing the zealotry of the converted, non-Spanish aficionados tend to be much more aggressive in their bullfighter love. There aren't many aficionados from nonbullfighting countries — perhaps about five thousand worldwide. Most of them seem to be American and British men in their forties, fifties, and sixties. Most were inspired by Ernest Hemingway. Many use bullfighting as a fantasy escape from their lives back home, and the most committed, the ones who return to Spain summer after summer, tend to chase matadors in a way few Spaniards would. Spanish fans, unless they are part of the bull business or have known a certain matador for years, tend to keep their distance. Instead, it is the foreign bullfight fans who are most likely to be found in matadors' hotel rooms, or consorting with bull breeders in restaurants, or offering impromptu commentary to television reporters.

And the amazing thing was, the bullfighting people ate it all up, relishing behavior in foreign fans they would have scorned had it come from Spaniards. But then Spain is a hierarchical country and the foreigners occupied a position comfortably outside the recognized hierarchy, and could therefore get away with strange behavior. Furthermore, as practitioners of a narrow folk art, bullfighters and bull breeders were always starved for recognition beyond the borders of their homeland.

As a non-Spaniard of Spanish sensibility, Noël was somewhat embarrassed by the behavior of his fellow non-Spanish aficionados. But as a non-Spaniard, he couldn't resist dabbling himself. Noël's great hero was Fran's grandfather Antonio Ordóñez, and Noël was proud that he and Don Antonio had exchanged letters and always greeted each other in bullrings. Noël was in the audience for Fran's historic debut in Sevilla, and given Noël's love for Don Antonio, it took him only seconds to fall for Fran. That first season, Noël attended eighty of Fran's ninety corridas, and eventually Fran and his cuadrilla began to notice Noël's face in the stands each afternoon. The two men met during Fran's second season, in the lobby of some provincial hotel. They ate dinner together and became friends. Kind of.

It was not a friendship of equals, because it depended on Noël's pursuit of Fran. Noël had managed to attend about four hundred of the six hundred bullfights Fran had participated in, but Noël maintained a certain formality around Fran. Noël rarely dropped by Fran's hotel rooms, saving that honor for special occasions, and when he did say hello he was careful not to act as though he and Fran were close. For his part, Fran tended to treat Noël with amused detachment. But he showed great respect for Noël's knowledge of bullfighting; he was always careful to refer to Noël as his "friend," something he did not do with everyone; and he showed genuine concern about Noël's health. Fran honored Noël each year by inviting him to the end-of-season dinner he gave for his traveling crew.

"I know Noël doesn't call me so often because he doesn't want to put me in a bad position," Fran explained. "But he is a friend of mine, so he doesn't have to call me all the time."

Noël Chandler was a tall man and well made. His head was large, oval, and bald, with a wreath of shaggy black hair. A bushy M-shaped brow dominated his face. Beneath this hairy cornice, each feature seemed to sag somewhat into the feature beneath. The eyes drooped into a downward-turning nose, which hung over a mouth that frowned its way to a strong chin. It was a face that might have given the impression that its owner was a timid, melancholy fellow, were it not for the ready smile that flashed in the mouth and the eyes, and the fierce crosshatched scars on each cheek, trophies of violent work done in Her Majesty's West Indies Regiment and on the rugby field. Seeing Noël on a fine spring morning in Madrid, happy and fit, you would not believe he was sixty-eight years old.

That afternoon Noël had to go see his scalper, whom I will call El Grande. "Why does my life revolve around this man?" Noël said.

El Grande and Noël did plenty of business, because the Madrid *feria* was the longest and most varied bullfight fair of the season, a marathon bull slaughter that ran from May 11 to June 8 and encompassed twenty-four regular corridas, three *novilladas,* and three *corridas de rejones*— thirty events in all, twenty-nine of them back-to-back. Noël planned to attend most of them, and as it happened had inherited the season pass of a journalist friend who was too ill with cancer to use it. But the pass was only a single seat, and Noël had promised to buy tickets for various friends from out of town, and that was where El Grande came in.

Each time Noël needed tickets from El Grande, he followed the same routine. Noël lived in the center of Madrid, in the old part of the city known as the Madrid of the Austrians, after the Hapsburg kings who ruled Spain in the sixteenth and seventeenth centuries. Making his way through tight, winding streets barely wide enough for cars, past spired churches and dusty little shops, Noël walked to the Plaza Santa Ana, a large square lined with tapas bars. On the square was an unassuming restaurant that was a notorious taurine hangout. (Any person, place, or thing related to bullfighting can be described as *taurino* in Spanish, taurine in English.)

Once inside, Noël went to the bar, ordered his first beer of the day, and waited. (Like many people who follow the bulls, Noël was a committed and accomplished consumer of alcohol.) At around two-thirty, the doors of the bar swung open and in marched a phalanx of about ten seedy-looking men engrossed in some argument, shouting theatrically, shoving and gesturing at one another, filling the small bar with their presence. These men were involved in the resale of bullfight tickets. They were part of a loose gray market comprising legitimate brokers dealing in tickets with a government-sanctioned twenty percent markup, scalpers who sold whatever tickets they could scrounge, and people who did a bit of both. At the center of this group was a tall, aging gray man in a tall, aging gray suit. He was bald and had the barrel chest and ham-hock fists and megaphone voice of an army drill sergeant. This was El Grande.

There was no way for Noël and El Grande to miss each other in that small bar, but El Grande made a great show of ignoring Noël, and Noël did not get up from his seat. Five or ten minutes passed. Finally Grande looked around, pretended he'd suddenly noticed Noël, rushed over, and clapped him on the back. "Ah, No-ayyyl," Grande shouted in his howitzer voice. "How's it going?" Grande insisted on buying Noël a glass of wine, and he launched into a discussion of his favorite topic, which was his own honesty and forthrightness.

"We are old friends, aren't we?" said Grande with a grin.

"Yes, we are," agreed a much less enthusiastic Noël.

"I always give you the best seats, and for good prices," Grande continued. "I never make an excessive profit on my friends."

"No, no, you always are very kind."

"Well, you see, I am from Aragón . . ."

Aragón is a landlocked region in the foothills of the Pyrenees, on Spain's border with France. Aragón is famous for being windy and sparsely populated, for the terrible battles fought there during the Spanish Civil War, for being the birthplace of the painter and printmaker Francisco Goya, and for breeding the most honest people in Spain—a bit of folk wisdom that has wider currency in Aragón than anywhere else.

After a half hour of everyone's life had ticked away, after the ignoring, the drink-buying, and the chatting, El Grande stopped and said, "So, you want some tickets for the corrida today?" This was a rhetorical question, since Noël had given Grande a wish list of tickets for each corrida of the *feria* some weeks before. But Grande liked to hear again what Noël wanted. So Noël ran through the information and Grande took out a sheet of paper and made extensive notes. Then he extracted a wad of crumpled tickets from somewhere within the folds of his suit, counted out the number and type Noël had requested, and pressed them into Noël's hands.

The process was nearly over, but not quite. Because at that very moment, when a price should have been set and money exchanged, Grande suddenly walked away from Noël and rejoined his pals. Noël went back to the bar. Time passed. Again Grande made a show of rediscovering Noël. Again he clapped him on the back. Again a glass of wine was shared. Then, and only then, did Noël ask for a price, and Grande told him, but briskly, as though the naming of a price and the proffer of money were a dirty piece of business and a distraction from a lovely afternoon's meeting between old friends.

Noël could now return home. It was exhausting, but he had to do it every time he wanted tickets, because El Grande sold only day by day. This was an involved type of relationship to have with a scalper, but it came out of El Grande's sense of personal honor. Personal honor is still an important thing in Spain, and it colors most dealings between people. Spanish culture is innately aristocratic. As one writer famously said, in Spain even taxi drivers behave like dukes. This means that no one in Spain will admit to doing anything for money alone. That would be unseemly. Work may be done for pride, for artistry, to strengthen bonds of kinship and friendship, to support society, and to uphold tradition. But it is never done solely for profit. El Grande was a scalper, and one supposes he did it for the money. Why else scalp tickets? To maintain his sense of honor, however, he felt the need to act as if he and his clients were old friends who happened to run into each other at their favorite bar, shared a few drinks, and, oh yeah, bought and sold tickets.

One day during that *feria*, Grande and Noël were in the middle of their ritual when a slender man dressed in a slick suit and coifed like a game-show host interrupted the proceedings. This was a man I'll call El Cabello, a rival scalper who dropped into El Grande's bar on a break from his usual post in another taurine hangout on the Plaza Santa Ana. When El Cabello saw El Grande with Noël, he came up and shot both of them an angry stare. Immediately El Grande glared back.

"Noël," said El Cabello, who looked hurt that Noël wasn't buying from him, "we've known each other for thirty years, haven't we?"

"Yes," Noël replied, "we have."

This was a direct challenge to El Grande, who couldn't let it stand. (Honor!)

"Well, I've known Noël for twenty-nine years myself," Grande insisted.

El Cabello shot Noël a sharp look, as if to say, "Is this true?"

Grande stared back at Cabello, as if to reply, "You bet it is."

Noël was besieged on two fronts. Cabello was right on the facts. Grande was doing a bit of exaggerating. But Noël wanted to keep El Grande in his good graces, because his sense of honor led him to charge comparatively little for his tickets, usually no more than the twenty percent markup. Whereas El Cabello was somewhat less encumbered in the Spanish-honor department and charged as much as he thought he could get. Later that day, Noël told an anecdote about El Cabello. One afternoon Noël was walking outside the bullring of some Spanish town when Cabello drove into view at the wheel of an enormous, shiny new Mercedes-Benz.

"That's a nice car you have there, Cabello," said Noël, not without a trace of condescension.

Cabello pulled the big car alongside Noël and leaned out of the driver-side window.

"Do you like it?" Cabello asked.

"Yes, very much."

"That's good," Cabello said, "because you paid for it."

10

Sun and Shadow

Madrid comes as a disappointment to the casual visitor. Its streets are congested with traffic. Its people can be gruff and unfriendly. The weather is almost always too hot or too cold. Most of all, Madrid doesn't look like the tourist's idea of a European capital. The predominant architectural style is modern and utilitarian. This is partly due to the fact that Madrid is a young city by European standards, not much older than Boston or New York, and so it lacks the quantity of beautiful and venerable buildings that adorn other Old World capitals. It is also due to the horrible damage Madrid suffered in the fierce fighting of the Spanish Civil War and to the rampant development carried out by the right-wing dictatorship of Generalissimo Francisco Franco, which lasted from 1939 until Franco's death in 1975.

Nevertheless, once a visitor knows Spain, he can't help loving Madrid, which manages to be the most cosmopolitan city in the country while reflecting the enduring essence of the Spanish people and their culture. Madrid is a desert town. It sits more than two thousand feet above sea level, atop the high Spanish *meseta*. The summers are ghastly hot, but summer nights are cool and the outdoor cafés stay open till dawn. The winters can be freezing, but the air is crisp and clear on cold days and the snowy mountains of the Sierra Guadarrama are visible in the distance. Madrid may be a young city with little indigenous culture in comparison to a place like Sevilla, but all of Spain is in Madrid, in its museums, its churches, its royal palaces, in its restaurants, and even in its people, a grand mix of immigrants from across the country.

Most cities come to a halt during their *ferias,* but not Madrid. The city is too big and too obsessed with business to slow down for the annual Feria de San Isidro. During the fair — which is dedicated to the local patron saint, a peasant who saw a vision — the city government sponsors exhibitions and performances at various venues. But apart from the deafening concerts in the city's vast main square, the Plaza Mayor, it is hard to see much evidence of a *feria* around town. Executives and secretaries continue to fill the bars for their traditional eleven o'clock breakfast break. Rich ladies go on shopping in the Salamanca neighborhood. Families stroll the Retiro Park. Ministers debate in parliament. Lines form to see the paintings by Titian, Rubens, Bosch, Veláz-quez, and Goya in the Prado Museum, and tourists and students wander the tapas bars in the old town.

Madrid's *feria* is most strongly felt at the bullring, the Plaza de Toros Monumental de las Ventas de Espiritu Santo. Las Ventas, as it is known, opened for business in 1931. It seats twenty-three thousand people and is the largest bullring in Spain. (The largest in the world is Plaza México, the forty-five-thousand-seat monstrosity in Mexico City.) Las Ventas is also the most prestigious ring in the world. A bullfighter who has taken the *alternativa* in another ring must repeat the ceremony the next time he performs in Madrid, to "confirm" his status as a matador. Despite its renown, most toreros dread appearing in Las Ventas, and would avoid it if they could, because it is an uncomfortable place to work. The wind gusts constantly on the arena floor, threatening to blow the bullfighters' capes in the air, exposing their bodies; the bulls purchased for corridas there are always the largest and meanest available.

But the worst thing about Las Ventas, from the torero's perspective, is the crowd. It is a big-city crowd, the kind that revels in its reputation for being knowledgeable and demanding. On an average day, a Madrid audience ranges in emotion from total indifference to raging hostility. Fran once said the people in Madrid don't come to the bullring for enjoyment, they come to give matadors a final exam. It is emblematic of the Las Ventas attitude that it is one of the only rings in Spain where the band doesn't play when a matador is doing well. In Madrid, music is seen as a frivolity. The bullfight may be an art form in the rest of Spain, but in the capital it is a bloody struggle, and the fans make it that way. Said Fran: "In Madrid you fight with the wind, you fight with the bulls, you fight with the people." Apart from its scale and the roughness of its fans, however, Las Ventas is a typical bullring. It consists of a circular stadium surrounded by outbuildings, which include corrals for the bulls, stables for the drag mules and the picadors' horses, an infirmary, and a chapel for the toreros to pray in. (By law, all bullrings must have chapels.) Like most Spanish rings, Las Ventas is equipped with an aging sound system that is almost never used — the music is provided by an unamplified band, there is no electronic scoreboard, and the interior of the ring is devoid of advertising. There is no law prohibiting advertising in bullrings, but by tradition the important rings refrain from spoiling the atmosphere with billboards. Bullrings in Latin America are much less fastidious on this front.

As in all bullrings, the sanded floor of Las Ventas is painted with two concentric circles, the first circle about seven and a half yards in from the fence that surrounds the ring, the second some ten yards farther in. These circles divide the sand into a three-ringed bull's-eye pattern, which provides some visual order to the geography of what would otherwise be featureless, and helps the picadors to correctly position their horses when receiving the bull's charge. The outer band of sand, between the fence and the first painted circle, is called *las tablas*. The narrow middle band is *los tercios*. The area generally corresponding to the inner circle is *los medios*.

The wooden fence around the sand is called the *barrera*. It is about five feet high and made of thick red-painted wooden planks set into grooved stone posts. A low, white-painted step runs along the base of the fence, inside and out. This gives the bullfighters a toehold when they need to vault in or out of the ring under duress. For more relaxed entries and exits, the *barrera* is broken by a series of narrow openings, each with a section of fencing set about a foot in front of it, leaving enough space for a man and not enough for a bull. These protected openings are known as *burladeros,* from the Spanish word that means "to trick" or "to joke." Between the *barrera* and the first row of seats is the passageway called the *callejón.*

Until the eighteenth century, bullfights mostly took place in city squares and palace courtyards, which may be why the Spanish name for bullring is *plaza de toros,* simply an open space in which bullfights are held. In Madrid corridas were mounted in the Plaza Mayor, which could accommodate fifty thousand spectators. From the beginning of the seventeenth century until 1855, around 250 so-called royal bullfights were staged in the Plaza Mayor to celebrate an event in the life of the royal family. These weren't like the bullfights we know, with a matador on foot, but the archaic and aristocratic type in which horsemen, usually nobles, used spears to kill bulls, with the assistance of commoners on foot.

As bullfighting on foot grew in popularity during the eighteenth century, Spaniards began constructing stadiums for their bull events. This does not seem unusual from a modern perspective, but it was viewed as a radical step at the time. The new *plazas de toros* of the eighteenth century were the first stadiums erected in Europe since the last great arenas of the ancient Romans fifteen hundred years before. One of the oldest active *plazas* is in Béjar. It was first used in the 1500s. Other early rings include the *plazas* at Campofrío (1718), Zaragoza (1764), Sevilla (1761), and Ronda (1785). These rings were built by charities, which held the exclusive right to mount bullfights, to raise money. In the nineteenth century rings were built purely for profit. Important nineteenth-century *plazas* still in use include those of Valencia (1851), El Puerto de Santa María (1880), and Valladolid (1890).

Despite the violent political upheavals of the twentieth century, the Spanish continued to construct bullrings at a merry pace. An 1880 government census found there were around 105 *plazas* in Spain; by 2001 that number had risen to about 350, with more being built. Most of Spain's bullrings are small, with an average seating capacity of 5,000, and a mere handful seat more than 15,000. The government classifies the *plazas* of Barcelona, Bilbao, Córdoba, Madrid, San Sebastián, Sevilla, Valencia, and Zaragoza as first-category rings, meaning they are large and each one mounts more than fifteen bull events a year, at least ten of those being proper corridas. (Though it isn't by law, Pamplona is also considered to be first-category.) The rings of provincial capitals, as well as a handful of other rings of some importance, are classified as second-category, with all remaining fixed rings as third-category. Portable rings are fourth-category. The regulations controlling bullfights are less stringent in the lower-category rings, and toreros and breeders are paid less to perform in them. Seats in bullrings are priced according to their proximity to the sand and whether they will fall in shade or sunlight during the corrida. Seats in the shade cost twice as much on average as seats in the sun. There are two reasons for this. First, when the bullfighters aren't in action they stand in the shaded half of the *callejón,* and this is where the bulls are pic'd. Second, most fans will pay top price to avoid the savage power of the Spanish sun. In the early evening, when most corridas are held, the sun sinks quickly, casting the ring in ever-increasing shadow, and the visual drama of the *plaza* bisected into sun and shade is a vital part of the aesthetics of the event. "The theory, practice and spectacle of bullfighting have all been built on the assumption of the presence of the sun," wrote Hemingway, "and when it does not shine over a third of the bullfight is missing. The Spanish say *'El sol es el mejor torero.'* The sun is the best bullfighter, and without the sun the best bullfighter is not there. He is like a man without a shadow."

The seating in a bullring is divided into pie-wedge sections called *tendidos.* The Madrid ring has ten of them. *Tendidos* one, two, nine, and ten are sold as *sombra,* meaning they are in shadow throughout the bullfight. During the season in question, the best *sombra* seats in Madrid cost $105 each. *Tendidos* three and eight are *sol y sombra* (sun and shade), meaning they begin the bullfight in sunlight and end it in shadow. These seats are priced less than *sombra.* The rest of the ring is *sol* (sun), the cheapest seats. They cost as little as $3.50 each, for the back rows. In Madrid, the *sol* sections are *tendidos* four, five, and six, as well as the notorious and reviled *tendido siete,* section seven, where the toughest hecklers in bullfighting sit.

Most bullrings do not have seats, in the commonly understood sense of the word. The standard bullring seating consists of rows of stone steps with numbers stenciled on them to mark a place for each spectator. The steps are cold, dirty, and unyielding to human flesh, and every *plaza* in Spain has a cushion-renting concession, usually run for the benefit of a local charity. For less than $2 you are given a small padded square to put between your backside and hard reality. The seating is hellishly cramped. Fans sit thigh to sweaty thigh, with knees pressing into the back of the person in the row ahead. In a different country this might provoke fisticuffs on a regular basis, but the Spanish are endlessly good-natured about this sort of thing and brawls during corridas are rare.

Given how expensive, difficult, uncomfortable, and unrewarding it is to follow bullfighting, it is amazing that anyone becomes an aficionado. Few forms of entertainment yield their pleasures as slowly or sparingly. To properly understand a bullfight, the spectator needs technical knowledge of the execution of scores of passes, of pic'ing, of banderillas, and of killing, as well as a grounding in the history of bullfighting and its multitudinous local traditions — not to mention a knowledge of bulls, which is a subject complex enough for a lifetime of study. Without a good bit of this information, the spectator will never view bullfighting as anything more than an intermittently thrilling, but mostly boring, spectacle that can also be a revolting bloodbath.

It is axiomatic among aficionados that bullfighting is almost impossible to comprehend fully, even for Spaniards, even for toreros. "This is a very difficult subject to know about," said Fran's great-uncle, the famous matador Dominguín. "I would say that only ten percent of matadors have any real understanding of bullfighting."

The technical side is just the start for the aspiring aficionado, however, because the only way to become a true connoisseur is to attend a large number of corridas — and that's a thing not many people can do. The fact is, there are few bullfights to see. In Europe, they are held regularly in Spain, France, and Portugal; in the Americas, Mexico, Guatemala, Venezuela, Colombia, Ecuador, Peru, and Bolivia mount corridas. But Mexico and Spain are the only countries with enough bull events to provide a steady diet, and even a Spaniard or a Mexican would have to do a fair amount of traveling within his or her country to see a large number of bullfights, since a mere handful of cities mount more than five corridas a year, and this travel would be too expensive and time-consuming for any save the idle rich.

Bullfights do appear on television, especially in Spain and Mexico, but a televised corrida is to a live corrida what pornography is to sex. You can learn a lot from video, but not what you really need to know, which is the emotion of the thing. Bullfighting is an art of feelings, and it depends for its effects on the charged atmosphere of the ring and the visceral impact of being in the presence of a large wild animal — things that are not well conveyed onscreen, and that's assuming the bullfight is a good one. In fact, most bullfights are awful. For a great bullfight you need ferocious bulls matched with matadors willing to risk themselves, a combination that rarely occurs. As a Spanish proverb goes, "When the bulls are great the matadors fail to show, and when the matadors are willing the bulls are lousy."

Despite its ornery nature, and in defiance of the millions of people worldwide who would like to see it banned, bullfighting thrives, even flourishes, around the globe. The most concrete evidence for this assertion is that the number of corridas mounted each year has been rising sharply throughout the past hundred years. According to the Spanish government, there were 864 corridas in Spain alone during the season chronicled in this book. That's up from the 513 corridas in 1990, the 323 in 1960, and the 209 in 1904. A similar sort of growth is chartable in France and Latin America, though bullfighting as a spectacle seems to be dying out in Portugal, where it is illegal to kill the bull in public.

In Spain, the surprising growth of the bullfight is usually attributed to three things. First, the Spanish economy boomed in the post-Franco years, and greater wealth has led to greater demand for leisure activities. Second, Spain joined the European Union during this time, and that internationalist move spawned a predictable backlash of interest in all things seen as singularly Spanish. Third, tourism has risen dramatically, making Spain the second-most-visited country on earth, and many tourists like to catch a bullfight.

Anti-bullfighting advocates are fond of claiming that the bullfight would die in Spain if not for the support of tourists, but the facts don't bear this out. Government statistics show that the majority of corridas are held off the tourist track — for example, in places like Murcia, Gijón, and Albacete, provincial cities that do not overflow with foreigners. And even in the big tourist centers it is still Spaniards who support the bullfights. Take Madrid and Sevilla. Both rings are packed during their spring *ferias*, the bullfights that the Madrileños and Sevillanos want to see. Yet both rings are virtually empty during their non-*feria* bullfights, even though these take place in midsummer, at the peak of the tourist season.

Bullfighting is everywhere in Spain. The newspapers cover it. Television broadcasts it. Posters for corridas fill the streets, as they have done since bullfighting was invented, announcing corridas in grandiose language that is familiar to aficionados everywhere. "With permission of the authority," the posters typically read, "and if the weather does not impede the spectacle, six wild and beautiful bulls will be pic'd, banderilla'd, and put to death by the sword." Restaurants and bars display bullfighting photos. Bullrings dominate city architecture. The countryside is riddled with bull-breeding ranches. Bullfighting is often called *la fiesta nacional,* and it has a semiofficial status. Most bullfights are presented with some financial assistance from the government, especially in small towns, and most bullrings are municipally owned. Political leaders are often seen at big corridas, as are members of the royal family. It is no accident that bullfights are held during *ferias,* which are civic celebrations. There's a sense that attending a bullfight is a way to support town and country, king and culture.

Yet it would be a gross distortion of reality to suggest that Spain is a land of bulls and bullfighters. Most Spaniards go about their lives in blissful ignorance of bullfighting, spending their leisure time and money on television, movies, music, the Internet, and professional sports, especially soccer. The so-called national festival of bullfighting isn't really. Polls taken on the Spanish public's attitudes toward bullfighting show that around half the country disapproves of the spectacle, with around thirty percent enthusiastically for it and the rest indifferent. But the people who say they are against bullfighting can't be very against it or they would do something about it, and the fact is that there is little organized opposition to bullfighting in Spain. It exists, but it fails to generate much of a response.

Bullfighting is not part of the local culture in every corner of Spain. The four great areas of bullfighting are the south (Andalucía), the center (Madrid, Castilla–La Mancha, Castilla-León), the northeast (Aragón, Navarra, and the Basque Country), and Valencia. There's hardly any bull culture in the northwest (Galicia and Asturias), and there is outright hostility to bullfighting in Spain's second city, Barcelona, which prides itself on being a pan-European capital, and where the bullfight is associated with *Españolismo* (always said with a sneer), which means anything having to do with traditional — read: backward — Spain.

Even in places where the people love bullfighting, the number actually willing or able to buy a ticket and see a corrida is relatively small. Sevilla, which has a population of around eight hundred thousand, may be the most bull-crazy city in Spain, but the Maestranza bullring seats fewer than thirteen thousand, and most of those seats are filled by fans with season subscriptions who occupy their seats day after day. Thus, in total, a small number of Sevillanos actually attend a corrida during the *feria*—certainly less than ten percent of the population. Nor is there a large television audience for bullfighting. The number of corridas broadcast on the national networks is tiny in comparison to soccer matches.

But for that haunted minority of fans, the bullfight is an overwhelming obsession. It is the only spectacle left in the world that offers such a mixture of beauty and violence, art and blood, national pride and primordial urge, the fascination of wild animals and of death. Both the bullfighters and their fans are addicted to the emotional buildup of the corrida day: the waiting and worrying; then the bullring with all its theatricality, ceremony, and music; the big crowd, the tension of the bullfight itself, and the moment when the tension breaks; when man and bull find their rhythm, and what was violence and ugliness resolves itself for a brief moment, perhaps, into something more.

11

❖——❖◦❀◦❖——❖

The Little Venom

Madrid, May 15. Silence . . .

The sun was high in the sky, but inside the two-room hotel suite the curtains were drawn and the double-paned windows blocked out the noise of the city. Everything was quiet and dark. There was a click at the door and Nacho padded into the luxurious sitting room, which was all done up in Christmas colors, reds and greens. Nacho held a teacup filled with olive oil, a candlewick floating on the surface. He put the teacup down on the table, went to the door that led to the bedroom, and eased the door open. A television glowed inside. Fran was curled up on the bed, a rumpled shape beneath the covers. Laid out on a chair beside him was a light blue bullfighter's costume.

Nacho puttered around a bit, and soon Fran stirred. He said something and Nacho replied and the two men took up the thread of what seemed to be a continuing conversation. After a few lazy moments Fran climbed out of bed, got down on the floor, and began his stretching routine. He wore blue pajama bottoms and one of those T-shirts sold in the tourist shops of Sevilla. The shirt read, *Joé, que caló!* (Fuck, it's hot!) Except the proper Spanish — *Joder, que calor!* — was spelled phonetically to render the sound of a thick Andalucían accent, in which certain consonants and all word endings are swallowed.

Fran sat on the floor, straightened his legs, and touched his toes. Nacho sat on the edge of the bed, watching his boss at work. Nacho was a heavyset man in his late thirties. He was dressed like an executive, in a dark blue suit, dress shirt, pink necktie, and brown tasseled loafers. The first of Fran's two afternoons of responsibility in the Madrid ring was about to begin, and Nacho knew better than to show up in anything less than his best clothes. The matador didn't tolerate personal sloppiness from his staff on a day like this one.

"I'd do some stretching myself," Nacho said, "but I'd split my pants."

Fran smiled and headed for the shower, and soon there was steam coming out from under the bathroom door. After a few minutes Fran emerged in his signature white towel, his wet black hair neatly combed. Fran dropped the towel. He took a pair of flesh-colored pantyhose and rolled them over his legs, thighs, and buttocks and up to his midriff. Then he slipped on a white tank-top undershirt. Fran sat on the bed and pulled on his socks. These were the traditional bullfighter's socks: salmon-colored with an arrow design over each calf. The socks went over the knees, where they were held in place with tight plastic garters. Then it was time to put on the bullfighter's costume itself, known as the *traje de luces* (suit of lights), because of the way the sun shines off the elaborate gold decorations, filigree, baubles, tassels, and beads.

Fran stood up, cupped his genitals in both hands, and shifted them to his left thigh. Nacho stood holding the knee-length breeches of the costume open and Fran stepped into one leg and then the other. Nacho hiked the pants up, holding them by the back of the waist, pulling hard until he had lifted Fran into the air, wedging the fabric into the crack of Fran's bottom, pressing Fran's penis and testicles against his left thigh like shrink-wrapped meat in a grocery freezer. Crammed into his pants, the fly still unbuttoned, Fran went to the writing table beside the bed and laid out the framed and unframed images of Jesus, the Virgin Mary, the Holy Family, an assortment of saints, and crosses, medals, and amulets. There were more than forty objects in total and they covered the table.

Fran took a clipper and cut and filed his fingernails—this to prevent a stray nail from getting caught on the fabric of the capes while he worked. Nacho set out Fran's shoes, the traditional black-leather pumps with a neat bow over the toes, and Fran stepped into them and then buttoned his fly. Slowly, so as not to muss his hair, Fran put on his bullfighter's hat. This was a deep skullcap of black woven fabric with a ball of the same material over each ear, which at some angles looked not unlike a Mickey Mouse hat. Nacho attached a fake pigtail to the hair at the back of Fran's head with a bobby pin, just beneath the cap. Then Fran slipped into a ruffled tuxedo shirt, tied a thin black necktie around his neck, and shrugged himself into the braces attached to his pants. Nacho wound a sash around Fran's waist and helped Fran into the vest of the suit and the heavy waist-length jacket with wide epaulets and holes in the armpits for greater mobility.

Silence . . .

Fran took a deep breath, blowing the air out through his nose. Then he did it again. Nacho closed the curtains in the bedroom, turned off the lights, brought out a bottle of cologne, and sprayed a few shots into the air. Nacho retrieved the teacup of olive oil from the sitting room and placed it in front of Fran's saints. Then Nacho retired from the bedroom, now bathed in cathedral gloom. The air was purified by the perfume. Fran stood before his saints. His back to the world, like a priest saying Mass in the old Roman rite, Fran crossed himself, took each saint off the table, kissed it, and laid it down again. Fran struck a match and lit the wick in the teacup. He bowed his head and prayed, slowly and with care.

The ritual was over. Fran turned and walked away, shutting the door behind him. No one would be allowed to enter the room or to disturb Fran's saints or the candle until Fran had returned safely from the bullfight. It was time to go. Nacho and Fran walked out of the suite and into the empty hallway of the hotel. The elevator arrived, and it too was empty. Nacho and Fran rode down in the elevator saying nothing.

Silence . . .

The elevator doors swung open and they were in the world again. Heat. Brightness. Mirrors. Lights. People shouted. Doors slammed. Cameras flashed. A group of Japanese tourists stared. Paparazzi and tabloid TV cameramen shoved each other, trying to get a good shot of Fran. Telephones rang at the reception desk. *"Hola, buenas tardes, Hotel Wellington."* Someone called to Fran in Spanish: "Fran, Fran, may I have your autograph?" Nacho and Fran made their way through the crowd and out the front door of the hotel. Air. Sun. Traffic. Shoes clicked on the sidewalk. More shouting. The lights of video cameras were in their faces. The minibus was at the curb and Fran's cuadrilla of assistant bullfighters was inside. Fran and Nacho hopped in and the doors closed with a thud.

Silence . . .

The minibus took off, heading north on the Calle Velázquez, and no one in the bus had much to say. The atmosphere was uptight, even a bit somber. The bus's engine hummed. Three paparazzi on motorbikes zigged and zagged around the bus, trying to get some footage of Fran through the windows. The sad story of Fran's marital troubles was still raging in the pink press. Eugenia was giving interviews, saying things like, "If Fran says he is the guilty one, then he must be." There was also news about Fran's mother. It seemed Carmen Ordóñez had checked herself into a Madrid clinic to be treated for addiction to sleeping pills, this following a television appearance in which she had seemed intoxicated to many viewers.

Fran sat in the center row of seats, strategically placed as far from the windows as possible, staring forward. His team of three banderilleros, Nacho, the assistant manservant Antonio, and the *apoderado* sat around Fran. The two picadors had gone ahead in a taxi. They needed to be at the bullring early, to choose their horses and get accustomed to them. This was the worst time of the corrida day for the bullfighters. The preparation — the liturgical progression of lunch, nap, the dressing, and saying one's prayers — had ended. The relaxation — the shower, the beers in the hotel lobby, and the dinner — was still far away. In between this alpha and omega was the bullfight, two hours of stage fright, risk, and violence. Some toreros thrived on it. Others dreaded it. Either way, they could lose themselves in it once it had started. But in the bus there was nothing to do except worry. There was no distraction except to stare out the window at the people in the streets. Regular people. People who were never bitten by what the Spanish call "the little venom of the bulls." People who strolled and shopped and sat in cafés, serene in the enjoyment of peace and safety.

The bus turned east through quiet streets of seven- and eight-story art nouveau buildings. Presently the road emptied into a wide avenue, the Calle Alcalá, which was jammed with rush-hour traffic. The driver, Pepe, did his best to inch forward in a herky-jerky progress until he broke through the jam and the buildings gave way and the bus was in a massive open space surrounded by highways on one side and housing projects on the others. In the center of this void squatted the hulking old ring. There were people all around it, swarming like insects, dwarfed by the scale of their surroundings.

The bus circled the ring until it came to the back entrance, the *patio de cuadrillas* (patio of the matadors' teams). A small crowd waited there. The minibus waded into the crowd and stopped. The people closed in around its doors.

Silence . . .

The doors opened and the bullfighters piled into the tumult. The wind blew. The picadors' horses smelled of animal and fear. They shied and fussed. Their hooves clopped on the stone floor. A siren wailed in the distance. Fans were everywhere. They shouted at the toreros, laughing and pushing, happy to be inside the bullring on the day of an important corrida, happy that the wait was about to end. Someone begged Fran for an autograph. People clapped him on the back. "Good luck, matador," they said. The bullfighters walked through the crowd and into the gate. The wait was over.

The band began to play, but you could hardly hear it in the vastness of the ring. The atmosphere of Las Ventas was distinct from that of the Maestranza. Everything in the Sevilla ring suggested warmth and intimacy, whereas in Madrid the palette was cool: gray sand, gray stone, and a wintry audience. The parade of bullfighters seemed tiny in the packed monumentality of the ring. The parade ended and the toreros strung themselves out along the *barrera* fence, making practice passes. It was a scene out of an impressionist picture. Degas would have done it justice. The circus costumes, the capes spinning like purple and yellow pinwheels, the sun and shadow, and the great throng rising in the bowl of the ring. This might have been an afternoon in Degas's time, or a century before that, or a century later. Apart from the clothes the audience wore, there was little in the panorama to give historical context, and Princess Elena and her husband were seated in the royal box.

The bulls were from the brand of the Heirs of Don Baltasar Ibán, raised just outside Madrid. Fran's first was black, a five-year-old that weighed some twelve hundred pounds. The bull marched out of the gate and looked around. One of Fran's assistants — hiding behind a *burladero,* across the ring from the bull — flicked his cape in the air, and the bull saw the blaze of purple cloth and made for it. Loose-muscled and sure, its small hooves beating muffled clops, the bull crossed the sand and skidded to a halt just before the *burladero* where the assistant bullfighter had ducked out of sight. Lacking a target, the animal turned away and made for the center of the ring. Then the assistant jumped up again, attracting the bull's attention and holding it near the *burladero.*

Fran, sheltered in his own *burladero,* just down the line from the one where his assistant was keeping the bull occupied, studied the bull in motion, watching how it responded to the cape and how it moved, formulating a strategy to deal with it. He slid out onto the sand, set himself near the fence, called to the bull, and gave a signature series of *verónicas*, which he closed with a sweet half-*verónica*. This would have met with an enthusiastic response in most other bullrings, but the Madrid crowd could hardly muster more than a few *olés* and scattered applause. The dominant sound from the stands was the rumble of thousands of people ignoring a bullfight.

Bullfighting can inspire strong passions, and throughout history there have been riots at bullfights, usually in response to bad bulls. But the most surprising thing about bullfighting crowds is how decorous they are. In Britain or the United States, a spectacle as violent as bullfighting would probably attract the kind of young male audience that would come to the arena to drink, see some blood spilled, and get into a few fights. In Spain, however, bad behavior is not part of the bullfighting culture. In big cities the audience tends to be drawn from the upper end of society, at least in the shaded seats, and from serious aficionados in the sun. Corridas are another place to see and be seen, to dress one's best and blow air kisses, or to prove one's devotion to the *fiesta nacional*. In small towns bullfights are a family affair, which in Spain means everyone from great-grandpa to the newborn baby. Non-Spaniards see the violence in bullfighting as transgressive and provocative; the Spanish don't share that view. They see the violence as part of the spectacle, not the point of the spectacle, and so are not aroused by it — at least in public ways.

The only part of the Madrid crowd that seemed engaged with this bullfight was seated in the sun, in section seven (*tendido siete*). These fans clapped in rhythm, whistled, jeered, mooed, stood on their seats, and made furious speeches. Their main target wasn't Fran, but rather the bull breeder and the bullring authority. The hecklers of section seven considered themselves to be fine judges of bull flesh, and having seen Fran's bull for a full sixty seconds, they had determined that it was a weak specimen and should be returned to the corrals. This was possible within the rules of bullfighting. Bulls were replaced all the time, especially in first-category *plazas* like Madrid's. This afternoon, though, the president of the corrida ignored section seven and signaled for the picadors to make their entrance.

The bull charged the horse, digging its horns into the padded overcoat and receiving a solid jolt from the spear, which the bull ducked away from, shy of the pain. Section seven increased its howling, whistling, and clapping. They weren't offended by the cruelty of the pic'ing for horse or bull. They were annoyed that the bull was so weak, and given that it was so weak, further annoyed that it was receiving so much punishment from the picador, punishment that might ruin the bull for the rest of the corrida.

Just then a voice—loud and high-pitched like a starter's whistle—swooped down from section seven in a way that could be heard throughout the ring. "Whom is the bullring president defending?" the voice said, implying that the official had refused to send Fran's bull back to the corrals because he was in cahoots with the breeder and the bullring management. Fran paid no attention to this, and brought the bull around in front of the picador again for another charge at the horse, the picador shooting his lance into the bull's back with energy.

"Enough, enough, enough, enough, enough, enough!" cried the same piercing voice from section seven, suggesting that this bull could no longer withstand more punishment.

The act of the horsemen ended, and Fran's assistants on foot placed the banderillas. Now it was Fran's turn. He walked onto the sand and bowed to the president, formally asking permission to kill the bull. Then he moved along the *barrera* to dedicate the bull to someone in the stands. Some matadors did this all the time, but Fran saved it for moments that meant something to him. This time he would honor the princess, since it was a rule of taurine etiquette that each matador should dedicate a bull to any member of the royal family in attendance. "I dedicate the death of this bull to our friendship," said Fran. He tossed his hat up to Princess Elena, who would hold it during his performance and toss it back to him at the conclusion, most likely with a small gift or card in it.

Fran turned to the bull. By then the whistling and clapping had slowed, because it was too late for the president to send the bull back. Fran started with right-handed passes to the right horn. The bull charged, but without meaning it, and the crowd continued to exude boredom. Some of the hecklers of section seven began to meow, suggesting the bull was no fiercer than a house cat. Fran switched to his left hand, and section seven started to moo, suggesting the bull was nothing more than a tame ox. Someone in the expensive shaded seats stood up and denounced the mooers, but no one could hear him.

Fran killed the bull, slamming the sword in well and good. The bull staggered and crashed. This was met with . . . nothing. Mostly there was silence, broken by a few bored handclaps. The band began to play again and the bullring servants came out, pulled the banderillas out of the bull's carcass, hooked its horns to chains, attached the chains to the harness of the mule team, and cracked a whip, causing the mules to drag the bull off the sand, leaving a bloody swoosh in its wake. Fran went over to the royal box and retrieved his hat with a shrug, as if to say, "Well, I tried."

Fran slipped inside the *barrera* and leaned against its smooth redness, staring out at the next matador, who was practicing his passes in anticipation of his bull's arrival. Slowly, deliberately, Fran grabbed the top of the *barrera* and shook it, rocking back and forth against it with growing ferocity, his face a snarl of frustration. Something inside him had snapped. There had been too many bad bulls and too much crap from the world. Nacho, concerned, rushed over and handed Fran a glass of water, which seemed to calm him down. The next bull was already in the ring, and section seven was already complaining about it. The voice wailed down again: "What does the Comunidad think?" In other words, what does the Comunidad de Madrid, the local government of the capital, which oversees the operation of the ring, think about this travesty of a corrida?

By the time Fran's second bull was released into the ring — the fifth of the afternoon — the mood in Las Ventas had slipped into a kind of lethargic detachment. A third of the spectators had already departed, because the local soccer team, the famed Real Madrid, was playing for the European championship in Glasgow at nine o'clock, and people wanted to be home to see the match on television. Fran's second bull exhibited even less fight than his first one did, and so Fran ran it around halfheartedly for a while, killed it, and went back to the *callejón* to wait out the corrida. The only fans who seemed to care about Fran's performance were the naysayers in seven. They let him have it.

12

Section Seven

Madrid, May 15. The bullfight ended as most bullfights do, with the slightly queasy feeling that comes at the end of a big feast, when the wine has soured in the stomach, the food has been reduced to rotten scraps, and the smell of stale smoke hangs in the air. The sand of the ring was disheveled and bloody. The dead bulls had been dragged off to the bullring butchery. Skinned, beheaded, and drained of fluids, their milky carcasses swung in the steamy cold of a refrigerated truck, ready to be shipped to local butcher shops, to end up on the dining room tables of Madrileños. The sun had set over the big city and the ring glowed in pale artificial light. Rumpled and sweaty and spotted with blood, the matadors saluted the president in turn and walked off the sand. What was left of the crowd applauded them. Everyone else had disappeared.

The bullfight had been over for thirty minutes, and the area around Las Ventas was deserted, when a small group of people walked out through an archway in the bullring's façade. There were ten of them, and they ranged in age from around twenty-five to sixty-five. They were dressed in casual clothes and chatted among themselves as they made their way to a nondescript corner bar. There was nothing outlandish about them, yet these were some of the hecklers from section seven, the infamous crew that had been called everything from hooligans to barbarians to killjoys by the Spanish press and by their fellow aficionados.

One of them was a pudgy, baby-faced man of thirty-three who

owned a small business in central Madrid. His name was Salvador Valverde, but he was known throughout the Madrileño bullfighting scene as the Voice, the man whose acerbic shouted comments could be heard in every corner of Las Ventas. Valverde was proud of his reputation and felt more than justified in sharing his dyspeptic view of the Madrid bullfights with his fellow fans. "When you buy a ticket to a bullfight it is a kind of contract," he said. "You are promised a real bullfight with big, wild bulls. And if that doesn't happen, it's like you've worked for a month and suddenly you aren't paid. It's awful."

Like most Spanish aficionados, Valverde was introduced to the bulls as a child by an older relative who was an enthusiast. But unlike most aficionados, Valverde was immediately as enraged by the spectacle as he was enthralled by it. When the bullfights were good, they were just about the best thing he had ever seen. The only problem was, they were hardly ever good, and when they were bad, Valverde got so damned mad about it he couldn't contain himself. He had to let his anger out, and when he did, he discovered that he was possessed of what a vocal coach might call "a powerful instrument," which got the attention of anyone within a wide range of his seat.

Valverde had purchased his first season subscription as a teenager, choosing to sit in section seven, which had been a recognized place for the disgruntled at least since the 1970s. Soon he became well known. He had certain favorite exclamations. In addition to "Whom is the president defending?" and "Enough, enough, enough!" and "What does the Comunidad think?," he also liked to shout "Don't stop your bullfighting lessons!" at struggling young matadors. If King Juan Carlos was in attendance, he'd cry out, "Say something to them, Majesty!" — the "them" in this case being the bullring management. Or if a bull looked small or timid, Valverde would cry with dripping sarcasm, "What a bull! What emotion!"

Valverde was convinced he had powerful enemies in the bullfighting establishment. He said there were years when the management of the bullring "lost" the renewal application for his season ticket, or "accidentally" sent him a season ticket far from section seven. He also maintained that he had been the victim of a sustained campaign of threatening phone calls telling him to quit the bullfights or else. One day, Valverde said, the "or else" occurred. His apartment buzzer rang, and when he went downstairs to answer it he was jumped and beaten by three men. The attackers might have killed him, Valverde said, but a dog-walking neighbor scared them off. No one was arrested for the crime and there was no apparent motive, since the attackers made no attempt to steal anything from him. Valverde needed fifty stitches in his head.

Valverde was also involved in a tussle with a leading bullfight critic. Apparently Valverde yelled something derogatory about this critic's late father, a man who had been a distinguished taurine critic in his day. Sometime after this, Valverde and the son ran into each other somewhere in the bullring and fists were thrown. Eventually a judge sentenced both men to a few days' house arrest as a punishment.

Whatever the truth behind Valverde's feelings of persecution, it was true that he and his fellow hecklers were detested by the greater part of Madrid's bullfighting public, who would have preferred to attend corridas without having to listen to section seven's incessant ranting. But the hecklers said they weren't shouting just for the sake of hearing their own voices. They were engaged in a serious protest against what they saw as the watering down of bulls and bullfighting. "People might be afraid of us or angry at us because of what we do," Valverde said. "But we are doing this with a sense of purpose they might not understand. We are defending the bullfight."

Just as there are breeders who breed easy bulls and those who breed difficult ones, so there are some bullfighting fans who are more interested in the work of matadors, and others who are more interested in the bulls. The bull fans are known as *toristas,* and the shouters of section seven were prime examples. All bullfighting fans love bulls, even though the spectacle they enjoy is one in which bulls are killed. This paradoxical attitude is not that different from that of the wine connoisseur who drinks great vintages into extinction. Both the wine lover and the bullfight aficionado accept the fact that to experience the object of their love, it must be done away with. But they do so knowing full well that the vineyards and the ranches will continue to produce new vintages and new bulls, and that if interest in fine wine and bullfights were to dwindle, then the bulls and the grapes would dwindle as well.

So, all aficionados love bulls, but the *toristas,* like those of section seven, take their bull worship to another level. For the *toristas* the *entire* bullfight is the bull, and the matador is nothing more than an anonymous conduit for revealing the bull's quality. There are even some *toristas,* a few old crusty men in Madrid, who'll go to the bullring on the morning of an important corrida, stare at the bulls in their corrals, and then head home, the corrida itself being of no interest to them. But being a *torista* doesn't mean just loving bulls; it also means having a particular view of history. *Toristas* believe there was once a golden age of bullfighting when the bulls were larger, faster, and meaner, and the matadors more brave in dealing with them. The *toristas* say the contemporary bullfighting bull has been bred into near docility by a cabal of breeders working under pressure from cowardly matadors and the *apoderados* and bullring operators who support them.

Many knowledgeable fans and critics dispute this idea. They argue that today's bulls and bullfighters are no worse, and probably better, than the bulls and bullfighters of earlier eras. They also point out that bullfighting has always been infected with a rampant nostalgia for a supposed better time when bullfighters were real men and bulls were monsters. Hemingway observed this phenomenon in the late 1920s, when people lamented the lost world of the late nineteenth century. "Historians speak highly of all dead bullfighters," he wrote. "Bullfighting has always been considered by contemporary chroniclers to be in a period of decadence."

Still, as crazy as the hecklers of section seven could seem at times, there was some method to their *torista* madness, because in the end there is no ruling authority in bullfighting except the fans. If the ticket-buying public demands fierce bulls and proper bullfighting, then they'll get it. Otherwise, for the same rate of pay most matadors would just as soon face mini-bulls and perform in safe and easy ways. Much as section seven's detractors would deny it, Madrid was one of the few rings in Spain where there was a good chance of seeing difficult bulls and matadors risking their all. García Lorca may have called bullfighting "the last serious thing," but as Noël Chandler once said, "Madrid is the last serious thing in bullfighting." And that was due in some measure to section seven.

One person who disliked section seven was Fran, a matador who represented everything the *toristas* despised. The great *torista* cities are in northern and central Spain, places like Bilbao, Madrid, and Pamplona, whose bullrings prided themselves on presenting big, ornery bulls. Fran was from Sevilla, in southern Spain, where people are more interested in the aesthetics of bullfighting than its danger or difficulty. *Toristas* are usually left wing politically, and admire bullfighters who came up from poverty. But Fran grew up in wealth, and his family was associated with right-wing politics. *Toristas* prefer bulls from the difficult breeders; Fran made no secret of his admiration for the matador-friendly Domecq bulls.

Fran also didn't help his cause with section seven when he said in a newspaper interview that the best thing to do with that part of the Madrid ring was to put a bomb underneath it and blow it up. Yet true to his stated indifference to matadors, Salvador Valverde said he was willing to let bygones be bygones. "You tell him that we don't have anything against him," Valverde told me. "We don't care about him more or less than anybody else. If he does well we'll cheer for him, and I hope he does well the next time he's here."

At around eleven o'clock that night old Madrid exploded into life. Real Madrid had won its match in Glasgow, defeating the German team Bayer Leverkusen to become European champions. Everyone was smiling and wearing the team colors, blue and white. Cars full of revelers raced along the Calle de Segovia, windows rolled down, the occupants singing, horns honking in disjointed rhythms. Perhaps this was a fitting end to a night on which a good portion of the public in Las Ventas, the greatest bullring in the world, had shown they cared more for a soccer match than for the last three bulls of a first-class corrida. It seemed emblematic of the way bullfighting had yielded to soccer and other more modern entertainments.

Just then three boys staggered into view, drunk and delirious with team spirit. They were carrying a large Real Madrid flag, and one of them grabbed it, jumped into the middle of the Calle de Segovia, and performed clumsy verónicas against the onrushing traffic. Here was a perfect illustration of bullfighting's place in Spanish society. True, bullfighting wasn't as popular in Spain as it had been in the nineteenth and early twentieth centuries, before soccer and television, movies and pop music. It was equally true, however, that bullfighting continued to exert a strong hold on the Spanish psyche. Despite its regional quality, and despite the many Spaniards who were hostile or indifferent to it, bullfighting remained an enduring symbol, perhaps the most important symbol of Spanishness.

Madrid, May 21. There were storm clouds in the sky and the ring was stormy with anticipation of Fran's second and last corrida in Madrid, his final afternoon of responsibility for the spring. Fran was on with José Tomás, the undisputed champ of anyone who claimed to be a sophisticated aficionado, and interest in seeing José Tomás couldn't have been higher. Just that morning one local paper ran a headline describing the bullfight as *"José Tomás y Dos Mas"* — "José Tomás and Two Others." As the ring began to fill it was apparent that most of the regular season subscribers weren't there: they had sold their seats, at a nice profit, to a better-dressed crowd. These were what the Madrileños called *gente clave* (key people), wealthy types who make it their business to be seen at every important event in town. They weren't bullfight fans. They had come for the spectacle of José Tomás.

Thirty minutes before the bullfight was scheduled to start, Noël was bellied up to one of the bars under the stands, nursing a cold beer and some dark thoughts about Fran. It hadn't been a rewarding spring to follow Fran around, and Noël was depressed by Fran's work in Sevilla and Madrid. He was also glum about the unhappy news coming out of the *prensa rosa* that a reconciliation between Fran and his wife looked less and less likely. Noël loved Fran and he also loved Eugenia, and he wanted them to make up. "It looks like Eugenia is leaving him," Noël said, "and I might do the same if he doesn't get his act together. Then again, I've said that a thousand times now, and every time I say it he does something beautiful that brings me back."

The bulls on this occasion were from the ranch of Martelilla, a Domecq breed from Andalucía. The less said about Fran's two performances the better. The first bull simply lacked the stamina for a full bullfight. It arrived at the act of the *muleta* in a state of exhaustion, and Fran did little more than peg a few lackadaisical passes and kill. The second bull was what the Spanish would call a *manso perdido* (a totally tame animal). It flew from Fran at every opportunity. Fran killed it, and it was *adiós*, Madrid.

In the end, Fran was a footnote to an afternoon that belonged to José Tomás, and it was striking to see how different the two men were. Fran was beautiful, tanned, and muscular. When he was performing well — "on song," as Noël would say — his cape work was natural, graceful, and direct. He stood still, reached out his hands, and brought the bull toward him, never contorting his body or exaggerating his gestures. Fran's art pleased because it conveyed a sense of harmony and honesty — of a lad imposing his will on a dangerous animal. Whenever Fran performed he was like the star of his own Hollywood action film. He risked himself but you always had the feeling he'd get out of the scrap somehow. His work was the abnegation of death and danger.

By contrast, José Tomás was gangly, pasty, and ugly. He had a sinister face composed of an old man's bushy eyebrows, hollow eyes, a flat nose, and a mouth in desperate need of orthodontia. When José Tomás worked he twisted and tortured his body into exaggerated attitudes. He bent his skinny legs, thrust out his groin and belly toward the bull, and hid his chin in his concave chest, scrunching his face into a scowl. Fran was as light on his toes as a boxer; José Tomás had a leaden stance. This was the very secret of his success. Through his heavy feet and his sickly look, he gave the audience the feeling that he lacked the will or the ability to get out of harm's way. This meant that every encounter with the bull was undertaken as an all-or-nothing gamble. José Tomás was a tragedy waiting to happen, and that was what his fans paid to see.

Describing his performance the year before in Madrid, José Tomás said a lot about himself as a matador. "I neither cut two ears nor ended up in the hospital," he told an interviewer from the magazine *6 Toros 6.* "Nothing! That is the worst for a bullfighter." Fran would never say something like that. He never showed an ounce of fear, but he was always clear that he had no desire to court injury or worse.

José Tomás's second bull of the afternoon was black with a gray stripe along its spine. It didn't show much promise during the first two chapters of the bullfight, and it charted a cautious way during the third of the red cape, especially when challenged to its left horn. But in a dramatic and unusual move, José Tomás began his performance by working to that very same left horn, in a series of dangerous *naturales,* the cape held in the left hand, the cloth hanging limp, without benefit of a sword to spread it. He was taking on the bull's more difficult horn and doing it with a minimum amount of protection.

He shuffled to the center of the ring and stood still, his feet flat on the sand. The bull remained in front of him, looking tired and not at all eager to charge. José Tomás spread his legs and held out his left hand for a *natural.* He shouted and the bull engaged. The bull was hesitant, trotting and meandering as it made its way into the charge. But José Tomás helped the bull along, persuading and cajoling and seeing the pass through to completion. *"Olé!"* came the response, a big one. José Tomás unspooled three linked *naturales.* He was about to finish the series with a classic chest pass when the bull flicked its big head in, chopping its horn at José's chest. Most matadors would have skipped backward, but not José Tomás. Feet rooted to the ground, he sucked in his stomach and the bull missed by inches.

"Ahyeee!" shouted the crowd. Then the people rose to their feet for a standing ovation.

After the corrida Fran's hotel suite was filled with friends, relatives, and admirers who shuffled around, waiting for a word from the great man. Fran was in the bedroom, spread out on the bed, naked apart from the customary white towel across his midriff. His body was limp; he looked exhausted. José Tomás had cut two ears that afternoon, something that was very hard to do in Madrid, and Fran had been a spectator, watching José Tomás take his victory lap around the ring. Fran's *apoderado*, Pepe Luis, was seated at the foot of the bed, trying to buck him up. Pepe Luis's main argument — as it would be all season long — was that Fran had drawn poor bulls, and the audience had shown poor judgment in not seeing the good in what Fran had done with them.

"Your bulls were terrible and so were José Tomás's," Pepe Luis said. "But it was his crowd. For me his performance wasn't worth two ears in Madrid. Maybe two ears somewhere else, but not in Madrid." (Pepe Luis's opinion was confirmed the following day in the newspapers. Most critics agreed that the Madrid crowd had been uncharacteristically generous toward José Tomás. But that is the way it goes in bullfighting: when you are the star of the moment, you get the breaks.)

One of Fran's friends poked his head in the door. He was a big fellow in a neat suit, a businessman of some sort, and he seemed blissfully unaware of any tension in the room. "You gotta hand it to José Tomás," the man said, a smile on his face. "That son of a bitch did well today."

Fran said nothing. He got up and went to the bathroom and turned on the shower. He looked glum, his body sagging. He'd pulled himself out of his post-separation funk just for the chance to do something wonderful in his two corridas in Sevilla and two in Madrid. He'd had eight bulls in the two greatest bullrings in Spain, eight chances to triumph, more opportunities than many matadors saw in a lifetime, and he'd failed to capitalize on them. There had been no ears, no successes, and no vindication. The best Fran could hope for from the rest of the season was a long campaign of small victories, cutting ears one corrida at a time, relying on the cumulative effect of many lesser bullfights to make up for what hadn't happened in the big ones. The season was beginning to look like a washout. Little did Fran know how much worse it would get.

13

Different Paths

Tolosa, June 16. The men assembled in the corrals behind the bullring. The cool mornings of spring were a memory by then, and the insistent heat of summer was baking the moisture out of the lush green hills that loomed beside the edges of the town. It was high noon. The men smiled and said hello in the Spanish way, grasping each other by the arms and giving stiff, back-patting hugs. Dressed in their jeans and short-sleeved shirts, the men looked like toreros. They were whippet thin, their hands were large and calloused, their faces weather-beaten. They walked like bullfighters too, arrogant and slouching, yet precise, in a way that was equal parts ballet dancer and gunslinger. And they had that quality of abstractedness, of not being entirely present, that is characteristic of people who do dangerous work for a living.

The corrals jutted out from the ring, forming a patchwork of rectangular enclosures separated by thick walls, with walkways running atop the walls. Some of the corrals were empty, but others contained bulls, and the bull smell was in the air. Six bulls were shambling around one of the enclosures, nosing in the muddy and dungy straw that covered the wet concrete floor. The bulls had been shipped in from a well-known ranch, Alcurrucén, but they were clearly the dregs of that year's herd. They were gangly animals with stubby horns more appropriate for oxen than bullfighting bulls, which was to be expected. This wasn't Madrid or Sevilla. This was Tolosa, a peasant town in the hills of the Basque

Country, with a third-class bullring that had just enough money for third-class bulls.

The men peered down at the six bulls in the enclosure and took notes on small pads. The men were banderilleros working for the three matadors scheduled to perform in the afternoon's corrida. They'd come for the *sorteo*, the ceremony of sorting the bulls into three pairs and assigning a pair to each matador. The *sorteo* is designed to ensure that a matador will not have to face a pair of bulls that are larger, fiercer, better, or worse overall than any other matador has to face. The banderilleros discussed the bulls, referring to each animal by the number branded on its withers. Their talk was rapid and quiet, meant for their ears only. One man suggested that number fifty-one was big and dangerous-looking and might pair well with the docile number twenty-six. Heads nodded, and soon the other four bulls were paired off. There was no need for argument. Everyone there was a pro, and it was in everyone's interest to make the three pairs come out equal.

When the pairs had been set, the men withdrew into the office of the bullring promoter, which was in the arena's bowels just behind the ticket booth. Old bullfight posters were taped to the damp brick walls, and the promoter, the herdsman of the bullring corrals, and a representative of the local government sat around a beat-up metal desk, smoking. One of the banderilleros tore three slips of paper off a large sheet and wrote the numbers of a different pair of bulls on each slip, crumpling and tossing them into the flat-topped Spanish cowboy hat of the corral herdsman, which sat upturned on the table. With everybody watching, the herdsman shook the hat to mix up the three balls of paper.

"Good luck, gentlemen," he said.

The banderillero of the matador with the most seniority reached into the hat, picked out a ball of paper, and read off the numbers of the bulls his matador would now have to kill in the corrida — and the bullring promoter recorded the numbers in a ledger and on some government forms. Then the banderillero of the second matador in seniority picked a piece of paper, and then the banderillero of the junior matador. When this was done the assistants left the room to tell their masters what had happened.

Two of Fran's banderilleros — gray-haired José Jesús Sánchez, whose nickname was Hipólito, and gangly José Antonio Gutiérrez, whose nickname was Joselito, walked out to the street. In 1903, when the ring was built, it was on Tolosa's outskirts. But the town had caught up with the ring since then, and was all around it, a collection of low-rise housing complexes nestled in the green hills. The toreros walked down a short avenue lined with apartment buildings, their windows shuttered against the midday sun. At the end of the avenue stood their hotel. Hipólito, who was known as Poli, and Joselito walked through the lobby to the parking lot out back, where they found Fran sunning himself against a wall. Pepe, the driver, was washing the cuadrilla's minibus nearby, and the two manservants, Nacho and Antonio, were running around doing errands.

"How are the bulls?" Fran asked, his eyes lidded against the sun.

"The first one is big," Joselito said, "with horns that go up like this." He gestured with two fingers, pointing them up in the air. "It's a fairly controllable animal," he concluded.

"What color is its coat?" Fran asked.

"Black," Joselito replied.

"And the second?"

"Larger, but with comfortable horns, a little up and in."

Again Joselito used his fingers to mimic the bull's armament. Horns that curve inward are thought to be safer — "more comfortable," in bull-fighting argot — for the matador because they hook away from the body and are less likely to catch him as he works with the cape. Just then, Fran's *apoderado*, Pepe Luis, appeared, took a quick look at Nacho, and clucked.

"Matador," Pepe Luis said, "look at those shoes."

Nacho wore a pink tennis shirt, blue jeans, and leather slippers with toes that pointed up in a vaguely *Arabian Nights* way.

"They are very comfortable," Nacho said defensively.

"And very ugly," Fran added. "How can you wear them?"

Everybody laughed.

Fran seemed to be in much better spirits, and the heaviness that had hung over him during the time of the important corridas in Sevilla and Madrid had passed with the spring weather. Not that his life was perfect. The April and May corridas were failures that would haunt him for another year; he'd slipped to ninth on the *escalafón*, with nineteen corridas; and his family troubles continued to receive top billing in the gossip press. Eugenia had just given an interview in *Semana* in which she said she still believed in love but was continuing the legal process of separating from Fran. A few days later the magazine *Interviú* hit the newsstands with a cover photo of Fran's mother, topless beside the pool of a North African resort. "Splendor in Tangiers" was the inside headline. Finally, *Sorpresa!* reported that Fran had lost his temper with some photographers who were stalking him on a playdate with his daughter.

"I would like to maintain, at least at the margins, my privacy," Fran was quoted as saying. "I am not my mother. You see, I have not sold an exclusive interview or photo to anyone, ever."

Three weeks had passed since Fran's second corrida in Madrid, and during that time Fran had performed in the cities of Granada and Toledo; in Plasencia, where he'd cut an ear; and in Elda, where he'd cut two ears. Then, in the three weeks following his corrida in Tolosa, he was scheduled to take part in nine bullfights in Spain and one in France, a series of dates that would culminate in his most important appearance of midsummer, an afternoon of responsibility on July 10 in the big ring in Pamplona at the height of the running-of-the-bulls *feria*.

The hotel in Tolosa had a cool basement restaurant, which was lined with bulging casks of hard apple cider, and Fran's cuadrilla assembled there for lunch around one o'clock. There were twelve of them, and Fran was paying every one of their salaries. Fran sat at a round table with his manservants Nacho and Antonio, the old picador Francisco López with his wooden-Indian face, Fran's driver Juani, the manager's driver Jesús, the junior picador Diego Ortiz with his big hands, and the *apoderado* himself, Pepe Luis Segura. The three banderilleros—Poli, Joselito, and slope-shouldered José María Tejero—arrived late, as always, and took a smaller table to one side with Pepe, who drove the team minibus.

Keeping track of a large group of Spaniards can be confusing. It seems that most men in Spain are called Juan, Antonio, Ignacio, Francisco, Manuel, or José, while most women are Ana, Teresa, or Maria. Last names too are limited. For this reason, the Spanish employ nicknames and diminutives and use the surnames of both mother and father. Without such measures it would be hard to distinguish people. In Fran's cuadrilla there were five Josés, but the banderilleros were called Joselito, José María, and Poli; the driver went by Pepe, a nickname for José; and the *apoderado* was a José Luis, who used Pepe Luis. Both the matador and the senior picador were Franciscos, but one was Fran and the other was often called Paco. Then there was a Juan, known as Juani, and an Ignacio, known as Nacho, and to round things out an Antonio, a Diego, and a Jesús.

Many books about bullfighting insist that toreros eat lightly before a corrida because of the fear, and because a full stomach would impede any surgical procedure that might be needed after an injury. It is a dramatic detail, and most writers repeat it. But it isn't true. At lunch after lunch, all season long, Fran's team consumed copious repasts before every bullfight, as did the cuadrillas of other matadors. In Tolosa they had a three-course meal consisting of soup, salad, and plates of asparagus and omelets to start; steaks, chops, and fish for the main course; and ice cream and cake for dessert. Many drank beer or wine. To be fair, Fran usually ate a bit less. That afternoon he confined himself to tomato juice and a plate of squid stuffed with rice in a sauce of its own ink.

The conversation at lunch was much like the conversation at any pre-corrida lunch. As with everything else in bullfighting, the way bullfighters relate to one another is governed by tradition. There was a well-defined hierarchy in a typical cuadrilla, and everyone understood his role. The matador was stern and aloof, a prince among his subjects. His banderilleros were his knights, his brothers in arms, and there was always a senior banderillero who acted as a trusted counselor. Picadors were a breed apart and kept to themselves. The *apoderado* might be a father figure, or akin to an older brother, or a mere employee, depending on the matador's age, his status in the profession, and the age and professional standing of the *apoderado*. Finally, the rest of the staff—the drivers and the manservants—often were the butt of jokes. They were considered lower-class buffoons, a recognizable stock character that has had an honored place in Spanish culture at least since Miguel de Cervantes created the manservant Sancho Panza in *Don Quixote*.

In Fran's cuadrilla, it was Juani who performed the main Sancho Panza role. Like Sancho, Juani came from a small town, and like Sancho, Juani's education and outlook were confined to what could be learned within the boundaries of that small town. Like Don Quixote, Fran was alternately exasperated and amused by the antics of his servant, and like Don Quixote Fran was sometimes bested in conversation and in life by the servant's street smarts. But while Don Quixote tended to treat Sancho Panza as he thought a knight should treat his squire, Fran teased Juani as an older brother does his younger sibling.

Juani was to be married that October, at the end of the bullfighting season, and he'd spent most of the spring sick with worry over the mounting cost of his wedding and trying to devise various schemes and strategies to make it a more economical event.

"One thing's for sure," Juani said. "I'm not inviting too many people."

Fran greeted this news with a look of deep concern. "But you have many, many guests to invite," he said.

There were knowing smiles around the table, and Juani looked more worried. Fran started running through a list of people whom Juani must invite or else court social disaster and perhaps expulsion from Fran's inner circle. The list included Fran's family, which was enormous on both sides, and the family of Fran's father's second wife, and all of Fran's many friends from around the world. As the list grew, Juani squirmed in his seat. Then he saw the others laughing at him.

"Okay," Juani said to Fran. "And you'll come with all your girlfriends."

Nobody laughed.

"I'll be coming alone," Fran said quietly.

There was another table of bullfighters across the restaurant from Fran and his cuadrilla, but they weren't laughing or fooling around. They were eating without talking, their heads down. At the center of their table was a clean-cut matador named Francisco Marco. He was twenty-eight years old, the same age as Fran, and was what the Spanish would call a *torero de la tierra,* a local bullfighter. This meant Marco had some fame in the region where he'd been raised, but nowhere else. Marco was from Navarra, the region next door to the Basque Country, and those were the two parts of Spain where he worked, performing, in a good year, eight or nine times. This was not enough work to support a fixed team, and so Marco used picadors and banderilleros hired by the day, men whose luck with the bulls had been as hard or harder than his own.

By contrast, Fran had always been among the top twenty matadors, those who appear in more than forty-two corridas a season in Spain and France and are thus required by Spanish union regulations to keep a full cuadrilla of five assistant bullfighters and pay those assistants the mandated top rate, about a thousand dollars a bullfight. The date in Tolosa was a minor one for Fran and his team, members of bullfighting's elite. For Francisco Marco and his struggling banderilleros and picadors, men who worked day jobs to feed themselves, this was a key afternoon of the year, one of the few days they could call themselves toreros — an afternoon of responsibility if ever there was one. The Marco and Rivera camps traveled on two different paths of the bullfight world. They did not speak to each other in the restaurant before the corrida, and there was no sense of foreboding when everyone finished eating and went upstairs for the siesta.

14

An Inherited Fortune

Tolosa, June 16. The bullring smelled of earth and wood. It was a pretty little ring of wooden beams and whitewashed plaster, and it seated five thousand, which felt painfully small after a week of corridas in big, old Las Ventas. It was also striking how different the fans were. In big rings like Madrid's, the audience was composed of adults, typically couples and groups of men. In small *plazas* like Tolosa's, however, whole families attended. It was not unusual to see babies, toddlers, and school-age children happily sitting through the bloody deaths of six bulls. No one had told them they should be horrified by it all, so they weren't. The bullfight should have been an attractive one to local fans: it featured Francisco Rivera Ordóñez, the local kid Francisco Marco, and Juan Serrano, called Finito de Córdoba, the matador who had led the *escalafón* the year before with 122 corridas. But the stands were only two-thirds full when the matadors paraded across the ring, perhaps because the World Cup soccer matches were on television that afternoon.

True to Joselito's prediction, Fran's first bull was a manageable creature and Fran gave it a fine performance that drew *olés* and applause and finally, when the passes came smooth and linked, a serenade from the band. But Fran blew his chance at an ear when it took him numerous sword thrusts to kill. His second bull was less accommodating than his first had been, and Fran couldn't piece together a satisfying performance with his *muleta*, and he failed with the sword again before ending the bull's life. Fran had always had problems killing, and this was shaping up to be yet another afternoon ruined by his lack of regularity in this facet of bullfighting.

Francisco Marco was the matador with the least seniority, so he faced the third bull of the day. It was the biggest animal in the corrals, a high-backed bull with full-sized armament and a good defensive intelligence. This was a bull that seemed to understand that the easiest way for it to defeat the bullfighter was to ignore the urge to charge the cape and attack only when the man had come in close enough to expose his body to the horns. Seeing that he had no choice, Marco moved into the bull's immediate vicinity and offered the cape for a series of shaky *verónicas* that opened the performance. Then the trumpet sounded and in marched the picadors, who took up their classic positions beside the *barrera* fence, one picador in the shaded half of the ring, the other on the sunny side.

Marco and bull were holding each other off in the center of the ring while the horsemen settled in. Then it was time for Marco to move the bull in front of the picador on the shaded side of the sand for the first pic. Marco raised his cape and swept it back and the bull followed, but it stumbled on its left foreleg and came up limping and in pain. In a first-class *plaza* the president might have sent such a bull back to the corrals in favor of a replacement animal. Tolosa, however, couldn't afford to replace bulls except in extreme situations, so there would be no such reprieve. Marco was going to have to make do with what he had, a defensive animal that was now injured.

He moved to within five feet of the bull, held out his *capote*, shook it, and gave a shout. The bull stood its ground. Its head lolled; its sad eyes stared at Marco in reproach. Marco shuffled toward it a few steps and offered the cape again, and again the bull stood its ground. Finally, Marco got right up in the bull's face and tried one more time. The bull thought for a second and attacked, thrusting its head down, then flicking it up, lancing its horn into Marco's thigh, sending him fifteen feet in the air.

This last bit is not poetic license. One second Francisco Marco was a matador citing for a pass, and the next he was an indistinct mishmash of limbs flung into the sky. He fell hard and lay like a dropped knapsack on the sand. The bull wheeled and raced at Marco's prone body, its battering-ram head lowered to send Marco skyward a second time. By then other bullfighters had entered the ring. Someone flashed a cape in the bull's face, and the bull, delirious from the thrill of having hit something solid, turned with the cape and charged away from Marco. Fran and a banderillero were the first to get to Marco, and they picked him up and ran him into the *callejón* and under the stands to the infirmary, with Fran's hand pressed on Marco's wound to stem the bleeding. The whole thing had taken less than a minute.

The bullfighters in a corrida are responsible for defending each other while there's a bull in the ring, regardless of which matador and team the bull corresponds to. During the act of the picadors the two matadors who are not in action stand to the left of the horse, ready to save either the picador or their fellow matador. During the banderillas there are numerous people in the ring, and during the matador's *faena* his banderilleros crouch in *burladeros,* waiting to spring to his aid should anything bad happen. At least that is how it should be. The reality is that over the course of a long and tiring season, many toreros let their concentration wander when they should be watching out for their colleagues, and so are often out of position when something goes wrong. One exception to this rule was Fran, who was famous in the bull world for his punctiliousness and concentration in the ring. For that reason, Fran made more saves than most of his colleagues.

A few minutes after Marco's goring, Fran returned from the infirmary, and Nacho washed Marco's blood off Fran's hands with water poured from a plastic bottle. During Fran's absence Finito de Córdoba had killed Marco's bull, quickly and without attempting to make a show of it. Since Marco was gone for the day and Finito had handled Marco's first bull, Marco's second animal, the final bull of the corrida, now belonged to Fran. The bull was named Heredado, which was appropriate to the situation, since it means "inherited." The bull looked like a winner out of the chute, red brindle in color, heavier in muscle than its fellows, and charging easily. Fran must have liked what he saw, because he ordered a gentle pic'ing and a fast act of banderillas. He didn't want to wear out the bull before he'd had a chance to perform with it.

The preliminaries finished, Fran came into the ring alone with his *muleta.* He cited the bull in the middle of the sand and gave it two series of passes with the right hand, working the right horn, working with conviction. The bull was willing to charge, but it didn't follow the cape well at first and the series were a bit disjointed. Fran stuck with the animal, passing it smoothly, holding the cape on a steady plane, trying not to jerk the bull's head up or down, keeping the cape in the bull's face, making the cloth seem just within reach so the bull didn't lose confidence and learned to enjoy the game of the cape. On the third series the performance jelled. Then the passes came in long rhythmic figures, Fran lengthening the passes out, pass by pass, slowing the bull down, and attenuating the moments of danger when the bull was passing close to his body.

The music started. Fran switched the cape to his left hand and took his partner through a classic set of *naturales,* bringing the animal across his legs with the red cloth dangling from the stick. It was one of those ecstatic moments that come rarely in bullfighting. It wasn't scary or tragic or moving. It was pure joy. Fran was in total control, and Tolosa loved it. Then he began passing the bull with his eyes on the audience and not on the animal. It was a parlor trick that his father, Paquirri, had liked to use, a trick that wouldn't pass muster in a first-class ring but was just the sort of thing to get a small-town crowd excited.

At the end of the last series, Fran walked up to the bull, dropped his cape to the ground, and thrust his chest at the horns. He was in front of the bull with nothing to protect him, no cape, no sword. There was nothing but an inch of air between Fran and the horn. The bull shook its head. Fran leaned into the horn, pressing its gray tip against his chest. All the bull had to do was chop and it would have popped a hole in Fran's heart, but the bull was fully dominated. Fran turned his back and walked away. While the ovation died down, he walked to the *barrera* and took the steel sword from Nacho. Fran lined up, ran in, and managed to sink the sword about halfway into the bull, the blade entering the body in a good place. The bull died and the crowd waved its handkerchiefs and Fran collected an ear and made a lap around the ring.

There was a sizable crush in the hotel lobby after the corrida, and a big crowd gawked in from the street. This was an event for the locals, since toreros were the only famous people who ever came to Tolosa. After a short beer at the bar and some autographs Fran and his team gathered again in the same hotel restaurant, at the round table they'd used at lunch. The group was alone in the room this time: Francisco Marco was in the hospital, and his cuadrilla waited there with the family until they had heard the outcome of his operation. When Fran sat down at the table he noticed that Poli and Joselito hadn't come downstairs yet. They were still in the hotel lobby, chatting up some girls. Fran waited for a while, growing increasingly irritated. He was in full prince mode this evening, expecting proper etiquette from everyone around him. Finally, Poli and Joselito appeared.

"We're always waiting for you two," Fran said, his voice harsh and loud in the empty restaurant. "It's rude."

Poli mumbled an excuse. Joselito stood behind him, looking terrified. Then Poli came over to sit down.

"You go and eat at another table," Fran said. "You are banned from this one!"

"Fine," Poli said. "I'll eat all by myself, alone."

"Poor baby," Fran said. Then he made a show of speaking to the person seated next to him.

The corrida had been a satisfying one, but Fran would never condescend to be happy about it. He was a star, a *figura* of the bullring, and an ear in Tolosa was not something he was going to celebrate.

After dinner the men headed to their vans and took off for Sevilla, a nine-hour drive. There was never any thought of spending the night in Tolosa. There were three full days until the next corrida, and the cuadrilla wanted to spend that time at home with family and friends. Meanwhile, Francisco Marco was nursing a sutured wound in his right thigh, a plastic tube sticking out from the stitches, draining the suppurating fluids. The terse report in the morning paper would describe his condition as "reserved," a good prognosis, and Marco's manager guessed his boy would be ready for his next scheduled corrida, which was in Pamplona on July 8, or the following one, also in Pamplona, on July 10, with Rivera Ordóñez on the card. Until then, Marco was in what bullfighters call *dique seco* (dry dock). It is a place most toreros are all too familiar with.

15

Death in the Sun

On July 9 in the bullring of Pamplona a young matador from Sevilla got it bad. Antonio Barrera was in the middle of his *muleta* performance when a big bull from the Santiago Domecq ranch jabbed its horn into Barrera's thigh and sent him skyward. Bullfighters spilled into the ring as Barrera fell to earth, landing hard on the sand. While some of the banderilleros lured the bull away from Barrera's prostrate body, a matador named Miguel Abellán picked him up and tried to help him to the infirmary. But Barrera wrenched himself free of Abellán and waved him away with a dismissive sweep of the arm. This was Barrera's first appearance in Pamplona, a big chance for him to earn his stripes with the fans up north, and he was going to kill that bull if it killed him to do it.

Serious gorings often take place after a matador has already been tossed, and the Pamplona crowd was worried about Barrera, with good reason. He was wobbly on his feet as he made a few final passes with the bull and went over to the fence to get his killing sword. Then he set himself and made a firm run at the bull, going over the horns and landing the blade between the shoulder blades, and everything looked fine — until, at the last second, the bull raised its head. Barrera went shooting off the horns. Later media reports would say that he had taken a direct hit to the scrotum and that one testicle was all but destroyed. This time Miguel Abellán had no problem getting Barrera to the infirmary, but when Abellán returned to the ring some of the fans heckled him for letting Barrera perform after the first tossing.

"What could I do?" Abellán said with a Latin shrug. "He's a torero."

Bullfighting's critics are fond of pointing out that the corrida isn't a fair fight at all, that the bulls are murdered in cold blood by matadors who work in relative safety. This is accurate, but beside the point. Bullfighting fans know the bullfight is not a fair fight, and they come to the arena assuming that the day's events will end with the bulls dead and the toreros unharmed. Far from being an embarrassment, it is this very imbalance in danger between man and animal that redeems bullfighting and makes it possible for it to exist in the contemporary world. Imagine if the bullfight were a fair fight — that is to say, a pitched battle that resulted in the deaths of half the bulls and half the men on any given day. Would such a throwback to the bloody death matches of the ancient Roman arenas be more acceptable to bullfighting's critics?

The modern bullfight is an artistic exhibition that results in the deaths of six bulls. While the death of the bull is the climax of the spectacle, it is not its dramatic focus. There is no suspense in the bull's death. Instead the drama comes from the possible death or injury of the bullfighter. In a sense, the bullfighter's medium is danger. The bullfighter takes danger, in the form of the bull, and plays with it, bringing the horns close to his body and sending them away again, creating patterns of danger and safety, standing near the horns, teasing them, avoiding them, until both the bullfighter and his audience are emotionally spent. In bullfighting any action the man takes, from placing banderillas to passing the bull with the cape to killing, is considered better and more interesting in direct proportion to how dangerous it is.

People attend bullfights for many reasons, but the biggest emotional reason is to be frightened. This is the same motivation that causes people to go to scary movies or ride roller coasters or walk through haunted houses, the only difference being that the danger in bullfighting is real and the audience has a role in creating it. Bullfighters like to say the most dangerous beast in the ring is the crowd. It is the crowd that urges the bullfighters to take greater and greater risks, and it is the crowd that voices its disapproval when the bullfighters play it safe. The crowd comes to the bullring hoping on some level for the ultimate thrill that a bullfight can provide: the death of the matador. And it is the crowd's ambivalence about this murderous urge that makes the bullfight so exciting and elevates the object of the crowd's aggression, the matador, to an object of worship.

According to Ramón Vila, the chief surgeon of the Maestranza bullring in Sevilla, there are around 120 major injuries suffered by toreros in the ring during the course of a typical Spanish season of 850 formal corridas. That's a big injury every seven bullfights, and it doesn't count pulled muscles, minor broken bones, cuts, bruises, and other small mishaps. Picadors suffer the fewest injuries, because the modern picador's horse rarely falls, since it is a big, healthy animal wearing padded armor. Banderilleros suffer the majority of injuries, because there are three times more of them than of matadors. But on a percentage basis a matador is more likely to be injured than a banderillero, and matadors' injuries tend to be more severe.

According to Dr. Vila, about seventy percent of all wounds suffered by matadors occur in the area between the belly and the knees, because that is where the bull holds its horns during most cape passes. But gorings in the eyes, head, neck, trunk of the body, and lower legs are also common, as are tossings that result in broken ribs, necks, backs, and limbs. One way or the other, most matadors spend a few weeks in the hospital each season, and many are punished cruelly by the horns year after year, coming close to death on multiple occasions. Interestingly, Fran hadn't been gored once in his eight seasons as an active matador, in spite of the fact that he had been tossed repeatedly, particularly at the beginning of his career.

Bullfighting histories tend to be both sketchy and inaccurate, but the history books suggest that there have been at least five hundred recorded incidents of toreros killed by bulls worldwide since bullfighting on foot came into vogue in the eighteenth century. The real toll is probably higher, given the number of bullfights that surely have been forgotten by history, especially in South America. Nevertheless, if we accept the figure of five hundred deaths and look back over three hundred years, that averages out to a little more than one and a half deaths in the ring each year. Of the bullfighters known to have been killed, a good 60 were full matadors, some 180 were apprentice matadors, 160 were banderilleros, 75 were picadors, and around 20 were Portuguese-style equestrian bullfighters.

Certain periods of history have been more lethal for toreros than others, but bullfighting has become less dangerous thanks to improvements in emergency medicine. For example, between 1900 and 1920 46 banderilleros were killed in the ring, compared to 9 killed between 1960 and 1980, a time when there were many more bullfights. Penicillin is credited with saving the lives and especially the limbs of many twentieth-

and twenty-first-century bullfighters who might otherwise have suffered horrible infections from dirty horns. For this reason, many Spanish cities have streets named for the man who first isolated penicillin, Dr. Alexander Fleming. There's even a statue of him outside the bullring in Madrid.

The majority of toreros who've died from injuries suffered in the ring have been anonymous types, but it is striking how many famous ones have been killed. Two of the three greatest matadors of the twentieth century died on the horns: José Gómez, called Joselito, was killed by a bull of the Widow Ortega, in Talavera de la Reina, on May 16, 1920; Manuel Rodríguez, Manolete, was killed by a Miura bull, in Linares, August 28, 1947. One of the greatest of the eighteenth-century matadors, José Delgado, called Pepe-Hillo, was gored to death in Madrid in 1801, as was one of the heroes of the nineteenth century, Manuel García, El Espartero, in 1894.

Pepe-Hillo, Espartero, and Manolete would be considered all-time greats even if they'd died in bed. Yet it has to be admitted that being killed in the ring does wonders for a matador's reputation. Fran's father was a fine matador and a star of his generation, but he became a legend in death. Or take Manuel Granero. He performed for less than two seasons as a matador, but he's famous to this day because in 1922 a Veragua bull named Pocapena (Little Pain) spiked him in the right eye in the Madrid ring, sending him into the history books. Being involved in a fatal incident is also good for the bull's reputation. No one remembers the names of most bullfighting bulls, but any good aficionado can tell you that Bailador killed Joselito, Islero killed Manolete, and Avispado killed Paquirri.

The deaths of important matadors have always been powerful national events in Spain and moments that the Spanish rather enjoy on some level. Of course they grieve. They wail, they moan, they write maudlin poetry, and participate in lavish funerals and ceremonies. But Spanish culture is deeply tradition-bound, and bullfighting is the most tradition-bound aspect of the culture, and it is a tradition in bullfighting that it is right and proper for a matador to die in the ring; that it is the matador's destiny and his calling. So when this happens, it is as though all the fairy tales were coming true.

"It is hard for Americans to understand why all this fuss about one bullfighter," wrote the American author Barnaby Conrad of Manolete's death. "Yet when he was killed, he died such a beautiful dramatic Spanish death that I swear, in spite of the great funeral, the week of national mourning, the odes, the dirges and posthumous decorations by the government, that in his heart of hearts, every Spaniard was glad that he had died."

At the same time there is also a strong tradition that a matador should never, under any circumstances, court death actively, or take risks in the ring deemed unreasonable by bullfighting standards. The essence of bullfighting is control. The matador must control his own emotions and the behavior of a wild animal, and as long as he stays in control of both, he'll be applauded for taking big risks. But when the audience senses that the man has lost his grip on himself or the animal and is simply throwing himself at danger, it will turn on him and beg him to stop. This is what happened in Pamplona. The people in the crowd wanted Antonio Barrera out of the ring after the first tossing because they could see he was in no shape to handle the situation. Sadly, they were right.

Barrera's goring was one of the 166 injuries sustained during that bullfighting season, according to *6 Toros 6*, making that year notably violent. There was no logical explanation for this. The bulls were no fiercer. The bullfighters were no braver. Perhaps it was just a run of bad luck. "The bull respected no one," wrote the editors of *6 Toros 6*. "He sunk his horn in where he could, with cunning or ferocity, with blind fury or self-assurance. This season has been one of the bloodiest in the last ten years, and without doubt it created more absences of important matadors than any year in recent memory."

The first top-level matador to go was Eugenio de Mora, gored in the buttocks in Sevilla on April 14, the same day Fran performed. That injury put Eugenio in dry dock for six weeks. Two days after that, in the same *feria* of Sevilla, the veteran matador José Ortega Cano was hooked into the air and came down on his left elbow, breaking it. He was out for two months. Later in the same corrida, Enrique Ponce, one of the top two or three matadors in Spain for more than a decade, suffered a foot-long wound in his left thigh and was knocked out for a month. He returned in mid-May and performed in another thirteen corridas, until June 23 in León, when a Zalduendo bull tossed him. The doctors thought he had sustained a broken rib and nothing more. Then Enrique stopped breathing, and they realized the rib had punctured a lung. Out another month.

The matador José Miguel Arroyo, called Joselito, broke his right leg in three places when a bull knocked him down during a spring corrida in the ancient Roman arena in the French city of Nîmes. The injury might have ended his career, but Joselito came back. He was still limping and his leg was a bit misshapen when, in the *feria* of Zaragoza, he took on a full corrida of six bulls by himself and the leg held. Then there were the trials of José Tomás. He was tossed in Granada, on May 13, breaking a rib and badly bruising a leg, which put him out until June 9. Then he was gored twice in Badajoz, on June 26, but stayed until the bullfight was over, a stunt that put him in dry dock for a month. He made his comeback, and in Huesca on August 10 a bull broke a bone in his left hand. In great pain, he continued his season. Five days later, he took a shallow horn wound in the chest. That autumn he retired from the ring, citing the constant pressure of danger as one of the reasons for his decision. He was twenty-six years old.

Fran's father was killed by a bull in 1984, and one of his companions in the Pozoblanco ring that day, José Cubero, El Yiyo, was killed by a bull in 1985. Six peaceful seasons followed. Then on May 1, 1992, in the Maestranza, a sometime-matador-turned-banderillero named José Manuel Calvo Bonichón, nicknamed Manolo Montoliú, was killed by Cabatisto, a 1,320-pound bull from the ranch of the Heirs of Don Atanasio Fernández. The bull lifted its head at the wrong moment during the placing of a pair of banderillas and punched its horn into Montoliú's chest, splitting his heart in two. Less than five months later, on September 13, in the same Maestranza, a bull named Avioncito (Little Airplane), from the ranch of the Conde de la Maza, killed a banderillero named Ramon Soto Vargas. From that day until the writing of this book, no torero has been killed in the ring in Spain — twelve years, the longest span in the history of bullfighting on the Iberian Peninsula without a death.

16

Peons

Tolosa, June 16. They had finished dinner, the cuadrilla bus was packed, and the last minutes of Sunday night were ticking into the first minutes of Monday morning when the bus pulled out of town. They headed west to Burgos, due south through Madrid and Córdoba, and west again to Sevilla, a six-hundred-mile trip that took less than nine hours, and by Monday afternoon José Jesús Sánchez, Hipólito, was out of bed and puttering around his house. Poli was Fran's *banderillero de confianza,* which meant he was Fran's senior adviser in the ring and the first among his assistant bullfighters. Poli was forty-two years old. He was tall and thin as a teenager, had blue eyes, a protuberant nose, a small mouth, and a fine head of graying hair. He was sharp and funny, formal in his dealings with the world, profane in speech, cynical about bullfighting, grumpy even when happy, and fierce about protecting his relationship with Fran, who he'd been with since Fran's first corrida.

"This is where I rest from the shit of this life," Poli said to me. "My house is yours and I am at your service."

Poli lived twenty minutes west of Sevilla, in Espartinas, which had once been a town but had become a dot in a sea of sprawl. Poli's white stucco home, built in what Americans might call Mediterranean style, was in a recently built community in a row of similar houses on a street that ended all at once in farmland. It was a landscape straight out of Southern California, antiseptic and rootless, thrown up at the last minute to meet the suburban aspirations of a growing populace. The house had two airy floors with bedrooms enough for Poli and his wife, their children, and an older relative, along with a kitchen, living room and dining room, an office space with a computer, and a den area centered around a flat-screen TV and DVD player. The family car was parked outside, and a luxurious swimming pool jiggled blue in the scorching back yard.

Espartinas is a poor place and bull-crazy, so by local standards Poli was both a financial success and a minor celebrity. He might not have been a star matador, but he was a torero, a bullfighter: a man who had escaped the workaday world to travel, consort with rich and famous people, and make a good living at the bulls. Banderilleros and picadors are hired and paid by matadors. They earn money on a bullfight-by-bullfight basis according to a scale established by their union, which is located in a small office on the Calle Fuencarral in Madrid. Because Fran had performed more than forty-two times the season before, he was classified by the union as a group-A matador and was thus required to retain a full team of two picadors and three banderilleros and pay them the top rate. This was about a thousand dollars a corrida for the picadors and the two senior banderilleros and about eight hundred dollars for the third banderillero. Everyone's pay doubled when a corrida was televised. Since Fran expected to perform in about seventy corridas that season, some of them on TV, Poli could earn close to eighty thousand dollars — which would go a long way in Espartinas. But Poli's story, like the stories of most banderilleros, was a story of failure.

Poli was born into a family that could boast toreros dating back to the beginnings of bullfighting in the eighteenth century. His childhood dream was to become a famous matador, and so he started out on that well-worn and treacherous path and became a *novillero*, an apprentice matador who takes part in junior bullfights called *novilladas*, which feature immature bulls. He began at the lowest level of *novillada*, the kind that has very young bulls and no picadors. After two seasons of performing in at least twenty-five of these, Poli was able to jump to *novilladas* with slightly older bulls and with picadors.

After this apprenticeship, a *novillero* is eligible to become a full matador and appear in a proper corrida with mature bulls. But a promoter won't offer a contract for such a corrida until the *novillero* has attracted substantial positive attention from fans and the industry. The afternoon of his first proper corrida, the *novillero* participates in a simple ceremony. At the start of the corrida the senior matador on the card cedes the killing of the first bull—which would be the senior man's responsibility—to the *novillero,* who would normally kill the third bull of the corrida. After the first bull has been caped and pic'd, the senior matador and the *novillero* stand in the ring and the *novillero* exchanges his *capote* for the *muleta* and sword of the matador, while the other matador on the card that day looks on. Then the *novillero* goes over and kills the bull. After this he is officially a matador—with one catch. If his *alternativa* takes place in a ring other than Madrid's, the new matador must confirm his status by repeating the ceremony in Madrid.

In most bullfighting programs matadors are listed with the facts of their *alternativas:* the date, the bullring, the name of the matador who performed the ceremony (the "godfather"), the name of the other matador on the card that day, the official witness, and the name of the bull, its weight, and its breeder. Fran's *alternativa* was on April 23, 1995, in the Maestranza. His godfather was Juan Antonio Ruíz, Espartaco, and his witness was Jesús Janeiro, Jesulín de Ubrique. The bull was Bocalimpia of the Torrestrella ranch, which weighed 1,155 pounds. Fran confirmed his *alternativa* in Madrid the following year during the Feria de San Isidro.

Most programs will also list the bullfighting genealogy of the matadors. This is like a family tree that traces the line of matadors who have given each other *alternativas* up to the matador appearing in that day's bullfight. Like most matadors, Fran traced his lineage from Pedro Romero, of the famous Romeros of Ronda, who helped perfect the modern bullfight (*alternativa* date, April 20, 1776); through four matadors to Francisco Arjona Herrera, called Cúchares, a nineteenth-century master (*alternativa* date, April 27, 1840); through five more matadors to Ernest Hemingway's early idol Nicanor Villalta (August 6, 1922); and through four more to Espartaco (August 1, 1979), who gave Fran the ceremony.

But most *novilleros* never take the *alternativa,* or if they do, their careers as matadors fizzle in short order. Bullfighting is as hard to break into as any part of the entertainment business, perhaps even harder, because the bullfighting industry is so small and there are so few opportunities. Bullfighting is a closed-off world dominated by a small and conservative group of powerful promoters and breeders, who are naturally prejudiced against *novilleros* and matadors they've never heard of. You cannot become a matador or even a successful *novillero* without attracting the attention of these people, but there is no way to attract these people's attention without performing in bullfights, so it is a bit of a problem.

Even if a *novillero* has establishment support and the large sums of money needed to launch a career, and even if he has the guts, the talent, and the luck in bulls to shine in the right rings at the right time, and even if he is given the chance to become a matador, he will then be faced with a much harder task, because as hard as it is to become a matador, it is even harder to make a living as a matador, much less become a star. Within the ranks of matadors, the competition for work is much stiffer, the bulls are more dangerous, and the public is more demanding than in the ranks of *novilleros.* That is why so few *novilleros* become matadors, why even fewer last as matadors, and why fewer still make it into that elite group of forty or fifty matadors who work — and why almost no matadors are admitted to the select club of two or three who are the true stars, the *figuras* of the ring.

"To become a matador is almost impossible," Poli said. "To become a *figura* is a miracle." Or as Fran's manager, Pepe Luis, put it: "It's easier to be elected pope than to become a *figura.*"

Sometime when he was a *novillero,* Poli stalled and never took his *alternativa.* It was the same story told by Joselito, José María, and countless others before and after them. None of them would go into much detail about what went wrong in their early careers. Instead each one slipped into the traditional, formalized lingo of bullfighters, giving the standard explanations that have probably been the refuge of banderilleros for centuries. "I had my good moments," Poli said, "but I lacked the circumstances to advance." "I didn't have the right help at the right time," said Joselito. "*Hombre,* to live your dream of being a matador is hard, very hard," José María said. "In my case, I didn't devote enough time and energy to it."

When a *novillero* or young matador fails he can opt for the banderillero's life, trading in his childhood fantasies and gold-encrusted matador's suit for the hard reality of a suit trimmed in silver or black and the role of the *subalterno* or *peón.* Even then, however, he is not guaranteed success. There are thousands of unemployed toreros in Spain competing for around one hundred banderillero jobs with the thirty matadors who work enough each year to pay their people well. So banderilleros know they are replaceable. They serve at the whim of their matador, and each season is a precarious dance to keep the boss happy, stay out of harm's way, hope the boss stays healthy, and try to make it another year closer to the age of fifty-five, when mandatory retirement and the union pension kick in.

Fran's team of matadors had consisted of Poli and two other men, both of whom departed at the end of the previous season. The first was a short, fat old-timer who knew his way around the bull world but disappointed Fran with his performance in the ring. He was asked to leave. The second was a proud young man, a kid who probably had the talent to be a matador, who placed banderillas with such skill and grace that he often received ovations for his work, and who quit Fran and joined forces with another matador. It was said that this young man clashed with Poli, but his likely motivation for leaving was money, since his new employer tended to perform twenty more times a season than Fran did, and thus was able to pay his banderilleros about twenty thousand dollars more a year than Fran was.

So Fran had two holes in his cuadrilla, and during the winter break he filled them. Joselito was available because his former matador, the great *figura* of the 1980s Espartaco, had retired following a devastating leg injury (suffered not in the ring but in a pickup soccer game). By contrast, José María had bounced from matador to matador, never sticking anywhere for long. Both José María and Joselito said they were thrilled to have been hired by Fran, and both said they were keen to impress their new boss. After years of moving around, José María was looking for some stability, while Joselito said he was glad to have landed with another star. He was also pleased because his job with Fran was a promotion. Until then Joselito had been the lower-paid third man on the team. In Fran's cuadrilla he was in the number-two spot.

"The matador took a gamble on me," Joselito said. "I have to respond. If I'm not up to the level, when the season ends he'll go out and find someone else."

Sevilla, June 18. Fran's manager, Pepe Luis Segura, worked out of a suite of rooms on the ground floor of a housing development in an undistinguished newer part of town. Pepe Luis was a short, florid man of fifty-six who wore his hair long and gelled into a thick blob at the nape of his neck. His face was expressive, his mouth was wide, and his tongue flicked to his lips as he spoke. He was clearly an intelligent man, and his way of speaking was wonderfully theatrical. He spoke high up in his nose, with great volume and at a rapid pace, repeating words for effect and making use of all the varied and complex rhetorical flourishes available in Spanish, which can have a grave, almost Shakespearean quality, even in everyday speech.

"Francisco called me one day in January and asked if I wanted to work with him," Pepe Luis said in his high whine of a voice. "And I thought, This is a *figura del toreo,* and I can make him into a *maxima figura del toreo.* I can give him hope and confidence. Not everyone can be the *apoderado* of a Francisco Rivera Ordóñez. Not everyone is afforded that privilege."

Pepe Luis had made it as a matador and had hung on for a number of years before quitting. He said he didn't understand why he hadn't been more successful, but had to admit that he lacked the charisma that excites fans. After he retired from the ring he went into business training and selling guard dogs. But the "little poison" of bullfighting was in his veins, and soon he quit the dogs to become an *apoderado.* Over the course of two decades Pepe Luis had managed the fortunes of a number of star matadors. In a profession not known for sensitive types, he was something of a psychologist, a motivator, who, as one newspaper writer put it, was adept at reviving sagging careers.

The telephone on Pepe Luis's desk rang. It was the promoter of a bull-ring that had a *feria* in August. "Well, why don't you have Francisco Rivera Ordóñez on your card?" Pepe Luis asked. The other man spoke. "Well, I know," Pepe Luis said. "But we want to be on with other *figuras,* with Ponce or El Juli."

One odd aspect of the bullfighting business is its last-minute quality. Although promoters may come to terms with big stars well in advance, most *ferias* are finalized only about six weeks before they're scheduled to begin. It is said this custom took hold following the passage of a law that mandates that anyone with a season subscription for a *feria* may ask for a refund if any of the matadors formally announced for that *feria* fail to show up. Since matadors are always getting injured, the promoters protect themselves by holding off announcing their lineups for as long as they can. But in truth, this style of planning couldn't be more Spanish. In Spain it is hard to get anyone to agree in advance to an appointment of either a social or business nature. Call a Spaniard a few weeks ahead to plan a meeting and he'll ask to be contacted a few days in advance. Call a few days in advance and he'll say, "Call me on the day."

If he happens to be around on the day you wish to meet, everything will be fine. But if he's decided to go somewhere else, well, better luck next time.

Pepe Luis and the promoter hung up without coming to an agreement, but Pepe Luis seemed unconcerned. He explained that it was his goal as manager to get Fran into the best *ferias,* making sure the bulls and the other matadors on the card with Fran were to his, Pepe Luis's, liking. Star matadors want to be on cards with other stars, and the bigger the stars, the better. Most matadors also like to be the matador of middle seniority in a bullfight, because the middle man performs with the second and fifth bulls of the day and never has to work in the first or sixth slots, when the audience is, in bullfight-speak, cold. As for bulls, all matadors have their preferences in this area, and it is always a source of negotiation, so much so that Pepe Luis employed a scout to go to bull ranches and look over any bulls that might appear with Fran.

At this point the sensitive subject of money came up. Matadors do not like to talk about their fees, because the money they earn per bullfight is perhaps the most concrete expression of their standing in the bullfighting community. Pepe Luis would not say what Fran earned. What he would say was that the top matador that year — Pepe Luis didn't name him, but it was El Juli — earned as much as two hundred thousand dollars a corrida in a first-category *plaza,* sixty thousand in a second-category *plaza,* and thirty thousand in a third-category *plaza.* The rates for the next ten or fifteen matadors were much lower, and then lower again for the twenty or thirty matadors after that. The matadors below the top fifty would take what they could get.

At the end of the season one of Spain's top promoters, speaking on condition of anonymity, said that Fran was commanding about thirty thousand dollars in a first-category ring, maybe half that in a second-category ring, and half again in a third-category ring. Those numbers were probably about right, according to a number of other taurine professionals who confirmed the promoter's estimate. That meant that in a typical season Fran could earn between one and two million dollars, from which was subtracted the ten to fifteen percent for his manager, the salaries of his cuadrilla, two drivers, and two manservants, and all of their traveling expenses. There was also the expense of his bullfighting costumes, capes, swords, and banderillas, which could amount to as much as fifty thousand dollars a year.

Despite Fran's poor showing in Madrid and Sevilla, Pepe Luis expressed confidence that Fran's season would be a good one. "As long as Fran kills well," he said, "he'll cut ears." It was his view that Fran was a great bullfighter and had the potential to be even greater, not just because of his prodigious talent, but because his art was informed and inspired by the essential tragic nature of bullfighting, which Fran inherited upon the death of his father. "Francisco represents bullfighting," Pepe Luis said. "He feels it in his bones. Bullfighting is the only theatrical production where there is true death. In the theater a man dies and gets up after the curtain falls. Here you die and you don't get up. Fran knows this in his heart because of the experience he had with his father. He thinks about the tragedy of his father. It passes through his head. And this is why he is a great torero."

17

Craftsmen

Alicante, June 20. The morning was hot and the sun was high over the old Arab fortress at the top of the hill, but a moist breeze blew in from the water and it made everything all right. Alicante is a seaside city, built on the side of a hilly range that divides the interior land from the shore. Along the shore are high-rise buildings that would not look out of place in Miami Beach, but the city becomes a nineteenth-century town as it moves up the hill. The local *feria* is dedicated to San Juan (Saint John); it begins each year in mid-June and is similar to the Feria de las Fallas, in nearby Valencia. There are fireworks, women promenading in peasant costume, and large statues that are burned down at the end of the festivities. That year ten bullfights of one sort or another were scheduled for the local bullring, a modern structure in the town's main square, and Fran was to perform in the fifth bullfight of the series.

Around eleven in the morning, Fran's assistant manservant, Antonio Marquez, strode out of the hotel, lighted a cigarette, and began walking up the avenue toward the bullring, checking out the goods in the shops and leering at every woman he passed who was between the ages of about sixteen and sixty. Antonio was forty-one. He was built narrowly, with dark skin, a head of wavy dark hair, melancholy hound-dog eyes, and the big-lipped mouth of a sensualist. He had a tough, street look about him, but he was a sweetheart. Unlike many people in Fran's entourage, who had little interest in the bulls and hung on with Fran because they were friends of his, Antonio had come up in the taurine world. His father had been a *novillero*. His grandfather also had been a torero, who had retired and made money renting used "suits of lights" to bullfighters in the Sevilla area. In the 1940s the grandfather had done business with Antonio Ordóñez, when the maestro was just starting out and too poor to buy his own costumes.

Antonio Marquez was as loyal to Fran and as hardworking on Fran's behalf as anyone on the staff. He was the one who solved all the little problems of the road and kept the Rivera Ordóñez traveling circus in good running order. Nacho, the chief manservant, was responsible for Fran and Fran alone. He would not lift a finger to help anyone but Fran and Fran's closest friends, and no one resented this because it was Nacho's job. Antonio, by contrast, was paid to look out for the other five bullfighters of the cuadrilla, and he was willing to help any friend or acquaintance of Fran's who wanted tickets to the bullfight or a hotel reservation in a town that was booked up for its *feria*. He did this sort of thing all the time and would never accept a tip for his troubles.

Antonio arrived at the backstage area of the ring, which was surrounded by a small crowd of rough-looking men. Some of them were scalpers and some were bullring officials and some were there because they had nothing better to do. Antonio marched up to the gate and then had to talk his way in, because the bull world had not adopted any of the kinds of security measures — ID cards or backstage passes — used in the United States and elsewhere. Once inside the ring, he made his way to the promoter's office, which was windowless and filled with noxious cigarette and cigar smoke, and asked for his money. The promoter reached under the desk and handed Antonio a small brick of euro notes, about seven thousand dollars. This was done without the slightest formality. The promoter did not ask for a receipt, but Antonio insisted, tearing off a shred of paper and signing it and handing it to the promoter.

This was a typical transaction in the bullfighting business, where written contracts are viewed with distrust and a man is supposed to be as good as his handshake and payments are made in hard cash. In this case the money was an advance against Fran's fee for the corrida. It would be used to pay the salaries of the cuadrilla and for some immediate travel expenses. On long road trips, a matador's manservant will go around collecting payment after payment in this fashion, and sometimes Nacho's briefcase was so full of cash that he looked as though he were on his way to a drug deal. Noël Chandler used to imagine that a successful career awaited some brazen criminal who waylaid matadors' manservants on the road, heisting the mounds of cash they always had with them.

Around midday the bullfighters gathered for lunch, and the subject of the September 11 terrorist attacks came up. Everyone agreed that it was a disgrace that a powerful nation like the United States had been unprepared to defend itself. "Such a thing could never happen in Spain," said the slope-shouldered banderillero José María. "Spain is invincible." The terrorist bombings of Madrid commuter trains were about two years away.

The bullfight in Alicante was twenty minutes old and the *plaza* was packed under an impossibly blue sky. The first bull entered the ring, and Fran gave it a solid series of *verónicas*. Then he let the bull go and it trotted back to the bullpen entrance, where it felt secure. When a bull picks a favorite spot in the ring and returns to it obsessively, that spot is called the bull's *querencia*. Bulls may choose *querencias* where they have gored a horse or a man, where the sand is cool, near the bullpen entrance, or anywhere else that suits their fancy. One natural *querencia* is the center of the ring, where bulls have the most available escape routes. A bull is hard to handle within its *querencia* because it will go on the defensive there. But a bull is less dangerous than usual when it is running toward its *querencia*, and a matador may attempt an impressive pass on such a bull, reasoning that it will ignore him in its haste to get where it wants to be. On the other hand, matadors are sometimes gored under such circumstances, since the bull is not paying attention to the cape.

A bugle sounded and the picadors sauntered in on their heavy mounts and stopped at their appointed positions in the outer band of sand near the wooden fence that surrounds the ring. One picador stood in the shaded half of the ring, the other across from him on the sunny side. Behind the picadors were the teams of ring servants, the *monosabios*. Dressed in matching smocks and berets, the *monosabios* are charged with assisting the picadors by keeping their horses in line and if necessary helping to save the picadors when they fell. In most rings the *monosabios* are regular people so addled by bull fever that they are willing to give up their time at very little pay and risk injury and death to be close to the action.

Fran went out and caped the bull to a spot in front of the picador who was standing in the shade, drawing it inside the two concentric circles painted in the sand. By the rules of bullfighting the bull must always charge the horse with the space of the painted lines between them. Seated in his saddle, Fran's picador Diego Ortiz shifted his horse so it was perpendicular to the bull, rattled his armored boot inside its armored stirrup, raised his spear into the air with one of his massive hands, and called out. The bull responded to this stimulus and charged, driving itself into the horse's padded flank, the horse twisting away its head, its pink tongue flicking around its lips in mute horror, as the *monosabios* whipped the horse's bottom with leather switches, forcing it to lean into the bull's horns.

The bull rocked forward and the half-ton horse slammed against the *barrera* fence, almost crushing a *monosabio* to death in the process. Meanwhile, Diego the picador leaned over and shot his spear into the bull, at the tail end of the tossing muscle that mounded out at the spot where the bull's neck met the trunk of its body. Feeling the pain of the spear, the bull tried to slide to its right and away from the horse. But Diego reined the horse toward the center of the ring, blocking the bull's escape route while he pressed the metal point of the spear into the bull's flesh with all of his weight behind it. After a few seconds of this Diego let the bull get away, and the spear popped out of the newly made wound, and dark molasses blood slicked down the bull's side. The audience whistled and jeered, wanting the bull punished as little as possible so that it would still have enough gas to charge the *muleta*.

In the eighteenth and nineteenth centuries, the act of the horses was one of the highlights of the corrida, and the picadors were the big stars. They got top billing, above the matadors, on posters (which to this day are the primary means of advertising corridas), they were paid more, and they were allowed to wear gold trim on their costumes, a privilege they still retain. In bullfighting's first centuries the picadors' horses were unprotected, and the job of picador was a skilled profession in which the performer tried to spear the bull as soon as it came into range, hold the bull off with the spear, and slide the horse out of the bull's line of attack, thus saving the horse and providing a show of equestrian and martial skill.

Nowadays the horses are so large and protected that there is only a small chance of a horse's being badly hurt and falling down, and because of this the art of pic'ing has degenerated to the point where most picadors simply let the bull hit the horse and shoot in the lance, a technique that requires much less skill than the work of the old-time pica-

dors did. Some fans still regard pic'ing as a fascinating test of the bravery of the bull. But most want it over with quickly, acknowledging that
the pic is necessary to wear the bull down, but hoping the picador
doesn't do too much damage, rendering the bull inadequate for the cape
work to follow.

As a top matador, Fran had two picadors in his traveling cuadrilla.
The senior man, Francisco López, categorically refused to be interviewed for any purpose. He was around six foot six inches tall, had a
craggy wooden-Indian face, was annoyed most of the time, and must
have been at least sixty years old, because he worked as a stunt double
for Charlton Heston in the movie *Ben-Hur,* which was filmed around
1958. López tended to pic with a heavy hand, bending into bulls and
doing a lot of damage. The junior picador, Diego Ortiz, was an amiable
man of about thirty-five with massive hands, a great help in his profession. He was happy to be interviewed, but his Andalucían accent was so
thick it was difficult for his cuadrilla mates to understand much of what
he said — and they were from Andalucía.

The picadors withdrew from the stage and the bull went back to the
center of the ring, bloody and too tired from charging the horses to
move unless provoked. At this point the banderilleros jogged in and
arranged themselves in the prescribed fashion. As the matador in charge
of this bull, Fran had little to do. He moved to the side of the sand, took
off his hat, and gave it to Nacho in exchange for a shiny metal cup of
water, taking a sip and handing it back to Nacho. Then he stood with
hands on hips and watched. The matador in line to kill the next bull was
José Pacheco, El Califa. He went over to the sunny side of the ring,
across from where the bull was, bunched up his *capote* in his arms, and
waited. Meanwhile, a banderillero from Califa's team and the third
matador of the afternoon, El Cordobés, moved into place across the
ring from Califa in the shaded sand. They were all in the ring to protect
the men placing the sticks.

Poli entered, holding his *capote* against his body as if he were waltzing
with it. Gray-haired Poli wore a pink costume trimmed in black. He
moved in front of the bull, offered the cape, and the bull engaged. But
instead of standing still and making the bull pass across his body as a
matador would, Poli bowed and then, like an ambassador taking his
leave of a king, shuffled away from the bull, tiptoeing backward in a
three-quarters circle. The bull, nose in the fabric of the cape, followed,

turning in a smooth arc, moving with Poli so that at the end of the turn the bull was in line with the center of the ring, in the right place and position to receive the first pair of banderillas.

This was the self-effacing cape work of the good assistant bullfighter in the role of *lidiador,* or man with the cape during the act of the banderillas. It was a sweet little piece of technical bullfighting, but the crowd neither noticed nor cared. Few Spanish fans understand bullfighting well enough to pick up on such details, and anyway the audience in a city like Alicante comes to enjoy itself, not to analyze. Fran, whose head is a computer of bullfighting minutiae, was pleased with Poli, but the act of the banderillas was of no interest whatsoever to him. His only concern was for the bull and what condition it would be in when it came to the act of the *muleta.* Like most matadors, Fran believed that a bull has a limited number of good charges in its body, and Fran did not want these wasted on unnecessary movement. Poli had brought the bull into position with a single delicate motion that did not tire or damage the animal unduly.

Gangly Joselito came out from behind the *barrera* and went to the sunny side of the ring, across the sand from the bull. Joselito was thirty years old, long and lean, leaner even than Poli, with a round face and surprised eyes. He was dressed in a suit of green with black trim. In his left hand Joselito held a matched pair of banderillas, wooden sticks about two feet long, each with a metal harpoon-like point at one end. They were festooned with shreds of colored paper, the top half yellow and the bottom half red, the colors of the Spanish flag. Joselito touched his right hand to his tongue and used the fingers to wet the harpoon points. The saliva is thought to help the metal slip through the bull's hide. Joselito took a banderilla in each hand, holding it by the blunt wooden end, balancing it against his palm, his fingers forming a tube around the shaft. Then he raised his hands high above his head.

The banderillas pointed outward in front of Joselito like horns. He called to the bull and it turned to face him, turning into the center of the ring. From the bull's perspective, Joselito represented a new threat, something it had never seen before: a man without a cape in his hands. Joselito screwed his face up in concentration, and maybe fear, and his breath came out in bursts through his straining lips. He stalked toward the bull with exaggerated steps that started on the heel and rolled to the toes, pelvis outthrust, back arched. A watchful moment passed. Then, as if by mutual accord, the man and the animal made their moves, running at each other. Except Joselito didn't come straight on, as the bull did. He ran in a circular pattern, making his way to the left of the bull's line of attack and then around into the line at a ninety-degree angle, running across the horns.

Joselito and the bull came together in midring, and the bull lowered its head to pluck Joselito into the air. Just then Joselito jumped — his back straight, his arms held high — and slammed his hands together above his head and drove them down over the bull's horns. The metal barbs at the ends of the banderillas lodged in the bull's thick hide, on the shoulder just behind the left horn. Joselito pushed off from the banderillas, pivoting away from the animal. He landed on both feet, like a gymnast dismounting the parallel bars, and threw his hands into the air, and the bull's momentum carried it past. The banderillas hung down off the bull, one right next to the other, clattering as the bull ran, and the crowd applauded.

Ernest Hemingway observed that no phase of the corrida is more pleasing to someone unfamiliar with the spectacle than the banderillas. For a newcomer to the art of bullfighting, Hemingway said, the first passes with the *capote* are hard to follow, the act of the horses comes as a shock, the matador's performance with the *muleta* is too complex, and the death by the sword is too fast-moving. But the placing of banderillas is just right for the new fan. It is easy to follow the action and enjoy it.

At first the fan wonders how the torero gets away with it. But, said Hemingway, the act of the banderillas is based on the simple premise that a four-legged bull cannot turn in a circle tighter than the length of its body, whereas a two-legged man can turn on a dime, twirling out of harm's way while the bull struggles to get around and take a stab with its horns. There are many ways of running up to the bull to place banderillas, but the most typical is the one described above. That is *al cuarteo,* or making a quarter-circle across the line of the bull's charge. The man can also choose to run straight at the bull: *poder a poder.* Or he can await the bull's charge, feint in one direction, then shift back as the bull reaches him: *al quiebro.* Or he can try any number of other strategies.

The placement of a pair of banderillas is judged on four criteria: the angle of attack (the more directly the torero comes at the bull, the better the pair); the manner in which the banderillas are placed (the man should jump high, keep his back straight, put the banderillas in over the horns, and make a clean landing); the terrain in which the banderillas are placed (in general, it is more dangerous, and therefore of greater merit, to place the sticks in a way that affords the man the tightest and least promising route of escape — for instance, an area of the ring where the torero is between the bull and the *barrera*); and finally, the position of the shafts, which should be sunk on the shoulders, behind the neck, and the shafts should be together, not spaced apart.

There is no single satisfying explanation for why banderillas are used at all. Some people theorize that the barbed sticks straighten the bull's charge by causing pain in the shoulders when pivoting; others say the act of the banderillas is purely ornamental. Whatever else they do, the banderillas are dramatic and fun to watch, and they aid in the process of wearing the bull down and focusing its anger for the final act of the matador and the red cape. Most bulls will be given three pairs of banderillas, though with a weak bull in a second- or third-class *plaza*, two or even one pair may be used.

A few matadors place the banderillas themselves, and some of them are great artists of this phase of bullfighting. When a matador places his own sticks, he does so alone in the ring, without help from his colleagues, and the performance is always accompanied by music. In many ways, the season when I followed Fran was the season of the matador-banderillero. The undisputed king of the rings that year was Julián López, El Juli, who placed his own sticks, and the new star was a former ski jumper from Granada named David Fandila, El Fandi, who was thought to be one of the best banderilleros to come along. Having said that, most matadors in Spain leave the task of placing banderillas to their assistants, and most assistant bullfighters are indifferent or even frankly cowardly in their performance with the sticks, which suits their matadors just fine, because it doesn't take the spotlight away from them.

When the banderilleros place the sticks, there is a strict division of labor. In Fran's cuadrilla it went as follows. For the first bull, Poli was behind the cape and Joselito placed the first and third pairs, with José María placing the middle pair. For the second bull, Joselito had the cape, while Poli took pairs one and three and José María the middle pair again. It is important that banderillas be placed on both the left and right sides of the bull, and most banderilleros specialize in working to a particular side. Poli and Joselito were left-side banderilleros; José María was a right-sider. Poli was a master with the cape, but the best thing one could say about his banderillas was that they were effective. José María was short and muscled with the slope-shouldered grace of a boxer, which he was in his spare time. He was a good athlete, but rarely thrilled with his work. Joselito lacked Poli's skill with the cape, but after a few rough spots early in the season he had begun to show that he was a classy performer in banderillas.

In public Fran was careful not to praise his cuadrilla, preferring to keep them a little off balance so they would work hard to stay in his good graces. In private, however, he admitted he was pleased with his new team. He always had Poli, the man who knew him best and could be counted on to lift his spirits with a well-timed joke or remark. José María was solid in the ring and a good man. Above all, Fran felt a special kinship with Joselito, who he thought exemplified the right way to be a torero.

The bullfighting business could be awful. It was filled with petty jealousies, fraud, and a kind of tacky, second-rate showbiz atmosphere. Still, many toreros carried with them a vision of what their profession should be. Fran believed that when you became a torero, you committed yourself as an artist in mind, body, and spirit. To be a torero was to conduct yourself with grace and dignity at all times. To be a torero was to carry with you the tragic spirit of your art, to study it, to live for it, and, if called upon, to die for it. This was a way of life that Fran found beautiful, and it was even more beautiful when encountered in a humble banderillero, who had given himself to bullfighting even though he knew the rewards would be small.

"I like the way Joselito thinks about bullfighting," Fran said. "It's the way I think about it. You see, bullfighting is very special. The bullfighter is a different kind of man."

18

They Eat Horses, Don't They?

Alicante, June 20. The red van and the green minibus pulled out of Alicante around two in the morning, and the wheels rolled through the misty night, up the Spanish coast, past Valencia and Barcelona and across the Pyrenees into France. From there the road took them farther north, skirting Perpignan and Béziers, and then east with the bending of the continent, past the ancient Roman provincial cities of Nîmes and Arles, and finally south to the shore and the small town of Istres, in the suburbs of Marseille, where there was a bullfight the next day. The toreros were not happy about having to spend time in the south of France, a part of the world that many people find rather congenial but Spanish bullfighters disdain because it isn't Spain and because they don't like the food.

"There's nothing good to eat there," Juani explained as he paid the toll on the first French highway after the Spanish border. "The only thing they have is duck, duck, duck, duck."

Fran had just woken up, and I asked him if he felt the same way. "Of course not," he said in English. "Look who you are talking to."

The Spanish are as intensely focused on their food as they are on their culture, language, and traditions, which means they are quite happy to eat Spanish cuisine all day, every day. Chinese restaurants, for example, have never done big business in Spain. But while they can be dogmatic about food, and they care about the freshness and quality of their agricultural products, especially those of their home region, the Spanish do not have it in them to be food snobs the way the French and some Italians are. They don't stand on ceremony when it comes to eating. They eat at all hours. Breakfast can be had anytime from dawn until noon, lunch from noon to five, and dinner from about eight until the early morning hours. Their cooking is rough and simple: good grilled meat and fish, fresh eggs, rice cooked with meat and seafood, soups, stews, and the famous cured Serrano ham. Contrary to what you read in books by Americans, the Spanish do not like spicy food. The wines and olive oil are underrated, but Spain does not have the kind of cheese culture one finds in France, and the bread is atrocious.

The big meal accompanied by big conversation is the central act of Spanishness, even more so than the Mass, the evening stroll, or the midday nap, three traditional activities that are fading. Spaniards love to chat, to argue, to opine and orate, especially over a table of good food. Both the Spanish language and the Spanish way of life contribute to this. The language is expressive, formal, yet poetic in a way that English is not. The Spanish lifestyle is structured to allow extended, unhurried time for meals and sitting in cafés and talking. Spain is a country where food and wine are cheap and plentiful, and a place to have a nibble, a smoke, and a sip can be found on every street corner. Much of life is taken up with sitting around such places, and a Spaniard would rather have one more drink or bite to eat than an extra hour of sleep.

Istres turned out to be a small municipality of medieval origin, situated on the shore of a large brackish lake with an outlet to the Mediterranean. Today it is best known for its proximity to a military airfield. Despite the efforts of the locals, Istres was not brimming over with charm, even during its so-called *feria*, an ersatz event inaugurated that year as a ploy to attract tourists. Fran and his entourage arrived in midmorning and settled into a brand-new motel off a highway on the outskirts of town. Built on the American model, the motel lacked a restaurant, which would be unthinkable at a European-style inn. But the dilemma of where to eat was resolved when a deputation from Istres's club of bullfight fans invited the cuadrilla to a celebratory lunch.

The meal was not a success. The day was swampy in a Florida Everglades sort of way. The restaurant was beset by flies and packed with red-faced Frenchmen drinking pastis, anise-flavored liquor that turns cloudy when water is added, as it invariably is. The proprietress didn't speak a word of Spanish, which turned out to be a blessing. The first thing to arrive at the table was a green salad. Plain and unadorned, it differed from the classic Spanish salad, which is always dolled up with bits of corn, onion, tomato, canned tuna, and egg. The bullfighters didn't touch it. Then came a generous plate of cold cuts with a pot of French mustard nestled in its center. This was also a no-go for the toreros, because the tray didn't include Spanish ham and Spanish sausage.

One of the Spaniards asked for cheese. The restaurant was probably saving it for dessert, but the waitress brought out a plate of soft, creamy French cheese. This was also rejected, since it didn't resemble the hard cheese from La Mancha that the toreros were used to. By the time the main course arrived, both the Spaniards and their French hosts were getting frustrated. In theory, the entrée should have been acceptable. It was steak and fries. Unfortunately for all concerned, Poli sniffed at his plate, looked around, and said in Spanish, "Maybe this is horse." The meal was done for. After a respectable amount of time the bullfighters retreated to their motel.

That evening everyone gathered to set out and find some dinner, and while he was waiting for the cuadrilla to assemble Fran talked about his upcoming corrida in Pamplona on July 10. Every morning of the Pamplona *feria* the bulls that are to be killed in the arena that afternoon are run through the streets of town, and anyone who wants to can run with them. Many people are injured each day, and once in a while someone is killed. The last time this happened, the victim was an American. Few professional toreros run in these *encierros,* as the bull runs are called. Bullfighters risk their lives with bulls for money, and don't need the added danger of being surrounded by amateurs, many of them drunk, many of them non-Spaniards. But like his father and grandfather before him, Fran often ran the *encierros,* partly to honor his forebears and partly because, like them, he enjoyed it.

"You must run with me this year," Fran told me. "It will be great."

I shuffled my feet a bit and said something about having a wife and child.

Fran smiled. "Don't worry," he said, the picture of reason and judgment. "I run far from the horns."

I asked him what he meant by "far."

"Oh, a few meters."

That sounded too close to me, so I mumbled more excuses.

Fran shot me a look, clearly exasperated with my un-Spanish show of fear. "I know!" he said with a wicked smile. "You will run with the bulls, you will get caught, and you will die. Then I will write a book about a dead writer."

We left it there. But I knew I was expected to run, and if I didn't, I'd be branded as the coward I was.

That evening, Fran decided to go to McDonald's for dinner. So there they were, a hardened group of matadors, picadors, and banderilleros, eating Happy Meals in a plastic picnic area in the south of France, where one can dine about as well as anywhere on earth. The night was cool and the meal pleasant, until the end, when Poli discovered that the big craggy-faced picador López had removed the desserts from some of the Happy Meals and eaten them himself. The two got into a shouting match, which had to be broken up by the *apoderado*. "It's just like summer camp," Fran observed.

Istres, June 22. The southern French border is closer to the great bullfighting land of Andalucía than New York is to Chicago. So it should come as no surprise that there have been Spanish-style bullfights in the south of France for at least two centuries. Today the bullfight is on the rise in France, and more corridas are given each year and more bullrings are being built. There are now about thirty *plazas de toros* on French soil, all of them in the south. Bullfights are held in the two-thousand-year-old Roman arenas at Nîmes and Arles. Béziers and Mont-de-Marsan have distinguished nineteenth-century rings, and there are a number of contemporary *plazas* in smaller towns, among them Magesq (opened in 1989), La Brede (1999), and Istres, which would officially open on the day of Fran's corrida.

Northern France has had its bullfights too. In 1889 a group of investors, led by the duke of Veragua, built a ring on Rue Pergolese in central Paris. It accommodated twenty-two thousand spectators and had electric lighting and a retractable roof, and the corridas held there led to a flowering of interest in bullfights in the north. There were strong protests as well. Animal rights groups brought many lawsuits demanding the abolition of the bullfight in France, and in the mid-1890s the national legislature passed a law banning the bulls. But bullfighting supporters worked to repeal the law, taking their case all the way to France's highest court, which ruled that the bullfight was indeed to be outlawed everywhere in France, with the exception of the south. The justices thought the bullfight was such a part of the indigenous culture there that it should be allowed to go on. This is the legal situation today.

The bullring in Istres was spanking new and rather pretty, with a graceful white awning that kept the expensive seats in shade. The program did not open with a traditional Spanish bullfighting march; instead the band played the "Toreador Song" from the French opera *Carmen*. Otherwise it was a regular corrida. The crowd was small. The bulls were bad. A young French matador cut the only ear. The six bulls died their deaths and the cuadrilla hurried back to the motel to shower, change, and get the hell out of France as soon as possible and back to the only real country in the world. For dinner they sent Juani to a supermarket, where he found ham and cheese and bread and beer that approximated the Spanish versions of those foods.

"Next year when we come," Pepe Luis said, "we can bring a barbecue and grill our own food."

As the cuadrilla minibus was being loaded, Joselito sat with his gangly frame draped over a chair in the motel lobby. He was studying a sheet of paper that had Fran's upcoming corridas listed on it. There were six dates left in June, then another ten in July.

"You have a lot of work coming up," someone said.

Joselito folded the paper and put it in his pocket. "*Hombre*, there's no point in worrying about the future," he said. "In this business you never know what is going to happen."

19

A Lapse in Concentration

Algeciras, June 29. In the days following the corrida in France, Fran and company drove back to Spain and made a tour of Castilla-León, the region just north of Madrid. They had no luck with a pair of Montalvo bulls before a half-empty *plaza* in Burgos on June 23, or with Luis Algarra bulls in the packed ring of León the next day. On June 25 they were down in the westernmost edge of Extremadura, in Badajoz, where Fran cut an ear off an excellent Jandilla bull, and it was back up to Castilla-León on the twenty-sixth, where Fran's poor showing with the sword in the bullring in Soria cost him any chance of trophies from the Arauz de Robles bulls he'd drawn. Next stop was Sevilla, for two days' rest, then on the road once again for a corrida of Núñez del Cuvillo bulls in Algeciras on the twenty-ninth.

It was a Saturday, and the air was oven-hot, with the terrible African heat of southern Spain that comes when the sun is large and the sky clear. But the heat was nothing more than a nuisance to the bullfighters. They were accustomed to it. What worried them was the treacherous wind that blew in from the water, a wind that would play havoc with their capes, blowing them up and revealing the toreros' bodies to the bulls. Algeciras is a blowy town. It sits at the southern tip of the Iberian Peninsula, where Spain and Morocco pinch within ten miles of each other, forming the Strait of Gibraltar — a stretch of water where the Atlantic and the Mediterranean come together, kicking up a sea wind.

Algeciras is also a Spanish city with a palpable Muslim presence, and signs on the grungy shops and coffeehouses down by the docks were in Arabic as well as Spanish. The bullring was a mile or so inland, atop a hill in the middle of the city's fairgrounds, which were filled for the *feria* with gaudy amusement rides and the booths of sellers of perfume knockoffs, fake NBA team T-shirts, greasy doughnuts, and all manner of plastic gewgaws. This schlockiness was the flip side of the elegance of Sevilla's *feria*. Up the hill, in direct confrontation with the coastal wind, was the bullring, which had the romantic name Las Palomas (The Doves). Inaugurated in 1969 with a corrida featuring Paquirri, the ring was decorated in red brick and white tile and resembled a municipal parking garage from the outside.

The stands were half full, the air smelled of sea and cooking grease, and the dying day was so hot you couldn't think straight when the toreros marched across the arena to open the bullfight. Fran was the senior man that day and he faced the opening bull of the spectacle, a black creature that was what the Spanish would call *anovillado,* an adult specimen that looked like the kind of immature bull used in *novilladas*. Fran chose a patch of sand to defend and began his performance with a confident series of *verónicas,* keeping the little bull under his thumb. Then the picadors did their business, and Poli, Joselito, and José María got the sticks well placed, and it was time for Fran to show what he could do with the red cape.

He began the *faena* with three series of right-handed passes to the right horn, running the bull with some success but without generating the emotion of good bullfighting. There was nothing technically wrong with Fran's performance, but the bull was too small, there were too many empty seats, and the people who were there were too hot to rouse themselves. Fran switched the *muleta* to his left hand and glided through two easy sets of *naturales* that elicited lackluster *olés* from the crowd. After this the bull showed signs of wear. Its sides heaved and it began charging with its mouth open, the bluish pink tongue lolling out.

Fran paused for a moment. He and the bull stood in the shaded side of the sand about six feet apart, and the bull was heavy on its hooves. Having completed an exploration of the bull's left horn, Fran decided to go back to working the right one. He transferred the cape to his right hand, set the sword behind it to spread out the fabric, and took his eyes off the bull to twist the end of the fabric down over the tip of the sword and fix the cape in place. It was a lapse in concentration of less than five seconds, and with most bulls on most days Fran would have gotten away with it. For some reason, however, this tired half-bull in Algeciras got excited at the wrong moment.

It might have been the motion of Fran's left arm as he twisted the cape down over the sword, or it might have been the gust of wind that blew, fluttering the cape at a key instant. Whatever it was, the bull surged forward, taking less than two seconds to get to Fran. If he had been paying attention, he might have escaped the situation one way or the other, but his head was down. By contrast, the bull, suddenly energized by the expectation of harming its tormentor, had its head up, and it drove its right horn into Fran at the level of his chest. It looked like the kind of goring that would kill. But there was no discernible puncture hole or blood as Fran blasted off the horn and fell backward onto his feet. The bull came again, chopped and missed, pounding Fran with its skull, slapping him down. As Fran collapsed he threw his left arm out behind him to break the fall. The arm shot out stiff, the hand struck the ground, and Fran's body went down on top of the hand, crumpling the arm in sickening fashion. The lower half of the arm, the part that can only bend forward, wrenched backward, popping the elbow from the socket.

The other bullfighters leapt into the ring and moved the bull away. Fran stood up and it was clear that the horn had missed his chest and hooked into his armpit instead. Otherwise he might well have been dead. But relief gave way to fear when Fran swooned against the banderillero standing next to him, holding his left arm and whimpering like an animal. They tried to carry him out of the ring, but he insisted on walking, and he sobbed as they led him around the *callejón* and into the infirmary while the audience gave him polite, ladies'-lunch applause.

In the small operating room the doctor shot Fran full of painkillers. Then he gripped Fran's arm and snapped the dangling lower half of the limb back into its socket. Two hours later Fran lay in the local hospital, easing his way into what would be a night of misery. "I thought the elbow was broken," he said. "Because I have never had pain like that. It was horrible, really, and I was asking for more drugs. And they said, 'We can't give you any more drugs, you've had enough,' and I was begging, saying, 'Please, give me something to end the pain. Give me everything you have.' It was a horrible night." The next day they flew Fran up to Madrid to assess the damage.

Madrid, July 2. The season was now in doubt. Soft-tissue injuries like the one Fran had sustained do not heal quickly, and a matador cannot get by with an injured elbow: he uses his elbows in just about everything he does. Back in Sevilla, Pepe Luis was trying to sound upbeat. Tests had shown that Fran had suffered nothing worse than a few strained ligaments in the one elbow, he said, adding that Fran would spend the coming weeks in Madrid doing physical therapy, under the care of Dr. Alfonso del Corral, the orthopedic surgeon of the professional soccer team Real Madrid. There was no way to predict how and when Fran would be able to perform again. *"Hombre,"* Pepe Luis said, "you never know. We'll have to wait and see what the doctor says. Right now we're hoping to come back on the twenty-first in Barcelona." That seemed optimistic.

20

Running the Bulls

Pamplona, July 8. The alarm rang in the darkened bedroom, but Miguel Angel Eguiluz was already awake and staring at the ceiling. It was six-thirty in the morning.

He swung out of bed. Short, compact, athletic, with a shaved head, a well-tended black mustache, and lively blue eyes, Miguel Angel was a forty-seven-year-old Pamplona native, a doctor who'd been running the bulls since he was a teenager. The famous running-of-the-bulls *feria* had been in swing for two days already, but Miguel Angel's suburban neighborhood was quiet as he dressed in white pants, white shirt, and running shoes, slugged down a sports drink, and descended the stairs to the basement parking lot to pound out thirty minutes of wind sprints. At seven-thirty he zipped into the city on his motorbike. As he parked he could hear the big crowd that had assembled in the bullring to watch the end of the bull run, and the band playing.

The route the bulls and runners took each morning snaked for a little more than half a mile through the streets and squares of the old part of town — the area was cordoned off with heavy wooden barricades. On a typical weekday during the *feria*, more than two thousand runners participated, and the number could double on weekends. Most of the runners were from somewhere other than Pamplona. Many hadn't slept the night before. Some were drunk. Almost none knew what they were doing. But within this ignorant mob (for that is what they were) was a small and anonymous group of a few hundred expert runners. Some were non-Spaniards—Noël Chandler, in his day, had been among them. Most were locals. These hard-core participants treated the *encierro* as a spiritual exercise and a serious competition. Their goal was simple: to put themselves just ahead of the bulls' horns and run there for as long as possible without touching or interfering with the bulls in any way.

Like most serious runners, Miguel Angel specialized in a certain stretch of the route. He began almost at the end, where the Calle Estafeta curved through an open intersection and down into the tunnel that led into the bullring. By law the runners were supposed to assemble back at the beginning of the bull-running route, at the Calle Santo Domingo, which sloped down to the makeshift corrals where the bulls were held. But Miguel Angel didn't do this. Instead he slipped into a shuttered bar on a side street behind the Calle Estafeta, walked through the bar and out a door and right into Estafeta, just about where he liked to begin his favorite part of the course. Then he settled in and listened for the rocket that signaled the release of the bulls.

"This is the worst time," he said. "It is just horrible. You are so afraid. You can't stop looking at your watch. You know eight o'clock is coming."

Pamplona's Feria de San Fermín is the most moving, horrifying, hard-drinking festival in Spain. It goes on for nine days and the pace is punishing. The bulls run each morning at eight, and then everyone eats breakfast, takes a short nap, then has drinks, then comes lunch with drinks, then the bullfight, then more drinks, then dinner with drinks, followed by more drinks, dancing and carousing in bars (still more drinks), maybe a few hours' sleep, and then it's time for the next bull run. The city runs riot. Revelers from local clubs called *peñas,* the marching bands of the *peñas,* lines of dancers, tourists, and drunks of all descriptions roam the streets at all hours, clashing together with mad passion.

The atmosphere of the corridas in the large ring is just as wild as the atmosphere in the streets. The *peñas* buy up most of the seats in the sunny sections, and they spend the entirety of the spectacle chanting insults and hurling sangria and flour while their house bands play over each other at full volume. There are true aficionados in Pamplona, some of the best in Spain. But the presence of these sober fans is wiped out by the cacophony of the sunny sections. "It is very hard there," Fran said.

"Because you don't know if the people like or don't like what you do. You can't hear if the serious people are clapping or booing."

But the Feria de San Fermín, rather like bullfighting itself, is redeemed by that amazing Spanish ability to reconcile the high with the low, the grotesque with the beautiful, the morbid with the joyous, the religious with the unholy, and make sense of it in a way that few other cultures can. The Pamplona fair blends a louche and seedy carnival with stirring church services, with bull sortings held in a spotless corral where tapas are served, with dinners in local homes where the cooking is as complex and well prepared as in any restaurant, with the people of a simple and elegant city trying to hold their annual festival in the middle of a tidal wave of rowdy foreigners.

Pamplona is the capital of Navarra, a square-shaped region in the foothills of the Pyrenees. Named for its founder, the Roman general Gnaeus Pompeius Magnus (Pompey the Great), Pamplona became a Roman garrison town in the first century before Christ. During the Middle Ages Pamplona was variously under the dominion of the Visigoths, the Franks, and the Moors. In the year 778 the future Holy Roman Emperor, Charlemagne, attacked the city, knocking down its walls. The Pamplonicas responded to this a few months later by ambushing the Frankish king's army, wiping out the rear guard, and this bloody bit of business became the basis for a popular and enduring epic poem, *The Song of Roland*, although the poet converted the Pamplonicas into Moors for dramatic effect.

Today Pamplona is a small city of the type that no longer exists in the United States, sort of like what Charleston or Baltimore must have been in the time before America was afflicted with the suburban scourge. Pamplona has a population of fewer than two hundred thousand, yet it is a center of banking and small industry; it has a university; and it is home to many wealthy and middle-class residents who support its restaurants, theaters, and shops and would never dream of fleeing the city center for split-level sprawl.

The only cloud over Pamplona is the ongoing violent campaign by some of its citizens to force the creation of a Basque state separate from Spain. The Basques are an ethnic minority, tall and fair, very Catholic, and with a strong agrarian tradition. They live on both sides of the French-Spanish border and in Spain are concentrated in the País Vasco (Basque Country) and adjoining Navarra. Although the Basques are a distinct ethnic group, they have almost never ruled themselves. They have their own language (of ancient and obscure origin), but it's been centuries since any significant population spoke it. You could be killed for saying such things in some parts of Spain and France, but the truth is that Spanish Basques are Spaniards, just as are the Catalan speakers of Cataluña, the Gallego speakers of Galicia, and the Valenciano speakers of Valencia. Spanish Basques live, speak, eat, and pray like Spaniards. They also adore bullfighting. There are three first-category rings in Navarra and the País Vasco — Bilbao, Pamplona, and San Sebastián — and a brace of smaller rings of great history and respectability. The aficionados in these rings are known for their *torista* tendencies. They are demanding of bullfighters and enamored of big, fierce bulls.

The Pamplona *feria,* as its name implies, is dedicated to Saint Fermín, a local priest who was beheaded in the second century after Christ by French pagans who didn't appreciate the good news of the Bible as much as Fermín had hoped they would. His namesake festival has been celebrated since at least the thirteenth century, and has long included religious processions, outdoor markets, fireworks, and bullfights. These days the festival goes from July 6 to July 14.

The bulls have been run in Pamplona for a good four hundred years, and in other places in Spain — especially in Navarra and around Madrid — in more recent times.

Most historians agree that the practice grew out of the fact that bullfighting bulls used to be herded on foot directly into whatever town square or palace was being used for the corrida. In order to minimize danger to life and property, the herdsmen would wait until the wee hours of the morning and dash the bulls in as fast as possible. One morning, way back when, some bright townsman decided to run along with the bulls, and this spontaneous activity hardened into a Spanish tradition.

The runs are now called *encierros*— "the enclosing of the bulls in a corral" — because that is what the runners are theoretically aiming to do, racing ahead of the bulls to lure them into the bullring. The average run lasts less than three minutes and results in the trampling and perhaps the goring of perhaps ten runners. From the 1870s to the 1970s, there were two dozen occasions when falling runners caused dangerous pileups that resulted in many injuries. Every so often a runner has died from being gored or trampled in a pileup. This has happened thirteen times since 1924, when people started keeping count. The most recent death was an American, in 1995, the only non-Spaniard to die in an *encierro*.

Pamplona, July 10. The buzzer echoed in the dark hallway of Noël Chandler's apartment and someone stumbled out of bed to let in whoever it was and stop the racket. There were four people staying in the apartment and they were all desperately hung over. Just then Noël shuffled out of his room, went down the hall, and opened the heavy wooden shutters in the living room, which gave out onto a city of gray stone situated in a green valley. The air was damp and cold. Down below was the Calle Estafeta. Apartment buildings lined the narrow street on both sides. Scores of people hung out of the small balconies on the buildings' façades, and ragged clusters of people wandered around on the street. All of them were dressed in the traditional costume of the *feria*: white pants, white shirt, with a red bandanna around the neck.

Noël was especially bleary that morning. He had been hard at the red wine the night before, something that he'd done frequently and with impunity in his younger days, but that had begun to play havoc with his close to seventy-year-old system. His blood pressure had spiked to vertiginous heights and he was worried about it. Of course that didn't mean Noël was willing to give up drinking or place himself in the care of a physician. Instead he did the best he could to moderate his alcohol consumption and was taking some blood-pressure medicine procured from a Miami cardiologist friend who was in town for the bullfights.

"At least I've got these new tablets," Noël said. "Last night my blood pressure was two-fifty over one-twenty; the doctor told me that by all rights I should be dead."

Just before eight o'clock, the mood in the Calle Estafeta quickened. The balconies were filled with spectators and the streets were mobbed with a sea of people in white shirts and red bandannas. Someone turned on the television in Noël's living room and there was a broadcast of what was taking place some three hundred yards down the street. A red-and-white throng had gathered beside a high stone wall with a small shrine in it, and they were chanting to the shrine: "To San Fermín we ask / because he is our patron / to guide us through the bull run / and give us his benediction. / Long live San Fermín! Long live San Fermín!" They chanted it again and again, the fear and anticipation rising in their throats.

Just then a mob came jogging below Noël's window. They had come from the spot where the people were chanting. They were the "valiant ones," who'd chosen to run so far ahead of the bulls that they were in more danger of losing their dignity than their lives. The crowd along Estafeta let out a lusty and sarcastic shout for the valiant ones, and the runners kept coming. Suddenly there was the cracking report of a single rocket. "They've opened the gates," Noël said. He waited, his long nose skyward, and then another rocket blast. "All the bulls are out," he said. "Watch now, you'll see them soon."

Pamplona, July 8. An old man touched the flame of his cigarette lighter to a wick and the rocket shot up leaving a cloud of white smoke. *Bang!* Someone opened the wooden gate and a thicket of gnarled horns emerged through the cloud. Behind the horns were steers: tame, lanky animals with coats of red, brown, and white blotches, cowbells around their necks. The steers ran the *encierros* every year. They knew where they were going and moved with a certain detachment, heads up, maintaining a steady pace. In their wake, crowding their bony hindquarters, scrambling with heads down, in a big hurry, came a knot of six bulls. The bulls were muscled and thick, and their heads bounced on stiff necks as they galloped.

Up the steep grade of Santo Domingo they ran, the clacking of the bulls' hooves and the lunatic music of the cowbells echoing off stone buildings. The runners were massed at the top of the hill, where the police had herded them. When the bulls came into view, the runners flew down to meet them, breaking around the bulls like a red and white sea over black rocks. The bulls kept moving. The runners stopped short, turned, and began running back up the hill, some ahead of the bulls, some right with them, and some behind them.

A man in a red shirt fell just in front of the pack of bulls. A chestnut bull lowered its head and, almost as an afterthought, punched its horn into the falling man's back. The man crumpled and didn't get up again. The bull moved on up the street, blood on its horn. "Oh, my God," shouted a pretty young American tourist, perched on a wall. *Bang!* The second rocket fired, indicating that all of the bulls were out of the corrals, but by then they were already over Santo Domingo and into central Pamplona. People stood on rooftops and balconies to see them. They hung off drainpipes, dangled over walls, and wrapped themselves on the wooden barricades to see the race go by.

Men and animals scurried through the Plaza Consistorial, where the Pamplona town hall was, and turned into the short Calle Mercaderes. The pack was running due east just then and the sun poured over them from between the buildings. Three bulls fell, but the madness of the herd was on them and they got up and kept running. Mercaderes ended with an almost ninety-degree turn into Estafeta. This was the notorious curve where there was always a spill. This morning four bulls went down, straining their necks forward and pawing madly as they lurched upright once more.

Estafeta was packed. The street was wall-to-wall runners, spectators, and hangers-on; there was nowhere for people to escape because the street was lined with buildings. The bulls plunged into the crowded street and the people gave way around the animals, falling, flailing, pushing with all their might into the stone walls. At this moment Miguel Angel appeared. He ran up from behind the bulls as they passed, out on the margins of the pack, gaining speed, dodging people, reaching the pace of the bulls, closing in. Runners surrounded the bulls. Miguel Angel lanced into the center of the street, toward the herd, moving laterally like an American football player, looking for a way to pierce the runners and get to the bulls. Then he saw daylight, shot to his right, hit the gap between two runners, and he was in with the bulls.

Knees pumping up and down almost to his chest, arms out, trying to maintain his balance, Miguel Angel Eguiluz ran in the small space between the hindquarters of the steers and the horns of a chestnut bull. He jumped out ahead of the horns a few paces, then slowed down again, then bounced off the horns, searching for the correct pace to stay within inches of the heavy bobbing horns. He ran looking back over his shoulder, watching the bull, heedless of what was going on ahead of him. For a moment he and the bull ran together, lost in their own form of communication in the middle of the mob. Then Miguel Angel lost steam. He slid across his bull, across the horns of two others, and popped out of the traveling herd and over to the safety of a wall. His run had taken less than ten seconds.

The bulls had more work to do. The three lead animals took the curve out of Estafeta, bounded into the tunnel, and came into the circle of the bullring to cheers. The rest of the pack straggled in behind, entering the ring one, two, three. As they entered they spread out, instinctively taking charge of the new, wider space they were in. Then they moved across the sand and were herded into the small entrance to the corrals. When the last bull had been stowed away, another rocket sounded. *Bang!* It was the end of an easy and uneventful *encierro* that lasted less than three minutes, with one goring and maybe two significant tramplings. Happy and exhausted, Miguel Angel went off in search of friends and some breakfast.

About an hour after the *encierro* of July 10, the day that Fran was supposed to have appeared in the afternoon corrida, Miguel Angel Eguiluz walked over to Noël's apartment to talk about being a bull runner. He was not eager to have his name in a book. His *feria* was a religious festival, he said, and the festival of the people of Pamplona as a group. It was not an excuse for one person to engage in self-promotion or bragging. Miguel Angel did not want to take too much time to talk about his exploits as a runner, or his injuries, or anything that he had done. What he did wish to do was to explain why he ran and how he felt about it.

"For me, the concept of the *encierro* is that it is for our saint, for San Fermín," Miguel Angel said. "For a Pamplonica, running with the bulls is the culmination of our *fiesta* and we honor our city by taking part in it. But it is hard to describe what it is like to run. It is a mix of fear, of anguish, of terror, and of joy. When you are running right there with the bulls, the world closes up around you, and it is just you and the bull. And sometimes you feel you are actually slowing the bull down, that he is running with you, and it is a kind of conversation between you and the bull."

21

Papa

For most of its history, Pamplona's *feria* was an obscure local festival, and its *encierros* were of little interest to anyone save the few men who took part in them. Anyone familiar with the overcrowded, spectator-sport atmosphere of present-day *encierros* would be shocked to see early photographs that show tiny handfuls of men, many wearing jackets and ties, running with bulls through streets otherwise devoid of life. Change came to Pamplona when Ernest Hemingway arrived, fell in love with the *feria,* and sold it to the world through his writing.

He was twenty-three, an unknown writer living in Paris, when he heard about bullfighting from his literary friends Gertrude Stein and Alice B. Toklas and from an American painter named Mike Strater. In the spring of 1923 he went to Spain and saw his first corrida hours after stepping off the train in Madrid. He returned to Spain a few months later for his first adventure in Pamplona. Those two trips altered the course of Hemingway's life and work. From that year on, he would return to the bullring again and again, both as a writer and as a fan. It is said that Hemingway called to reserve tickets to the Pamplona corridas in the weeks just before he killed himself. The first rocket of the 1961 *feria* exploded four days after the self-inflicted gunshot that blasted off Hemingway's head.

Bullfighting is one of the predominant subjects in Hemingway's work. It crops up in his early newspaper articles; in the short sketches that interlard his first story collection, *In Our Time* (1925); in his Pamplona novel, *The Sun Also Rises* (1926); in *Death in the Afternoon* (1932), which at the time was the only philosophical explanation of bullfighting in any language; in the Spanish Civil War novel *For Whom the Bell Tolls* (1940); in short stories like "The Undefeated" (1927) and "The Capital of the World" (1938); and in the last work Hemingway published during his lifetime, the three long articles for *Life* magazine about the series of one-on-one corridas in 1959 that starred Fran's grandfather Antonio Ordóñez and Fran's great-uncle Luis Miguel Gonzáles Lucas, Dominguín, later published in book form as *The Dangerous Summer* (1985).

Hemingway has done more than anyone to foster worldwide understanding and appreciation of the bullfight. Nearly all bullfighting enthusiasts born in a nonbullfighting country were either drawn to the bullfights by Hemingway or read him as their interest in bullfighting grew. So why is it that most bullfighting people dislike him? You'd think Hemingway would be a hero in taurine circles, but he isn't. The Spanish dismiss him because he doesn't translate well into their language and because many of them refuse to accept that a non-Spaniard has become, in effect, the spokesman for their national *fiesta*. He embarrasses English-speaking aficionados because he reminds them that what they like to think of as their private obsession is actually something found in books that are read by most high school English classes.

"Look, Hemingway was the first kid on the block," said Jesse Graham, a Hollywood screenwriter and aficionado of Anglo-Irish descent. "So you have to declare independence from him. There is a defensive thing that happens. When you say you are interested in the bullfights, people immediately assume you were inspired by his example, and then you just feel like saying, 'No, I never read him.' "

Whether they are Spanish, English, or German, bullfighting fans don't like Hemingway because they feel competitive toward him. Like most religions and many hobbies, bullfighting inspires a tedious snobbism among its adherents. Hemingway was the worst when it came to this sort of thing. From the know-it-all tone of much of his writing on the subject, it seems obvious that part of what attracted him to bullfighting was that it was virgin territory from a literary standpoint and he could have it all to himself. The Scottish novelist A. L. Kennedy sums up Hemingway's attitude in her 1999 treatise *On Bullfighting*. "The Hemingway bravado did nothing for me," Kennedy writes, "the menopausal bar-room stories, the foreigner trying too hard to be part of Spain, but, all the while, hoping to keep it exclusive, defining the country, for the first time, as one vast DT-haunted tourist club."

But Hemingway is by no means the only offender in this department. Since the very beginnings of the spectacle, Spanish commentators have consistently written about bullfighting fans as though they were divided into a vast ignorant crowd that comes to the arena for cheap thrills and an elite minority of aficionados who understand what they are seeing and can make intelligent judgments. Taking their cue from this attitude, most non-Spanish fans like to think of themselves as members of the elite. Visit any bar in Pamplona at *feria* time and you will find an American going on and on about his near-death bull-running adventures, how many corridas he's seen, how many matadors call him friend. If anyone else at the bar makes a comment about bullfighting, this guy will disagree for the sake of it. If anyone mentions Hemingway, he'll say Hemingway didn't know blankety-blank about bullfighting.

The standard rap on Hemingway is that he didn't know as much about the subject as he claimed; that he saw a relatively small number of corridas in his life compared, say, to an aficionado like Noël Chandler; and that his *Life* articles of 1959 contain some grossly unfair criticisms of such important matadors as Manolete and Domínguin. The critique is fair, but it misses the point. Hemingway wasn't a bullfighting expert or a journalist, even when he was ostensibly writing bullfighting journalism. He was a fiction writer and a prose stylist who used the corrida as raw material for his larger artistic purposes, dramatizing and warping bullfighting as he needed to for effect.

Yet in looking back on Hemingway's work—particularly *The Sun Also Rises* and *Death in the Afternoon*—one is struck by how quickly and fully he understood his subject. He makes few if any factual errors. More important, he manages to zero right in on bullfighting's peculiar nature. As Hemingway said, bullfighting is an ephemeral art. The work of a great matador disappears as soon as the bull dies, and nothing can preserve the feeling of it as it happened—not painting, not sculpture, not film, not video, not words on a page. It is gone. Which is part of the reason why bullfighting fans are almost always nostalgic, their memories of bygone corridas being so much sweeter and more exciting than the corridas they are able to see in real time. It is also part of the reason why no two fans can ever agree on anything except that Hemingway didn't know what he was talking about.

Bullfighting fans love to argue, even about what should be simple facts. Ask how many first-category rings there are and some people will say eight, as does the Spanish government; some will say nine, including Pamplona, which is considered first-category by the bullfighters' union; and some will say eleven, adding Nîmes and Arles, the first-category French rings. Mention the well-known statistic that the noted matador Juan Belmonte performed 109 times during the 1919 season and someone will object that two of these weren't formal corridas. Ask a roomful of fans the meaning of any bullfighting term and each person will offer a different definition. The discussions of bullfighting experts compare in complexity with those of Talmud scholars. As Hemingway himself once wrote, entire books of controversy have been written in Spain on the subject of how to define a single cape pass.

Hemingway's other major insight might seem simple, but it is not one shared by many aficionados. Hemingway understood that death was bullfighting's primary subject. Many aficionados, including Noël, are quite uncomfortable with this. They are so wrapped up in the culture of bullfighting, so interested in it from a technical point of view, that they can no longer see it clearly. Seated in a bullring, surrounded by well-dressed couples and families munching on snacks, it's easy to forget that large creatures are being slaughtered down on the sand. But Hemingway never forgot it, and he praised Spaniards for taking an intelligent interest in death and having the common sense to pay a small fee to see it given, avoided, refused, and accepted during an afternoon's entertainment.

Well, Hemingway could be an annoying guy. He was highly impressed with himself and always had to be the smartest man in the room. In his final years he was a drunk and a bore, he preferred to play the role of "Papa" that he had created for himself, and he perhaps judged the toreros of the 1950s by the standards of the 1920s. He was certainly the product of his time, and many of his interests and attitudes seem out of date these days. Even people who enjoy his writing concede that when he wrote poorly — which he did with increasing frequency as his life progressed — the results read like a parody of his more successful early style.

Yet Hemingway was perhaps the most influential writer of the twentieth-century and, along with Goya, Picasso, and a handful of others, was one of the artists whose interest in bullfighting elevated it from an obscure folk art to a topic of international discussion. He was also an important figure in Fran's life, because the matadors that mattered most to Hemingway, the ones to whom he assigned starring roles in his books, the ones who defined what Hemingway wanted to be as a man, invariably bore the last name Ordóñez.

22

❧⟡⟐⟡☙

Dry Dock

Madrid, July 12. Fran groaned in agony, his breath coming in tatters through clenched jaws. The day outside was scorching, and Fran was in a small clinic in a neighborhood north of the city center. Madonna's "Like a Prayer" played on a small radio. Fran sat on a stool in a booth-like room, his left arm perched on a padded table. A physical therapist pressed the forearm down as far as it would go, which wasn't far. When the forearm reached about sixty degrees above the table, Fran couldn't take the pain anymore. "Stop, stop, stop!" he said, and the therapist let go, and Fran breathed a sigh of exquisite relief.

Two weeks had passed since the tossing in Algeciras, and Fran had already missed a half-dozen corridas, including the July 10 date in Pamplona, a tough loss. On that afternoon Francisco Marco, El Juli, and Fran's replacement, Manuel Caballero, cut a total of five ears off a cooperative and easy-charging string of bulls from the ranch of Gutiérrez Lorenzo. This was the greatest number of ears cut in a single corrida in Pamplona that year and a wonderful opportunity for the matadors on the card to make a splash in the most important bullfighting cycle of midsummer. Fran was still chewing over his bad luck.

"The bulls were the best ones of the *feria*, weren't they?" said Fran. "That sucks." And then, "This fucking arm."

But if Fran was depressed, he didn't show it. Like all matadors he expected to be knocked out of action for a part of every season. Although he'd never been gored in his career, he had strained or broken a knee, a wrist, or an ankle during previous seasons, and he knew that after such an injury his job was to keep evil thoughts at bay and get better as soon as he could. "Not only have I lost many fights," Fran said, "but the real problem is that I will not see a bull for a month and I'll lose my touch. Then I have responsibility for all of my people. I have insurance for myself, so they pay me for every fight I lose after three. But my men don't get anything. They are losing a lot. A couple of them are looking for a big tree to hang themselves."

Tossings and gorings change bullfighters. It is said in the bull world that you do not know how much potential a young torero has until you see how he reacts to his first big goring. Some matadors never recover their composure after a serious wound; some lose it for a while and then get it back again. But every injury in the ring has its effect on the bullfighter, and over the course of a long career such incidents can mount up and give him a sense of doubt when he is in the ring, which can be more debilitating than a broken bone or an open horn wound.

Fran's injury wasn't a serious one, but the afternoon of the tossing was still on his mind. "The bull wasn't fierce," Fran said, "but it was unpredictable and it surprised me. At one moment there was a lot of wind, and just then I moved the *muleta* from one hand to the other, and when I did I lost sight of the bull. And the bull came at me. He attacked me and I couldn't do anything." But Fran had come to terms with the injury by explaining it. "I made a mistake. You cannot take your eyes off the bull, ever. All the time you have to keep him in the corner of your eye. All it took was one second for the bull to surprise me. I shook the *muleta* at him, but he ignored it. He wanted me. Sometimes the bull just catches you, but most wounds come because of your mistakes."

Fran led a boring life in Madrid. His hangers-on had all gone back to their homes around Sevilla and Córdoba, and he was staying in the apartment of an honorary aunt, which happened to be near his physical therapist. He awoke each morning around nine and made his way to the clinic for a few hours of painful stretching, followed by weightlifting and thirty minutes of sprinting on a stationary bicycle. Then it was back home for lunch and a nap, and then another two- or three-hour session at the clinic. Evenings he ate dinner with his aunt or caught a movie. At twenty-eight, he had two arthritic knees, resulting from various injuries and overexercise, and a left arm that might never hang straight again.

"I'm a wreck," Fran said.

The only bright spot during this time was the few days Fran had spent in Ronda, where he was the promoter of the local ring. Ronda was the stunning mountain town where the Romero dynasty of matadors established bullfighting on foot in the eighteenth century, and where the Ordóñez dynasty sprang up in the twentieth. Fran had inherited the right to manage the historic and beautiful bullring there from his late grandfather Antonio. The bullring was home to a three-bullfight *feria* each September, and the centerpiece of this cycle was the Corrida Goyesca, one of the important dates of the bullfighting calendar. A *goyesca* is a corrida in which the participants wear costumes resembling those worn by toreros in the late eighteenth and early nineteenth centuries and depicted in the prints and paintings of Francisco Goya.

Fran's grandfather Antonio and his great-grandfather Cayetano Ordóñez, El Niño de la Palma, founded the first *goyesca* of Ronda in 1954, to honor the two hundredth birthday of Pedro Romero, the most famous of the Romeros. The *goyesca* was always one of the most popular bullfights in Spain and tickets were hard to come by, but the *novillada* (junior bullfight) the day before and the *corrida de rejones* (equestrian bullfight) the day after never attracted as many fans. So that year, for the first time, Fran had offered a subscription for *goyesca* seats, giving preference to fans who had purchased season tickets, and as a result sales had shot up for the *novillada* and the *corrida de rejones*. The upcoming *goyesca* was scheduled for September 7, with Fran, El Juli, and an uncle of Fran's, the matador Curro Vázquez, on the card. Fran hoped that he would be well enough by then.

Fran finished his physical therapy and moved to the stationary bicycle. Injured or healthy, he was always careful to keep himself in good shape. During the off-season he practiced martial arts, rode horses, ran, lifted weights, stretched, and did pushups and sit-ups. Like most matadors, Fran was young and fit, but toreros did not have to be great physical specimens to perform well. In fact, sickly and elderly bullfighters often continued to practice their trade with success. During Hemingway's heyday, Manuel García López, called Maera, dazzled crowds in 1924 before dying of the tuberculosis that had been killing him all that season. In 2000, Francisco Romero López, Curro Romero, at the age of sixty-five performed seventeen times, including four dates in Sevilla and a major triumph in Jerez.

As one famous bullfighter is said to have remarked: "Why do I need to be in good shape? It is the bull that makes all the effort."

That afternoon in Madrid, I asked Fran why he had decided to become a matador. Fran didn't answer my question except to say that he had always wanted to be one. Then he launched into a series of anecdotes from his childhood, each of which had the same basic plot: the young Fran expresses his desire to become a torero; someone tries to dissuade him and this only increases his ambition. The last of these stories took place when Fran was already practicing with his grandfather. Someone gave Fran two video collections of the most terrifying gorings in bullfighting history and told him to watch them from beginning to end.

"I saw them a couple of times," Fran said, "and after that I still wanted to be a bullfighter."

This talk of videos and gorings led me to ask Fran a question I had been putting off until the end of the season for fear of antagonizing him. Had he ever seen the video of his father's goring and the footage in the infirmary as the doctors tended to his wounds?

"Ah," Fran replied. He paused for a moment, then turned to me. "Yes," Fran said, "I saw it. But many years later."

I expressed sympathy for Fran's loss, something I had never had the chance to do. But Fran was uninterested in such sentiments. As he had with his tossing in Algeciras, Fran had reduced his father's death to something explainable. It was an accident, he said, and no worse than any other accident that takes a young man from his family, and it certainly wasn't the reason Fran had become a matador. Paquirri's death was just something that had happened. Not a tragedy. An accident.

"I am sure my father preferred to die in the ring," Fran added. "Because I think I would prefer that too. Of course I want to die in bed with my great-great-great-grandchildren around me. But if I have to die tomorrow, what would I prefer, a heart attack or the ring? I prefer to die in the ring. This isn't just a profession. It is a way of life. My father was a bullfighter, and bulls kill bullfighters. I think he died the way he wanted to. I don't want to be a bullfighter because my father was one or my grandfather was one. I do it because I like being a bullfighter."

23

The Kid

Cayetano Ordóñez y Aguilera, Fran's great-grandfather, was born in Ronda on January 4, 1904, a single day shy of seventy years before Fran's birth. He had no bullfighting pedigree. His father was a cobbler in Ronda with a shoe store named La Palma, at 8 Calle Santa Cecilia. The store failed when Cayetano was thirteen, and the family moved to La Línea de la Concepción, near Gibraltar, where work was easier to come by. Cayetano got a job as a busboy in a local restaurant. He learned English there from the tourists, and about the bulls from the many breeders and toreros who frequented the restaurant and bar.

This was a real perk, because like most Andalucían boys of his time, Cayetano was besotted with the idea of becoming a great matador. Bullfighting was one of the few forms of mass entertainment in turn-of-the-century Spain, and it was going through what is now thought of as its Golden Age, thanks to the competition between two toreros from Sevilla. José Gómez y Ortega, known as Joselito, became a matador in 1912 at the age of seventeen, skipping the long apprenticeships that were common then. He was tall, elegant, and handsome, and he made bullfighting look easy, placing banderillas with style, commanding the bull with his *capote,* and killing like a cannon. It was said that there was not a calf born that José couldn't handle.

Joselito was the best of his day, but it is important to remember that his day was a primitive one. Picadors' horses wore no protection. Many died each corrida, and spectators in the front rows were often splattered with the horses' blood and viscera — something that was portrayed as comic relief in contemporary newspaper accounts. The act of the horses and the killing with the sword were the key elements of this earlier, more brutal form of bullfight. The art of passing bulls with the *muleta* and the *capote* was still quite crude. The prevailing practice was, you waved your cape at the bull and then got out of the way or the bull would get you. There was a concept that matadors could stand still and use the cape to direct the horns past their bodies, but few were able to practice it.

The development of modern bullfighting was a complex process. Many toreros contributed to it, and aficionados love to argue over who contributed what. For sure, one major figure, perhaps *the* major figure, was a matador named Juan Belmonte. He was born three years before Joselito but became a full matador in 1913, a year later than Joselito. Belmonte was as unlikely a matador as Joselito was a classic one. He was short, ugly, and sickly, with twisted legs that could barely run. Still he drove himself to be a matador. Legend has it that as a child Juan would sneak out of Sevilla into the countryside where he would strip nude and cape bullfighting bulls in their pastures by moonlight. In his ignorance of how to use a cape and in facing the limitation of his bad legs, Belmonte adopted a revolutionary style of *toreo*. He proved that if he stood still and swung his cape, the bull would follow the cloth and leave him alone.

It took Belmonte years of blood and struggle to perfect his style, but when he hit the arena, he hit it like an earthquake. People thronged to see him, and one prominent matador of the old school said that people had better see him as soon as they could, because he wasn't going to be around long. In fact, Belmonte improved each year, and over time his success with his style helped to change bullfighting forever. After Belmonte, the work with the *muleta*, which had been perfunctory, became the longest, most dangerous, evocative, and dramatic part of the bullfight, until it became the point of the bullfight.

Many of the other matadors of Belmonte's day had a hard time keeping up with Belmonte, but not Joselito. He'd been a genius of the old school, and he brought all of his grace and ring science to mastering Belmonte's technique. From 1913 to 1920 he and Belmonte performed together more than 250 times, driving each other to excellence, creating their golden age.

Sometime during those years, or so the story goes, Belmonte was in a restaurant in La Línea de la Concepción, where he was presiding over a table of *taurino* types, when a thin busboy in an apron, bloody from cutting sides of beef, walked up to him. "Can I help you, son?" Belmonte asked. "Yes, Maestro," said Cayetano Ordóñez. "I want you to give me the *alternativa* and make me a matador in the bullring of Sevilla." "Excellent," Belmonte replied with a laugh. "When you can kill a bull more cleanly than you can cut him up for steaks, I'll make you a matador."

Meanwhile, aficionados were sharply divided between those who admired Joselito's elegance (the Joselistas) and those who loved Belmonte's tragic intensity (the Belmontistas), and often when the two performed together the feelings aroused in the stands were so strong that fans would riot. But by 1919 the public began to turn on both men. Like many matadors before and after them, Joselito and Belmonte were the victims of their own success. Every time they appeared they were expected to perform miracles. They'd excelled for so long that they had begun to compete with the public's memory of their greatness, and the memories were always better.

By the spring of 1920 many crowds treated them with open hostility. Their last performance together took place in Madrid on May 15. According to Belmonte's semifictional memoir, the crowd screamed at them both, and Joselito was taking it badly. "Listen, Juan," Joselito is supposed to have said to Belmonte. "We might as well face it now. The public is furious with us, and the day is coming when we won't be able to go into the ring at all."

The next day, in the village of Talavera de la Reina, on the road from Madrid to Badajoz, Bailador, a bull of the ranch of the Widow Ortega, gored Joselito. The matador's midriff was sliced open and his innards spilled from his body. As he was carried to the infirmary, he cried out, "Mother, I'm smothering!" Then he died. Although audiences had harassed him to an early grave, forcing him to take greater and greater chances to please them, all of Spain went into mourning over Joselito, including Belmonte, who was devastated by the loss of his rival. Belmonte went on for another season, but his heart wasn't in it, and in 1921 he fled to South America. Bullfighting's Golden Age had ended, and for the next few years the world of the bulls languished as the search began for a new savior who could reinvigorate the spectacle.

In 1924 wild rumors began to circulate that the new idol had been found. He was a *novillero* named Cayetano Ordóñez, who performed under the name El Niño de la Palma (the Kid of the Palm), after his father's old shoe store. El Niño, as he was soon called, had worked his way into the bull world and up the ranks year by year until he erupted onto the national stage with two triumphs in Sevilla. The day after the second of these, which took place on May 4, 1925, the noted critic Gregorio Corrochano, of the newspaper *ABC,* published a review that contained the most famous line of praise ever written about a bull-fighter: *"Es de Ronda, y se llama Cayetano"* — He is from Ronda, and his name is Cayetano.

The full impact of this sentence doesn't come across in translation, but it was magic to many Spaniards, because it summed up the hopes of their generation of aficionados. Joselito was dead, Belmonte had retired, but here was a new hero. He came from Ronda, the town where bull-fighting was born, and his name was Cayetano — like Cayetano Sanz, one of the nineteenth century's great matadors. In many ways El Niño found himself in the same position that Fran would seventy years later. By virtue of circumstances neither one had any control over, each of these young men was thrust into the role of the anointed one, the mata-dor who was going to live up to the legend of a dead hero or be judged a failure.

Like Fran, El Niño took his *alternativa* ceremony in Sevilla before he'd gained enough experience and skill to justify the elevation in rank. (As it happened, Juan Belmonte returned to Spain just in time to give El Niño the ceremony.) And like Fran, El Niño had the talent and bravery to defy his own inexperience and justify everyone's expectations of him in his first season, his one true season of brilliance.

Mythologized by a Spanish bullfight critic in May of 1925, El Niño would have the luck — good or bad — to be mythologized by an Ameri-can novelist two months later. By then Hemingway had published his first short story collection and was launched as a writer. The next step in his career would be a novel, and he was on the prowl for a subject. He found one in Pamplona that summer. Hemingway had brought along a ragtag band of friends to the *feria* that year, including a doomed blonde and her alcoholic boyfriend, a Jewish writer who'd slept with the blonde, and some bohemian types. There was tension over the girl, and Hem-ingway would take that tension and build a novel around it, adding a single crucial character to the mix, a young matador who catches the blonde's eye and brings the plot to its climax.

In that novel, *The Sun Also Rises,* the matador is Pedro Romero —

Hemingway giving his bullfighter the name of the revered Romero family of Ronda matadors. But as Hemingway would later write, the model for his Pedro Romero was El Niño, and all the bullfighting sequences in the book are true to what Hemingway saw Cayetano Ordóñez do in the ring in Pamplona in 1925.

"Romero never made any contortions," Hemingway wrote in his novel. "Always it was straight and pure and natural in line. The others twisted themselves like corkscrews, their elbows raised, and leaned against the flanks of the bull after his horns had passed, to give a faked look of danger. Afterward, all that was faked turned bad and gave an unpleasant feeling. Romero's bullfighting gave pure emotion because he kept the absolute purity of line in his movements and always quietly and calmly let the horns pass him close each time. He did not have to emphasize their closeness."

El Niño had a kind of innate wisdom about bulls. From the beginning he knew just how to approach each animal, and he combined this with a natural panache in performance wedded to the serenity to pass the horns close to his body. That was on his good days, however, and El Niño was never a consistent performer. He was a mercurial figure, happy and giddy and ready for a party one day, melancholy and lethargic the next.

During the 1926 season, his second as a full matador, El Niño did well, but not as well as he had in 1925. He also caused a stir that year when he stated openly what everyone in bullfighting knew, that many critics accepted bribes in return for favorable reviews. But El Niño refused to name names, which alienated the entire bullfighting press. The crooked critics hated him for exposing their scam, while the honest critics were furious because, by refusing to say who was on the take, El Niño had cast doubt on the innocent as well as the guilty.

The 1927 season, El Niño's third, was also a successful one for him, but not as successful as 1926, and even less so than 1925. There were days when he had the spark. Yet there were more and more days when it seemed the whole thing bored him, and when the crowds complained, El Niño would retreat into a resigned stubbornness that pleased neither himself nor his public. That July he married a part-Gypsy silent-movie actress and flamenco dancer named Consuelo Araujo de los Reyes. By all accounts the couple was happy, too happy, as Consuelo had a taste for all-night parties that did El Niño's bullfighting no good. Midway through the 1928 season, his reputation as a matador falling, El Niño retired. He was only twenty-four, already starting to look old, and was roundly judged to be a failure because he couldn't live up to the legend of Joselito.

He returned to the bulls in 1929 and clung to the wreckage of his career for another two decades, eventually sliding into the role of banderillero when the public would no longer have him as a matador. During this time Gregorio Corrochano, the writer who had made El Niño's reputation, became his harshest and most persistent critic. Hemingway went the same route. "If you see Niño de la Palma," Hemingway wrote in *Death in the Afternoon,* "the chances are you will see cowardice in its least attractive form; its fat-rumped, prematurely bald from using hair fixatives, prematurely senile form." El Niño appeared in his last bullfight in 1950. He died, broken in body and spirit, in the autumn of 1961, a few months after Hemingway's suicide and a few weeks before the death of Gregorio Corrochano.

The parallels between El Niño's life and Fran's were notable. Both sprang onto the scene with impossible legacies to live up to and little experience. Both had success for three seasons, only to watch their reputations decline. Both were distracted by high-profile marriages to strong women, and both forged hostile relations with the press. But Fran had one thing going for him that his great-grandfather did not: he was still alive. There was time for Fran to write a different ending to his story — not as much time as there had been, but time enough.

24

A Traveling Season

Málaga, August 10. "We're all so tired," said gray-haired Poli, lifting a cold bottle of Heineken to his lips, "and we shouldn't be, because we've had so much time off."

"I think we're tired *because* we've had all this time off," said Pepe the driver. "You need to accustom yourself to this life."

Fran's cuadrilla was eating its post-bullfight dinner in a neighborhood restaurant near their businessmen's hotel downtown. Fran wasn't with them. He preferred to stay in the fancy hilltop resort hotel with its commanding view of the old bullring and the high-rises around it and the bay in the distance. It was midnight, and two days had passed since Fran's return to work following his June 29 injury in Algeciras. The strained elbow had kept him out of action for forty days, a layoff that had caused the predictable disruption to pocketbooks, bullfighting skills, and psyches. The team had missed twenty corridas, Fran had slipped to twelfth on the *escalafón*, and they'd lost the invaluable opportunity to rack up a consistent stream of successes and get in mental and physical shape for August and September — the traveling season when the corridas would come every day.

In retrospect, the first half of August, the weeks after Fran's return, were the absolute low point of the season. The joyous anticipation of the winter, the grim determination of spring, and the resigned concentration of the injury layoff had all dissipated, and in their place a kind of disengagement with the task at hand had set in. There was nothing acute about it, but Fran didn't seem motivated. He was distracted and lifeless in the ring, giving up on bulls that might have yielded ears with a little effort from the matador. He no longer mixed with his cuadrilla during off hours, but spent his free time locked away in hotel rooms, going to the movies with Nacho, or flying off to fit in short visits with his daughter, who was staying with her mother at the duchess of Alba's summer retreat in Marbella.

The cuadrilla members were also in a dark mood. They'd lost a lot of money during their enforced summer holiday, and when they started performing again the matador wasn't cutting ears the way a top-ranked matador should. This upset them on many levels. As businessmen they were worried that if Fran kept going on this way he would fall from the top rank and there wouldn't be as much work for them in the future. As toreros, they wanted the pride of being able to say they traveled with one of the elite matadors in Spain and the pleasure of working in the first-class rings and big *ferias*. And simply as people, it hurt them to see Fran not doing as well as he could. "Please, God, let him cut a few ears!" said the assistant manservant, Antonio, one evening. "Let him cut a few ears!"

Fran returned to the ring on August 8 in the shockingly large *plaza de toros* of Palma, the capital of Mallorca, a Spanish island in the Mediterranean off Valencia. For the only time that season, Fran and his assistant bullfighters took a plane to a bullfight, leaving Pepe to drive the cuadrilla minibus overland and hop a ferry from Barcelona. The corrida took place on a soft summer evening. The arena was full of people on holiday, and King Juan Carlos was seated in the first row. As is customary on such occasions, Fran dedicated his first bull to the monarch, but killed badly and lost an ear. He was better on his second bull and did cut an ear. It wasn't much of a result given the indulgent crowd that night, which had granted two and three ears to the other matadors on the card.

Palma de Mallorca was everyone's first look at how the injured left elbow was going to hold up under bullfight pressure, and it was not a promising sight. Even at a distance it was easy to see that Fran was still in a lot of pain and favoring the arm. It was unable to bend the way a healthy arm should. It hung at Fran's side at a funny angle, and he held it against his hip when he wasn't using it, and tried not to use it too much. To reduce the load the arm had to carry, Fran had taken to hugging his *capote* to his chest during downtimes in the ring and carried the *muleta* as much as possible in his right hand. These were things Fran would continue to do until the end of the season.

On August 9, the day after Palma, Fran was down in the southern tip of Andalucía for a bullfight in the grand old *plaza* at El Puerto de Santa María, perhaps the largest and most impressive small-town ring in Spain. Fran drew bad bulls that evening and couldn't be bothered to put in the effort to make something out of them. That brought him to August 10 and the first of two corridas he was scheduled to take part in that month at La Malagueta, the venerable ring of Málaga. On that evening, with a small, ugly, but willing bull from the ranch of Daniel Ruiz Yagüe, Fran snapped out of his prevailing funk, only to have a fine effort spoiled by a stubborn bullring president who, for some unaccountable reason and in defiance of bullfighting rules, ignored an arena full of handkerchiefs and denied Fran the ear he deserved.

(As the crowd spilled out of the ring that night, one local aficionado explained that this president — the aficionado actually referred to the president as a "son of a bitch" — was trying to raise the reputation of the Málaga ring by making it harder to cut ears there.)

Fran's cuadrilla had already had three corridas in as many days, and the week ahead was going to be just as grueling. They were in the thick of the typical inhuman schedule of a working team of toreros in the late summer of a Spanish bullfighting season. During the eight days from the tenth to the seventeenth of August, they would perform in seven corridas, driving overnight on six nights and passing two in hotels. Their shortest overnight journey would be about 240 miles, from the Mediterranean coast at Málaga to Ciudad Real, in the central plain of La Mancha. Their longest overnight trip spanned 620 miles across the very length of Spain, from Gijón, hard by the Atlantic Ocean, to Málaga, on the Mediterranean. In all they would travel some 2,200 miles that week. This was approximately the distance from New York to Los Angeles, or from Madrid to Moscow by airplane. But they were not flying; they were driving in cramped vans through the second-most-mountainous country in Europe.

"How long is the trip to Huesca?" asked José María. They had a corrida the next day in Huesca, in the region of Aragón.

"It's about nine hundred kilometers," Pepe said — about 560 miles.

"I couldn't drive that overnight," José María said. "I've never driven that far before, least of all when everyone else is asleep."

"You could, you could," Pepe said. "You learn how to do it."

"No," said José María. "You have a special skill."

"When I started out in this, no one in the business paid much attention to who they hired as a matador's manservant," the big picador Francisco López said. "The drivers were the ones who got all the respect."

Fran's team of three banderilleros, two picadors, two manservants, and a driver traveled in a Mercedes minibus that was a bit taller and wider than the average American van. Most matadors plastered their name, face, and Web address on the sides of their cuadrilla bus, but Fran's was painted a plain forest green. It had three rows of seats and storage space in the rear. Each night after a corrida, Antonio and Pepe loaded up the back of the bus with nine suitcases of everyday clothes, five or six of Fran's bullfighting costumes, another six or eight costumes belonging to the banderilleros and picadors, the heavy armor the picadors used to protect their legs from the horns, three bags of heavy *capotes,* five *muletas,* the leather case for Fran's swords (the case had belonged to Paquirri), and many boxes of banderillas, in white and in the red and gold of the Spanish flag. The picadors' lances were provided by the arena.

Fran's costumes were made to order for him by Santos, one of the handful of bullfighting tailors, all of which were located in Madrid. The handmade suits cost around three thousand dollars apiece, and Fran ordered at least three or four new ones each season. The colors of the suits are mentioned each morning in newspaper accounts of any corrida, and the colors have evocative names such as *verde manzana* (apple green), *celeste* (heaven, a shade of blue), and *sangre de toro* (bull's blood). A top matador like Fran would wear a suit no more than ten or fifteen times before giving it away to a less fortunate torero. Fran always wore a new suit when he appeared in Sevilla and Madrid, saving the used ones for lesser arenas.

Fran also ordered his bullfighting shirts, his ties, his socks, his slippers, and his fake pigtails from Santos, as well as his *capotes* and *muletas.* Each cape came from the tailor's with Fran's name stenciled into it in black ink. As Fran did with his suits, he used newer capes in the better rings, saving the worn ones for smaller *plazas.* To keep the capes straight, Antonio wrote pet names on them, such as Princesa de La Pizana (La Pizana was the home Fran had shared with Eugenia) and San Juan Evangelista. It could cost as much as fifty thousand dollars a year to

keep Fran fully stocked with costumes and gear. The care and maintenance of all this was one of Antonio's main jobs on the road. After a corrida Antonio, and sometimes Nacho, would fill a hotel bathtub with
cold water and soak the jacket, vest, and pants, working on any blood-
stains with soap. Once the suit was clean, Antonio would hang it next to
the front seat of the minibus to dry. It rode there next to Pepe like a
ghostly reminder of the owner of the bus.

Most members of the cuadrilla brought pillows with them to make
the ride more comfortable. But more important to one's comfort on the
bus was being seated in a spot with something close at hand to prop the
pillow on. Seating was assigned by seniority. Pepe, of course, drove. As
the employee closest to Fran, Nacho rode next to Pepe in the shotgun
seat, which provided ample space for him to put up his feet and sleep
against the window. The craggy old picador López sat just behind Pepe
in the coveted second-row left-side window seat. Next to him was Antonio, who endured life in a middle seat, which meant he was forced to
sleep upright. Then came the junior pic, Diego. He had a window seat,
but the seat was an uncomfortable few inches from the window, to allow
access to the back row. Poli had the left-side window, third row. More
often than not he'd stretch out on the floor, leaving the other two banderilleros to share the back seat.

Pepe had estimated that the 560-mile drive to Huesca would take at
least seven hours that evening. But this haul did not seem to factor into
what the toreros ordered for dinner. They sat down around midnight
and ate their typical massive meal, washed down with plenty of wine
and beer. Whether it was due to practice, professional pride, or something in the water, they were all able to get through long overnight trips
without a rest stop, even after big boozy feeds.

They left the damp Mediterranean soup of Málaga at one o'clock in
the morning, heading from palm trees and sand toward the interior.
There was little talking. Pepe chewed on sunflower seeds as he drove,
spitting out the shells like a baseball player. The old picador snuggled
his massive craggy face into his puffy pillow and began snoring. Antonio smoked. Diego looked out the window. Joselito arranged his gangly
frame in the back seat and listened to headphones. Poli was down on the
floor and José María leaned against the wall in back. Within an hour
everyone except for Pepe was asleep.

It was the height of summer by then, and the days were as hot as you
would imagine Spanish summer days to be. But the nights were fresh

with the windows open and the mountain air rushing into the minibus. This was fortunate, because the bus's air conditioning had broken down the season before, and everyone had voted not to fix it.

The miles began to pile up. After a few hours the van climbed through a dark wood of piny trees, coming over the top of it and down the other side. This was the famous pass of Despeñaperros, the only practical route through the mountains of the Sierra Morena, which divide Spain into north and south, separating sunny Andalucía from the arid plains of La Mancha and Castilla. (Partisans of the Andalucían bullfighting tradition love to say that no great bull or matador was ever born north of Despeñaperros.) Then came the flatness of La Mancha with its massive farms and warehouses, and then the suburbs of Madrid.

"That's Las Ventas," Pepe said, pointing to the vast empty bullring perched over the network of highways.

The way bullfighters travel raises many questions at first, but these are all answered when you ride with them. Why don't they fly? Planes are expensive and impractical: vans would still be needed to take the men and equipment from the airport to the bullring, and bullrings are usually not near airports. Why do they travel at night? Summer nights are as pleasant in Spain as summer days are boiling, the roads are empty at night, and it saves the matador money on hotel rooms if everyone sleeps in the van. How can matadors nap before corridas? After many nights in a car, the human body will take any opportunity to stretch out on a long, clean bed. Why do all toreros stay in one or two particular hotels in a given city? Bullfighters don't use hotels the way other travelers do. They check in at four in the morning, check out at eleven that night, and expect to pay for only one night's lodging. They want their laundry done on the spot and need cold beer, large portions of traditional food, and a staff that will keep unwanted fans away.

Northeast of Madrid the land rose again, but this time it was rocky and bare, like the highlands of Scotland, and the night was crisp and dry. The van had passed out of the province of Madrid and into Aragón. After a couple of hours of mountain roads, past great fields of windmills harvesting the power of the air, the bus entered a city and came to a gentle stop.

They were in a small square that had been built on the side of a hill, and the blustery wind of Aragón announced that this was Huesca. Fran's red Chevy van was already parked in front of the hotel. The half-asleep bullfighters poured out of the minibus. Poli went in to get the room keys while Antonio unloaded the bus and everyone else watched and helped out a bit. It was a lot of work after a night of driving. The sky was turning from navy to royal blue, and the clock above the check-in counter read eight A.M. Everyone took his suitcase upstairs and collapsed. They had only a few hours. The sorting of the bulls was set for eleven-thirty that morning.

25

❖———◄►ᵣ✿✿ᵣ◄►———❖

The Supreme Act

Huesca, August 11. Huesca is a typical Spanish town, a tightly packed collection of stone buildings huddled in the middle of an empty wilderness. Spaniards are a relentlessly urban people. They do not share Americans' romantic view of an awe-inspiring nature. The Spanish see nature as a malevolent force, and prefer to live cheek by jowl with their neighbors, even when there is more than enough space to get away from them. This aversion to the natural world is one of the metaphors underpinning the bullfight. The corrida is a passion play in which civilization is redeemed by its champion, the matador, in his oh-so-stylized and urbane suit, who tames and then destroys nature's champion, in the form of the bull.

The corrida that afternoon took place in an autumnal chill. The sun was brassy and the wind blew gusts that swept the sand off the arena floor and into the audience. The Aragonese crowd was harsh, especially toward Fran. When he appeared for the opening parade chants rose from the sun seats: *"Guapo! Guapo!"* (Handsome! Handsome!) This was not meant kindly. Lewd remarks about Fran's mother were audible throughout the arena, and a group of young men came down to the front row and waved *prensa rosa* magazines in Fran's face. Fran did not react; he never did in such situations. He was too proud, too conscious of his role as a matador and a public figure, to give in to whatever he felt when someone jeered him in a ring or printed a story about his family.

"I've been famous since I was born," Fran always said, "so I am used to it." And that was that.

The bulls were from the ranch of Don Javier Pérez-Tabernero of Salamanca, and Fran drew two good ones. They were both well muscled and they were chargers. The first was black with a white underbelly, the second was all black. They were the kind of bulls that let a matador shine, and Fran took advantage. He gave the first bull a *faena* of long, drawn-out *derechazos* (right-handed passes) and worked the short-charging second bull with choppier and faster passes to the left and right. The crowd chanted *"Olé!"* in all the correct places, the music played, and Fran came to the end of each *faena* in the happy position of needing nothing more than an effective sword thrust to guarantee him one ear, maybe two.

The first bull of the afternoon was ready to die. It stood on heavy feet beside the wooden *barrera,* head down, defeated. Fran moved over to the fence, handed the lightweight dummy sword to Nacho, and received the steel killing sword in return. The standard matador's sword is a rapier with a thirty-three-inch blade. The handle and cross-guard are wrapped in strips of red cloth, and the lead-weighted pommel is covered in red-dyed chamois or leather to prevent slippage in the hand. Most matadors carry at least three swords with them, and the blades are kept deadly sharp by the matador's manservant, who hones them on a stone before each corrida. Each blade curves at the tip. This curve is known as "the death," because it is designed to help drive the blade down into the bull's body, where it has the best chance of severing the pulmonary artery or other major blood vessel. The sword is not meant to pierce the heart and almost never does.

Fran chopped the *muleta* back and forth across the bull's nose, getting the bull to step forward and stop with its front legs parallel. When the bull stands this way—"squared up," in bullfighting parlance—its shoulder blades spread, creating the space into which the matador can put the sword. When Fran was ready to kill, the band stopped playing and the fans hushed each other into silence. The ring was quiet. Fran stood directly in front of the bull, in profile, his feet perpendicular to the animal, his left shoulder facing it—the *muleta* in his left hand, held out to the bull. Then he swiveled his hips and feet, pointing his toes at the bull, left foot first, right foot just behind it, like a figure in an ancient Egyptian wall painting.

Fran raised his right hand behind his head, bringing the sword up to eye level, pointing the blade at the bull, sighting along the blade to the target between the bull's shoulders. He stepped up onto the toes of his left foot. He bent his left knee and shifted his weight back onto the right foot, which was flat on the sand. He rocked back onto the right foot, rocked forward onto the left, and launched at the bull. Fran shot forward, lowering his left hand, bringing the *muleta* down, ahead, and away from his body, and the bull strained its neck down in pursuit of the decoy, leaving the spot between its shoulders unprotected. Fran brought his right hand forward, jumped up, and leaned down over the bull's horns, driving the sword into the target.

For an instant Fran and the bull were joined together in one pose: Fran bent over the bull, the sword going into the bull's back. Then the pose broke as the sword hit bone and Fran flew backward and the bull charged away to the center of the ring. The sword was stuck in the bull, but only at the very tip. It stood upright as the bull ran, teetering for a moment, then spilling onto the sand. The crowd groaned. "What a shame," someone in the stands said. Fran had lost his ear.

In the old days of bullfighting the kill was the climax of the spectacle, and matadors were prized for their skill in what was known as "the supreme act." As already noted, the word *matador* means "killer." But after Belmonte's era in the early twentieth century, bullfighting became preoccupied with the danger and beauty of proper *muleta* work, and the kill diminished in importance. A great kill must fell the animal quickly. It must be performed without cheating, the man going right over the horns and exposing himself to their peril. Finally, the thing should be done with style and dramatic flair, the killer taking his time to set it up, building anticipation before the execution. Unfortunately for the toreros of today, the kill is more often a negative than a positive act, botched kills being the primary way that today's matadors ruin their performances.

There are two basic ways to kill a bull. In the modern era the technique that is almost always used is the one described above. It is named the *volapié*, or flying feet. To kill *volapié*, the matador runs at the bull, using the cape in his left hand to direct the horns down and away from his body, while guiding the sword to its target with his right hand. The second method of killing is called *recibiendo* (receiving). In the *recibiendo*, the matador stands still and uses the cape to induce the bull to lower its head and charge and impale itself on the stationary sword. *Recibiendo* was the standard way to kill in the eighteenth and early nineteenth centuries. It's hardly ever used now. The only modern bullfighter to kill *recibiendo* with any frequency was Fran's grandfather Antonio. In both the *recibiendo* and the *volapié* the cape is really what does the dirty work, which is why the Spanish say, "It is the left hand that kills."

The matador aims his sword at a patch of fur that lies between the shoulder blades. This target is oval-shaped and the size of a dime, a nickel, a quarter, or a balled fist, depending on whom you speak to. In Spanish it is called the *cruz,* or the *rubios.* Hemingway called it the "death notch." This isn't the only place on a bull's body where a sword wound would be fatal. In fact, there are dozens of easier and more effectively lethal spots to aim a blade. But high up between the shoulders is the only place the bull has a fighting chance to defend with its horns, because a correct sword thrust takes the matador over the horns, exposing his entire body — head, neck, torso, and thighs — to maximum danger. For this reason, the rules and traditions of the bullfight dictate that between the shoulders is the only acceptable place for a matador to kill a bull.

Many, if not most, sword thrusts fail to kill the bull outright. It is common to see a bull stumble around the sand with a sword in its back, taking its time to die — or not die, the sword having failed to slice through any crucial blood vessel. For this reason, a matador should be judged not by the effectiveness of the sword thrust, but by the frankness and style with which he attacked the bull and by the position of the sword once he has sunk it in. The sword should be driven at a little less than a ninety-degree angle. Any sword sunk in less than halfway, or at a shallow angle, or placed in front of, behind, or to the side of the correct target, is considered to be an invalid kill and may cost the matador an ear. Failing to stick the sword in at all is considered to be even worse than getting it in badly.

Fran bent down and picked up the fallen sword from the sand. Once again he faced the bull in profile, swiveled his feet to face the bull, ran at the bull, leaned in . . . and hit bone again. Up went the sword on the bull's back and down to the ground. That made two attempts with no result. The crowd grew restless. The goodwill Fran had earned with his cape work was growing into resentment. Mutters rumbled in the air, and there were disapproving whistles. No one enjoys watching a matador who can't close the deal. Bullfighting audiences want the kill over fast. A drawn-out kill is a sorry spectacle. It's bad for the poor animal and it reminds the crowd of how brutal and ugly bullfighting can be. A bad kill forces the viewer's attention on the nature of what he or she is watching. Whatever else it may be, a bullfight is a bull killing. It isn't done for sport or food but for fun, and there are many bullfighting fans who don't want to think about that.

Fran lined up for the third time, ran in, thrust the sword, but came away from the encounter with the sword still in his hand; this is known as a *metisaca* (a take-in/take-out). The audience stirred some more. Fran lined up for the fourth time, ran up, leaned over, and finally, finally, the sword slid into the bull's flesh like a hot knife in ice cream. That's the way it is with killing: when it works, it's easy. When it was all over, the audience applauded, but there were no hankies. Fran had lost another ear with his ineffective sword — a problem that had plagued him throughout his career.

Fran's performance with his second bull was much the same as with his first. He won over the crowd with his *muleta,* heard music, and lost another ear, or maybe two, when he took five tries to kill. On the fourth attempt the president of the corrida authorized the sounding of a warning. This is a trumpet blast that is played if the matador has not killed the bull ten minutes after the first *muleta* pass. A second *aviso* is blown at thirteen minutes, and a third and last one at fifteen minutes. If the bull is still alive at this juncture, it will be led out of the arena, to the shame of the matador. Fortunately for Fran, he killed before the second *aviso.*

Like the pitch in baseball or the swing in golf, the sword thrust in bullfighting is a somewhat mysterious process, even to the professionals who do it well on a regular basis. This has to do with the fact that to throw a major league curveball or drive a golf ball three hundred yards down a fairway or kill a bull with a sword in the prescribed fashion, you must perform a complex sequence of movements correctly, with rhythm, and in a relaxed manner. If any of the movements is off, if the rhythm is wrong, or if the body flinches, then the whole thing will fall apart. That is why so many talented pitchers and golfers and toreros suffer unexplained and seemingly incurable slumps, some of them career-ending.

Of course, killing a bull is more problematic than pitching a curveball, because the bullfighter must risk life and limb to do it right. It's one thing to learn how to relax and throw a baseball; it is quite another to relax when you are throwing your body across a bull's horns and one upward jerk of the bull's head can kill. Hemingway famously referred to the kill as "the moment of truth," because it is the time when the matador's bravery is tested, just as the bull's bravery is tested during the act of the picadors, when it is pierced by the lance and has the choice to keep up the fight or back away. There is a truism of bullfighting that says the kind of bravery required to kill well tends not to show up among artists with the cape, and vice versa. In other words, great killers are often found among those known for their ability to dominate bulls, not among the artistic types.

Fran's trouble with the sword had kicked in just when his reputation had begun to fail. In his early years he was an effective killer, but his grandfather hadn't trained him properly, and he lacked technique, and this led to frequent tossings. In his third year as a matador Fran decided that he could not sustain a career by being thrown into the air every two or three corridas, so he resolved to find a way to kill without getting killed. He began asking for advice from other matadors, and they were happy to fill his head with numerous tips, many of which were contradictory. As so often happens in such situations, Fran found himself in worse shape than he'd been in before he tried to get better. "One moment came and I said to myself, 'I just don't know how to kill a bull anymore,'" Fran recalled. From then on, he had been an inconsistent swordsman.

Fran's second bull in Huesca died the slow death that most bulls die, even when the sword is placed correctly. With the sword in its entrails, the bull weaved about the ring, sluggish, tossing its head up and down in pain. Its back was covered in blood where it had been pic'd, and the banderillas that had been pegged underneath its hide were slick with the blood. The hilt of the sword was between the bull's shoulders, and it bounced up and down in the wound as the bull walked. The bull's mouth was closed (the Spanish take this as a sign of bravery and good genes in a bull), but blood bubbled in the black nostrils. On instinct the bull looked for somewhere secluded to lie down—a *querencia* to die in. But there is no shelter in a bullring, and when it dawned on the bull that its life was finished, it had nowhere to go but the *barrera,* where it sank to its knees under the heartless sun and the eyes of the crowd.

Even then the bull was alive. Its head was up. Its eyes were open. And as the junior man in the cuadrilla, it was José María's job to finish off the bull. For this he carried a short fat knife called a *puntilla*. José María stood behind the bull and jabbed the *puntilla* into the nape of the bull's neck. One jab and the bull was still alive. Two jabs. The bull shook its head. On the third jab the bull stiffened and rolled over. The spinal cord had been severed. The bull was dead. The crowd stood up. People stretched, talked to each other, and looked around as though nothing much had happened. The band played. The bull was on its side in a growing pool of blood. The bullring servants hooked the bull to the mule team and dragged it out of the arena. As it exited the stage, its eyes were open and its mouth worked up and down as if it were trying to tell the crowd something. Bullring veterinarians insist that this phenomenon, which one often observes, is a post-death spasm and nothing more.

Many aficionados claim that bulls do not feel much pain in the ring, since their wounds come in battle. While it's true that many wounds suffered in the heat of combat don't start to hurt right away — at least in humans — and most bulls are surprisingly calm in the ring even as they are being killed, it is also true that bulls exhibit clear signs of suffering in the ring. They shake their heads, they bellow, they cough and sputter and weave around. They also seem to be in some kind of emotional anguish, if such a term can be applied to a bull. As stated before, bulls attack as a last resort, otherwise most would prefer to retreat. The bullfight works because the bull, enclosed alone in a ring, is frightened for its life and will keep charging as long as that fear persists. As one writer put it, the famous attack of the Spanish fighting bull is really nothing more than a forward retreat.

People in the Spanish bullfighting community are not adept at defending their spectacle from charges that it is cruel. Their standard rationalizations are that the bulls are bred for corridas and that it is better for a bull to die in glory in the ring than to be slaughtered anonymously for food. Neither argument carries much intellectual weight, but then neither do most of the arguments made against bullfights. Bulls suffer and die in the bullring. Either you believe this is justified, or balanced somehow by the supposed beauty, history, and cultural significance of the corrida, or you don't. Cattle and other animals suffer and die in the food industry. Either you believe this is justified, or balanced somehow by the human desire for nourishment from meat and by the tradition of meat-eating, or you don't.

All fancy arguments aside, most people's beliefs about bullfighting are formed in the same way as their beliefs about religion. That is to say, most people believe, or at the very least tolerate, what they were brought up with. Most people raised in a certain religion tend to stick with that religion for the rest of their lives, with varying degrees of commitment. The same is true of the bullfight. People who were not brought up around bullfighting are much more likely to be shocked and horrified by it than those who were raised in an environment that had bullfighting in it. This does not absolve bullfighting from charges of cruelty. It is cruel. But it does mean that most people's reaction to bullfighting says more about their culture than it does about the morality of bullfighting.

26

First-Class Standards

Huesca, August 11. The evening after the corrida was a rare one without travel, and some of the bullfighting people in the hotel where Fran and his crew were staying decided to use their free time to visit a brothel. These people did not want their names used in a book. But it should be said that most of them weren't bullfighters working for Fran, and Fran wasn't with them.

Someone in the group suggested they visit a well-known whorehouse outside of town, on the highway to Zaragoza, but no one wanted to drive there. So they asked a waiter in the hotel restaurant and he pointed them toward the downtown red-light district. Sometime after midnight a small group of men slipped out of the hotel, crossed the darkened square in front of the hotel, and made their way through streets filled with *feria* revelers until they came to a seedier neighborhood and found a small tavern with a pink and blue neon sign in the window.

This tavern was a whorehouse. In the front was an open room with a bar, where a woman was selling drinks to a group of beaten-down men, most of whom were senior citizens. Ten women lolled against a wall at the other end of the room. They wore nothing but underclothes and appeared to have come, or been brought, from North and Central Africa. By the looks on their faces, they seemed bored. Some of the men at the bar leered at the women, but no one was making use of the small rooms in the back that were clearly set up for assignations. It was a slow Sunday night in Huesca, and the brothel was kind of like an eighth-grade dance: boys on one side, girls on the other.

Like professional entertainers everywhere, bullfighters are known for their sexual exploits. Being successful with women is part of the classic torero's persona, and many bullfighters do their best to live up to it. It is said that many matadors cannot relax after a corrida without releasing some of their built-up tension with a woman, and there is no shortage of women willing to help out. Groupies haunt the hotels where bullfighters stay, and if the amateur talent is lacking, there are always professional ladies available. For centuries Spanish society maintained a strict, almost Koranic control over its women, especially in matters of sex. As a result of this, some might say, prostitution was always a force in Spanish life. A study conducted in the mid-1960s found that two thirds of Spanish men said they'd lost their virginity to a prostitute.

Forty-odd years later, things had changed a great deal. Spanish women had won a large measure of liberation, and studies have shown that fewer and fewer men were having their first experience with a hooker. But Spanish culture persisted in the view that women were either Madonnas or whores. It was no accident that the word *puta* (whore) figured prominently in Spanish putdowns and curses. However, to call something *de puta madre* (whore-motherish) meant it was wonderful — the Spanish idea being that anything that combined maternal comfort with the pleasure of illicit sex must be fantastic. The sex trade was big business in Spain. Prostitution was legal, and even though pimping and operating a brothel were illegal, they were much on display. The Spanish euphemism for whorehouse is *club*, and there were a few such *clubes* on the highways outside any Spanish city.

Despite the expected locker room boasting about sex, and despite ample opportunities to put words into action, there was little evidence of womanizing in Fran's crew. It seemed that Fran was going to bed early and alone that season and did little but talk about his estranged wife. The banderilleros and picadors sometimes chatted up women in public places, but it never seemed to go further than that. They might have been hiding their bad behavior because I was writing a book about them. That would have been hard to do, though, given the intimacy of our travel arrangements. In Huesca that night, no one did anything more than have an expensive beer. They had no interest in black women, they explained. Most of them went back to their hotel. A few of them hit the bars.

San Sebastián, August 12. Rain fell and clouds hung low over the skyline when Pepe guided the minibus into this beautiful and modern city. San Sebastián ("Donostia" in Euskara, the Basque language) spreads out from a crescent-shaped bay dotted with impressive green hills. The scenery recalls Rio de Janeiro, but San Sebastián is on the northern coast of Spain, up near the French border. It is the capital of the Basque Country and is famous for its cuisine, both traditional and experimental. Fran and Pepe Luis checked into the luxurious Hotel María Cristina in the center of town, while the cuadrilla settled into a straightforward businessmen's hotel on a quiet street near the bullring. This hotel had just opened, and the owners, a husband and wife, were in the lobby to greet the toreros when they arrived. The couple, both aficionados, were excited to have bullfighters staying with them.

It may seem unjust that Fran got to stay in a five-star hotel and put his men — men charged with defending his life — in a more modest establishment. But this was in keeping with bullfighting tradition. In the days before the toreros' union, matadors treated their subordinates shabbily, paying them meager wages and housing them in the cheapest fleabags — or, whenever possible, saving the price of lodging altogether by letting them sleep on the road. Things were much fairer in Fran's day, but no one objected to his staying in a fancy hotel. As the matador Fran paid the bills, and as the matador he ran most of the risks in the ring. If any of Fran's men had possessed the luck, talent, and guts to be matadors themselves, they would have treated their employees exactly as Fran did, or worse. In fact, Fran was known among the top matadors for treating his team well. They ate better and slept in greater luxury than many of their colleagues.

There was no bullfight that night, so the cuadrilla looked forward to an unhurried dinner at the hotel restaurant. As always, their behavior was quite formal. Each newcomer greeted the table with *"Buen provecho"* ("Good appetite") as he sat down, and bullfighting was not discussed, because it was considered to be impolite to mix business with food. A waiter came by and delivered menus. The men studied them and placed their orders. Time passed. The drinks were late in coming, which produced some consternation. The first round was consumed, then another, and still the food had not arrived. The waiter was summoned, and the craggy-faced picador López gave him an earful of complaint.

The waiter apologized and eventually plates of food were set on the table. The toreros were pleased at first, until they looked down at what had been set before them. Then their faces darkened. The style of presentation at this restaurant was pure nouvelle cuisine, and that meant one thing: small portions. The steak was around four ounces. It came with three bites of potato, each one carved to resemble a mushroom. The rice with squid in a sauce of its own ink was formed into a hockey-puck-sized disk that sat forlorn in a sea of empty porcelain. All of it was pretty, but it was not enough food for the bullfighters. Most of them looked unhappy but resigned. Poli seemed as if he were ready to explode.

San Sebastián, August 13. On the outskirts of town, atop a hill, stood the Illumbe entertainment complex, home to a nine-theater multiplex cinema, a food court, video-game rooms, and a first-category bullring that seated around ten thousand spectators. The seats in the bullring were honest-to-goodness seats with backrests. There were aisles between sections that led to refreshment stands and clean, modern bathrooms. Best of all, given San Sebastián's rainy climate, there was a retractable roof that could open or close in twelve minutes. The Illumbe ring opened in 1998 with a corrida of Torrealta bulls that were dispatched by three matadors, including Francisco Rivera Ordóñez. It was the most comfortable bullring in Spain and had all the atmosphere of a midwestern hockey arena.

The San Sebastián corrida would be Fran's crucial summer date. Given the lost bullfight in Pamplona, this was his only opportunity to triumph in one of the big rings up north. It was also his only scheduled appearance in a first-class ring between May and September. On this afternoon Fran would have to perform in a different way than he had in the small towns he'd been visiting during the prior months. In small towns the crowds just want a good show. They don't come to judge bullfighters but to cheer them. They aren't great connoisseurs of the ring and don't want to be. They applaud any pass that looks flashy and risky. They enjoy all the flourishes: the matador staring at the audience while the bull runs by, or passing the bull on his knees, or kneeling in front of an exhausted bull and tossing away his cape, or leaning his forehead against the bull's horn.

By contrast, fans in big cities like San Sebastián come to the arena, in large measure, to display their bullfighting knowledge. They may not know anything more than the people in the small towns do, but they think they do, and what they think they want is their vision of what classic bullfighting should be. This means each bull should be pic'd just enough to tire it, but not enough to exhaust it; the banderillas should be placed in proper style; and the matador should lower his hands and give deep, measured *verónicas* with the *capote.* In addition, the matador should favor his left hand in his *muleta* work—with no sword behind the cape to spread the fabric—and lure the bull just past his body, prolonging the moment when the horns are close by, slowing the bull down, then curving the bull behind his back to link the next pass. Finally, the matador must kill on the first try, going straight over the horns and leaving the sword in the right place.

Aside from his well-publicized traumas with the sword, the thing that hurt Fran the most with the fans in the first-class *plazas*—and the newspaper critics whose columns they studied—was his *muleta* technique. Fran was often criticized for failing to "cross" at the beginning of each pass. That is, he didn't start each pass between the horns, right in front of the bull, but instead from a position parallel to the bull. The concept of crossing had come into bullfighting during the 1970s and was championed by certain critics. Like many matadors, Fran rejected crossing as an unworkable fantasy technique, because the matador had to forgo linking his passes in favor of shuffling in front of the bull between each pass. Fran was also criticized for failing to complete his passes by bringing the bull around his back; he had a tendency to allow the bull to run out and away from him at the end of each pass, something the press-box pundits called "vulgar."

The bulls in San Sebastián were from the ranch of the brothers García Jiménez of Salamanca, in central Spain, and Fran drew two of the better ones. The first was a red-coated creature of twelve hundred pounds named Voluntario (Volunteer), an apt name for a bull that was more than willing to get into the fray. Voluntario charged and charged, asking for as much action as Fran had to offer. As always, Fran began well, with a handsome set of first-class *verónicas* that were met with applause and *olés!* When the horsemen and banderilleros had run their course, Fran came out with his *muleta* and worked a fine opening stanza of passes with his right hand, lunging forward on his left leg to pass the bull low, forcing the bull's head down, bearing down on its charge, and bringing it under control.

Three sets of right-handed passes followed, each one an improvement on the one that preceded it. The passes of the second series were elongated, with Fran "running the hand," as the Spanish say, pulling the bull through drawn-out circles of movement. The audience called out *olés* and clapped in rhythm, demanding music. The president resisted at first, but then relented, and the next series was all anyone could have asked for in *derechazo* passes: Fran drawing the bull across his body in stretched-out straight lines, then bending those lines into tense angles at the end, dragging the bull behind his back. He ended this series by switching the cape to his left hand in midpass, bringing the bull whence it had come, pushing the cape up at the end, wrenching the bull's head up with it and out past Fran's shoulder.

"*Olé!*"

The band played. Fran kept the *muleta* in his left hand, the cloth hanging down, offering only a minimum of protection. He stalked the bull, stopped about ten feet from it, and offered the cape from there, gambling that Voluntario was enough of a bull to accept a challenge from a great distance. The gamble paid off. The bull attacked, making a dramatic run across the sanded circle of the ring. The pass connected. The bull was sucked into the draw of the cape. But the pass was incomplete. Somehow Fran couldn't keep the bull under control, and instead of following the cloth, it ran right through the cloth, spoiling the line Fran was sketching, spoiling the tempo Fran was creating, and cutting off the tension, the energy, and the beauty.

Fran cited with his left hand again, but the pass ended much the same way the first one had, with the bull running through the cape. On the third pass the bull blew past him, making its way to a *querencia* near the bullpen gate, forcing Fran to pursue it. Most of the audience applauded after each pass. Even in a place like San Sebastián, most of the fans were the kind who would applaud anytime the bull ran past the man. There were, however, more and more jeers and whistles after each pass. The hard-core experts in the audience, or those who thought they were, seemed to agree that this was a good bull, and they were annoyed that Fran couldn't quite contain the animal's prodigious energy and channel it into satisfactory left-handed *muleta* passes.

The third series of *naturales* went much the same way as the first two had, and the whistles picked up. Seemingly defeated by his left hand, Fran returned the cape to his right and did another solid set of *derechazos*. But this did nothing to mollify the part of the audience that had been waiting for grade-A work with the left hand, and they jeered with feeling.

Fran ignored them and went over to trade the lightweight sword for the steel. He hit bone on the first attempt, got a little of the blade in on the second attempt, did a take-in/take-out on the third try, and sank half the blade on the fourth. The bull died. When the time came, the crowd reacted to Fran's performance in silence, which was better than whistles but not good. Obviously, there was no question of awarding an ear, and Fran did no better with his second bull.

In the next day's newspapers Fran was admonished for what the critics called his bad *muleta* form. In *ABC*, the critic Zabala de la Serna wrote that Fran's bulls had been good ones, "but there is nothing a matador can do with a bull when that matador never crosses in front of the horns, and sends the bull out and away from himself at the end of each pass, and fails to kill with sincerity or conviction."

Noël Chandler had been staying in his Pamplona flat and driving up the A-15 highway each afternoon to attend the day's corrida in San Sebastián. "As I've been saying all year," Noël said, sipping a post-bullfight beer in a bar underneath the arena, "instead of reaching out and bringing the bull into his body, he's holding the *muleta* near his body and sending the bull away from his body. Very depressing."

Back at the hotel that evening, the cuadrilla assembled for their meal in a terrible mood. The corrida had been a bad one, they had a long ride ahead of them, and they feared they were going to be cheated out of their one remaining pleasure, a big meal. They ordered, and again the food was a long time in coming, and again when it came the portions were small, and finally the frustrations of the entire season boiled over into insurrection. The old picador López began cursing and yelling in indecipherable Andalucían. Then Poli took over. "This is a *vergüenza!*" he said. "A disgrace! This is why we need to go to *taurino* hotels, places that know what we like." The men decided the time had come for a formal protest, and Poli pulled out his cell phone.

He dialed Pepe Luis Segura's number and waited. When Pepe Luis answered, Poli went into his litany of complaints about the service and food in the hotel restaurant. When he had finished there was a pause on the line. Then Pepe Luis began to speak, and everyone at the table could hear that he was shouting. There was a pause, and the voice changed. Fran had come on the line (Pepe Luis and Fran had been sharing dinner in their hotel), and then he shouted for a while too. Poli's face lost its color. When Fran gave Poli a moment to think, he backed down somewhat from his aggressive posture and Fran hung up. After that, no one was in any mood to complain about the food.

27

Good Luck, Bad Luck

Gijón, August 14. Something had to give in Fran's season, and it finally did on a gentle evening in Gijón, a summer resort town about 185 miles west of San Sebastián along the Atlantic coast. This was a different kind of bullfight than the one in San Sebastián had been, before a different kind of crowd. Gijón has a proud taurine tradition. The annual Feria de Nuestra Señora de Begoña (Our Lady of the Begonia) has been an important August stop for toreros for a long time — the impressive and unusual sixteen-sided bullring first opened in 1888. But Gijón is a second-category ring, a provincial ring, and the audience there has a second-category attitude. The fans are not interested in being tough on matadors, or in proving their superior knowledge of the subtleties of the art of bullfighting, or in watching sober demonstrations of bull-fighting essentials. This was a crowd that wanted to be entertained with all the bells and whistles.

Fran was angry after San Sebastián and he put that energy to use, coming out and giving the good people of Gijón exactly what they wanted. He won their hearts at the outset by dropping to his knees and passing the bull with a one-handed flip of the *capote* over his shoulder in a series of three *larga cambiadas* — red meat for the provincial crowd. When it was time for the *faena,* Fran skipped to midring, took off his hat, stretched out his arm, and slowly turned around the ring, dedicating the bull to the fans of the city. This was not the sort of theatrical gesture he usually indulged in, but it went over big-time with the crowd.

Fran was just fine with the *muleta*. The aficionados in a first-class *plaza* might have quibbled about his technique, but he passed the bull every which way, spinning with the animal as it moved by, passing it while staring up at the audience, standing in front of it with his cape folded and taunting it with the sword, and then he killed it on the first try.

The stands were aflutter with white handkerchiefs. The president awarded an ear, and the cheering and waving continued, and eventually he gave Fran another ear. At the president's signal, one of the two *alguaciles* knelt over the bull's carcass and cut off both the ears, yanking each one up and hacking at the skin and cartilage to separate it from the skull. Then the *alguacil* went over to where Fran stood and placed the ears, still warm, with the flaps of hairy skin hanging off, in his palm, giving him a big hug. Fran held an ear in each hand and began to walk the circumference of the ring, holding up his new trophies for inspection, smiling and bowing before each section of seats. As he approached a section, the fans sitting there rose to their feet and threw flowers and cigars and wine skins and hats down to him, and the cuadrilla ran behind to collect the stuff. When Fran had completed his circuit, he headed for the center of the sand and grinned as the audience cheered him one last time. He hadn't seemed as happy in a bullring since his *faena* in Tolosa, back in June.

Fran did another good job on his second bull, killed effectively, and cut another ear. When the corrida ended Fran was not allowed to walk out. Instead he was gathered up on the shoulders of a few men who'd come down onto the sand and carried through the main gate of the arena and over to the cuadrilla bus. Fran was the only matador of the day to cut a single ear, much less three, but still, the following morning the critics were dismissive of his achievement. "Francisco could have been better, given the quality of his rival [the bull]," wrote *ABC*'s local critic, José Luis Suárez-Guanes, "but one cannot dispute his desire, his persistence, his bullfighting with the *muleta* — a performance out of his early career." It was this sort of review — of which Fran was so often a victim — that led him to stop reading the papers.

Alfaro, August 17. Fran's August 15 corrida in Málaga, his second in Málaga that week, had gone badly. The bulls were awful and the seats half full. And if Málaga was bad, then Ciudad Real, the next day, was worse. Ciudad Real is a boring, dusty town in the middle of the La Mancha plain, and the ring was smaller and also half full, and who cared about the bulls anyway? After Ciudad Real came Alfaro, which was nothing more than a village on the upper edge of the winemaking region of La Rioja, where La Rioja meets Navarra. (Pamplona is less than an hour's drive to the north.) It was late at night when the bus came to a stop in Cintruénigo, a village just up the road from Alfaro in Navarra proper. For some reason someone had built a boutique hotel there, which would not have seemed out of place in Madrid or New York. It was called the Maher and was not the kind of hotel where you'd expect Fran to put his people up. There was a cheap and cheerful hotel in Alfaro, across the street from the ring, and most matadors would not have spent the money.

Next morning there was nothing to do, so I hung out in the hotel lobby with Jesús, the *apoderado*'s driver. Jesús was middle-aged, tall and shy, and had a good head of black hair. He was a real *taurino* type and boasted of many decades of work in the bull world. Jesús and I had been friendly on the rare occasions when we bumped into each other, which was almost always in hotel lobbies. That morning I detected something in Jesús's voice that was not familiar to me. There was an edge. It seemed that he wanted to tell me something, but was having a hard time getting up the nerve to do so. Finally his theme emerged.

"You're very lucky," Jesús said. "You know, in all my years of doing this, I have never heard of a journalist being allowed to ride along with toreros the way you are with Francisco. It just doesn't happen."

I agreed. It was indeed unusual and I was indeed lucky.

"Well, you may be lucky to have this experience," Jesús said, "but I must tell you, Eduardo, there are some people who think you are bringing bad luck to Fran."

I laughed this off. I told Jesús that I wasn't trying to bring Fran bad luck and I didn't think I was bringing him bad luck. Jesús smiled along, but his eyes were serious. The whole thing seemed preposterous to me and I promptly put it out of my mind.

I should have known better. Bullfighters are a superstitious bunch, as superstitious as any group of people who risk their lives regularly and come from a religious country like Spain. Most bullfighters try to preserve their good luck by praying to their saints before each corrida and by wearing medals of their saints. They try to avoid bad luck by starting the opening parade of each corrida on the right foot, by not wearing yellow costumes, and by making sure to keep all hats off beds.

The speech of bullfighters is riddled with references to *suerte* (luck), both *mala* and *buena. Suerte* is often used as a face-saving device. Matadors will say, "I had *mala suerte* in my career and didn't advance." Or "I had *mala suerte* in the bulls I drew." Or "I had *mala suerte* with the sword and hit bone on a good try."

Fran came down from his room just before lunch; he was still angry about the food revolt in San Sebastián and promised he would exact some punishment from the cuadrilla in the coming days. Fran was carrying his reading glasses and the book he'd been reading. It was the Spanish translation of *Black Hawk Down,* a nonfiction account of the disastrous 1993 American military operation in Mogadishu, Somalia. He had bought the book after seeing the movie version, which he'd enjoyed. Fran asked if someone was going to make a movie of the book I was writing about him. I said I hoped so, and by way of a joke suggested that Fran could star as himself in the picture. In fact, I said, with his looks he could go to Hollywood and start a new career in the movies.

Fran agreed that this would be a great idea.

"But," I added, "you could never go back to bullfighting. No one would take you seriously. They would laugh you out of the ring."

"Oh, and that would be a shame," Fran said in his characteristically dark fashion. "Then I'd miss all the fun in places like Ciudad Real."

The bullfight in Alfaro did not go well. It was a rustic little arena, and the two other matadors and their cuadrillas walked to the back door of the *plaza* from the motel across the street. The audience was drunk, rowdy, and disrespectful, and the bulls were like oxen. That night we all sat down to dinner in the hotel — the cuadrilla, Pepe Luis, Fran, the manservants, the three drivers, and the American. It was the first time everyone had sat at the same table all season. While we ate our appetizers Pepe Luis looked around, did a head count, and announced that, all together, we made thirteen, which was *muy mala suerte* indeed.

Fran was a religious man. He was a believing Catholic, went to church when he could, and belonged to a religious club in Sevilla that participated in that city's Holy Week processions. He was, however, not superstitious the way many matadors were. He kept his pre-corrida rituals fairly short and simple: he prayed to his saints and that was that. Half the time he didn't cross himself before the opening parade. In many ways Fran's entire career was based on proving that fate didn't exist, that the legacy of Paquirri did not spell doom for his son. But Fran was angry with his cuadrilla for their behavior in San Sebastián, and he was even angrier with himself for the way he'd been performing. What he did not need at that moment was to have the idea of bad luck introduced into his mind.

"Fine!" he shouted. "If that's the way it is, I'll go eat by myself and then you'll be twelve." Poli and Joselito went over to sit with Fran at the small table he moved to, but he was still seething, and everyone ate in silence with heads down — especially me, since I was obviously the thirteenth person and therefore the cause of all the trouble.

Sometime during the meal my cell phone rang. It was my mother-in-law calling me from New York. My wife, Megan, had fallen and broken her big toe and needed me at home. We had a large and floppy baby boy, and we had stairs in our house, and Megan wasn't sure she could carry my son up and down. I couldn't speak to her just then because she was in the emergency room, but the message was: book a flight and call her later with the details. I hung up and told everyone what had happened, and they began giving me a hard time. Mostly this was a joke. Everyone was laughing. But it was serious too, the way it had been with Jesús. They wanted to know why I wasn't more upset. My poor wife had hurt herself — where was my sympathy? I pointed out that a broken toe wasn't exactly cancer. With some sarcasm I said my wife had broken her elbow in about fifteen places a few years before, a much worse injury, and we had somehow weathered the storm. She would probably survive a broken toe.

Pepe Luis was sobbing with laughter. He called me over to him. "You aren't a very lucky fellow, are you?" he said as everyone else laughed along. Then he pulled out his wallet and handed me a small card with a photograph of a statue of the Virgin Mary, a talisman to raise my *buena suerte* quotient. I turned to Fran and asked him in English if I should mention that I was Jewish. He was not laughing. He was sitting quietly at his table. He smiled at me and said no. I thanked Pepe Luis and went upstairs to pack. I had a flight out of Pamplona that morning at five.

All the Roads Home

Being a *matador de toros* is much more difficult than I had imagined it would be, but also much more beautiful.

— FRANCISCO RIVERA ORDÓÑEZ

28

❖━━❖❦❖━━❖

Master of Masters

Ronda, September 6. The moment I left Spain, Fran began cutting ears like a demon. There was no single explanation for this. It was a confluence of several factors. He was beginning to achieve some emotional detachment from his marital situation; he'd nudged his elbow back into usable shape; he was back in practice with real bulls and live audiences; and he was having *buena suerte* in the bulls he was drawing. Fran cut three ears in Játiva on August 20, two ears in Antequerra on the twenty-third, and a single ear in Alcalá de Henares on the twenty-fourth. In Linares, on August 28 — the fifty-fifth anniversary of Manolete's fatal goring in that ring — Fran clicked with his second bull and cut two ears. Noël was there and said it was Fran's best performance of the season. After Linares he got two ears in Requena on the thirtieth and an ear on the first of September in Ejea de los Caballeros.

I returned to Spain as fast as I could, switching planes in London for a direct flight to Málaga. The local *feria* was over by the time I arrived, and it was odd to see the streets quiet and the old bullring empty. Noël picked me up the next morning and we headed for Ronda, where Fran was scheduled to preside over the Corrida Goyesca the following day. My plan was to see the bullfight in Ronda and hop on the cuadrilla bus for the last few weeks of the season. Things seemed to be going Fran's way again, and the end of the season was shaping up to be a happy time. In the month since Fran's return from injury, he had climbed two steps up the *escalafón* to tenth place, with forty-six corridas and thirty-three ears. Best of all, he was triumphing again and September was a month packed with important *ferias*. If Fran could cut some ears in Valladolid, Barcelona, Murcia, Sevilla, and Logroño he might be able to turn the season around.

Whatever happened, September was going to be interesting, because Fran would be forced to confront his complicated history in two emotionally charged corridas. The first was the *goyesca* in Ronda on the seventh; the second was a bullfight in Pozoblanco on the twenty-sixth. The *goyesca* was important to Fran because of the great bullfighting history of Ronda, his family connection to Ronda and the *goyesca,* and because this bullfight took place each year in the ring where his grandfather's ashes lay buried, under the sand where the bulls emerge from the bullpen gate. The Pozoblanco corrida meant a lot too, because it would take place where Fran's father had been fatally wounded, on the eighteenth anniversary of his death, and because the bulls Fran would face that afternoon came from the same ranch that had bred the killer bull Avispado.

Noël eased his black Audi sedan out of the snarl of Málaga's morning rush hour, traversed the hills that divide the coast from the interior, crossed the plain behind the hills, and came to Serranía de Ronda, the rough mountain range with the old city perched atop two peaks, like a fortress. When the road began to twist up into the mountains toward the gates of the city, I tried calling the cuadrilla to see about hooking up with the bus. Antonio was not answering his mobile number. Nacho picked up right away, but when I announced myself he told me to call the *apoderado.*

That was odd.

"I don't want to bother Pepe Luis with my travel plans," I said.

"Just call the *apoderado,*" Nacho said. Then he hung up.

Something about calling Pepe Luis felt wrong to me, maybe even impolite. It seemed to upend the natural hierarchy of the cuadrilla. Surely, my presence on the bus was something for Nacho or Antonio to arrange. This was all far below Pepe Luis's pay grade. I phoned Nacho again.

"Call the *apoderado,*" he repeated, his voice rising. Then he hung up again.

I put the telephone in my lap and stared out at the mountain scenery for a moment, gathering my thoughts. The phone rang. It was Pepe

Luis, and before I could get a word in, he began to speak. "You are a good person," he said in that high, nasal, air-raid siren of a voice of his, clipping off the ends of words in his deep Andalucían accent, "but you know that bullfighters have their superstitions."

Pepe Luis said certain people in the cuadrilla — he wouldn't name names — were worried that I was bringing Fran bad luck. When I was around, Fran did nothing, nothing, and more nothing. And the minute I went away, Fran started cutting ears. So, Pepe Luis said, it would be better for everyone if I got around on my own. "You may continue with your work," he said. "But traveling with us? No way."

He apologized. He said he was sorry it had to be like this and assured me it wasn't personal. I told him it was no problem. Then I asked how severe my quarantine was going to be. Was I banned from speaking to the cuadrilla? From saying hello? Pepe Luis told me not to worry. He said he and the boys were happy to sit down with me and have a few beers anytime we crossed paths. But I was bad luck and they were throwing me off the bus for good. End of story.

We pulled into Ronda and Noël and I stored our gear in our respective hotels and went for a walk. Ronda is small, and within minutes we had bumped into various members of the Rivera Ordóñez entourage. When we asked them about my banishment, Nacho, Juani, Antonio, and Poli swore up and down that they didn't think I was bad luck, didn't want me off the bus, and furthermore denied that anyone in the cuadrilla wanted me off. Then we went to see Fran at his hotel, and he too pleaded ignorance of the situation — although he seemed not at all surprised by it and quite amused as well. In full prince mode he took pains to assure me that as far as he was concerned I'd done nothing wrong, and he would be glad to call Pepe Luis and have me reinstated on the bus. I was tempted, but said no. My presence was causing more of a stir than it should have. The time had come to travel on my own.

We left Fran and meandered around the hard and lovely town. Ronda's two halves were set on plateaus atop facing mountain peaks, separated by a brooding ravine with only a narrow stone bridge to join them. The view from the bridge was dramatic. Tumbledown houses rimmed the sides of one peak, then came the deep cleft of the ravine, then the other side of the ravine with an open square and the bullring, with its white walls and red-tiled roof and its statues of El Niño de la Palma and Antonio Ordóñez in front. Wreaths lay on the statues with ribbons that read, *In memoriam, your grandchildren and great-grand-children.* Gardens ran down to the edge of the plateau. The view was of the glum mountains all around, the pleasant farmland in the valley, the fields spreading in patches of burnt yellow and green, and all of it grow-ing smoky as day blurred into evening and glimmering lights came on in the farmhouses below.

It was exquisite and sad. Ronda was changing. Germans were buying up the fields and farms, and the historic *goyesca* was not what it had been. The Ordóñez family had founded the *goyesca* to celebrate Pedro Romero, but the corrida quickly became a celebration of the greatness of Antonio Ordóñez. He had performed in the *goyesca* most seasons from 1954 to 1980, and during that time it was one of the signature events in Spain, a lure for celebrities, jet-set types, and hard-core bull nuts like Noël Chandler. But the *goyesca* had lost some glamour after Antonio stopped appearing in it, and even more so after his death in 1998. By the start of the new millennium many of the chic people had forgotten about Ronda, and the aficionados that Noël had known were too old, too tired, or too dead to show up anymore. It seemed that eve-ning that Ronda was full of ghosts. Most imposing of all was the ghost of Antonio Ordóñez.

The wall along the main passageway under the seats in the monumen-tal bullring in Madrid is lined with plaques commemorating famous matadors. Some of these toreros were minor stars who, for whatever reason, had been favorites of the Madrid public. Others were big stars in their day whose accomplishments have faded from the minds of all but a few history buffs. Still others — a bare handful — were true *figuras de epoca,* so great that they have come to define their eras and are re-membered by aficionados everywhere. Each of these plaques features a portrait of a matador and a small statement about him. Most of these statements say generic things such as, "He was the pride of [insert hometown here]." The text of the plaque for Antonio Ordóñez is a bit different. It reads, "Antonio Ordóñez y Araujo, master of masters, the pride of bullfighting."

As Kenneth Tynan wrote in his 1959 *Sports Illustrated* profile of Anto-nio, the title *figura de epoca* is not bestowed on the man who earns the most money during his career, or is the bravest, or has the best tech-nique. A *figura de epoca* must have all of these, and endure at the top of his game for years, and have his own inimitable style. In the twentieth century there were no more than a half dozen matadors who might be considered *figuras de epoca,* and only four would make everyone's list. In the teens there was Joselito, the greatest practitioner of the old technique of the first two centuries of bullfighting, and Juan Belmonte, who discarded that technique and changed the game. In the thirties and forties, Manuel Rodríguez — Manolete — overwhelmed Spain with the brutal, tragic force of his personality. Then, in the fifties and sixties, there was Ordóñez, a matador who seemed to be in touch with the essence of classic bullfighting.

He was tall, handsome, and knock-kneed, with a commanding personality and a style that was at once forceful and refined. Antonio did all the passes without an ounce of posturing, fakery, or guile. He did everything by the book and made it look new again. After seeing Antonio for the first time, in Pamplona in 1953, Hemingway made this oft-quoted assessment: "I could tell he was great from the first long slow pass he made with the cape. It was like seeing all the great cape handlers, and there were many, alive and fighting again except that he was better."

Like his father, El Niño, and his grandson, Fran, Antonio was a complex person. He dropped out of school at fourteen, saying that a great matador needed to write just well enough to "sign checks," but he loved opera and spoke French. He was as Spanish as Spanish could be, but he was one of the only international Spanish stars of the Franco era. He killed bulls for a living, but more than any other matador in history, his performances expressed a sense of collaboration between man and animal. "For me the bull is a friend," Antonio once said, "a great friend, who I am mortally afraid of in the ring." Or, as Antonio's good friend Orson Welles once said, "With Antonio, each pass asserts not 'How great I am!' but 'How great we are!' "

Like El Niño and like Fran, Antonio was shy by nature but had an absolute belief in his own brilliance, and would lapse into a cold fury when he thought this was being questioned. He could be kind one minute and cruel the next. Pepe Luis Segura remembers an evening in the 1970s when he found himself on a drinking binge with Antonio. They weren't friends, just taurine acquaintances, but as the night wore on, Pepe Luis was moved to unburden himself to the older man. Pepe Luis was still working as a matador then, but was failing to convince the promoters, critics, or fans that he was a great matador. Unable to earn a decent wage in the ring, he'd been forced to develop his side business of breeding and selling guard dogs. "Why has this happened to me, Maestro?" Pepe Luis complained.

Antonio, who was already retired and a legend, patted him on the shoulder and told him things were not as bad as they seemed. "Whatever you do in life, it is important to be the best at it. So don't worry, Pepe Luis. I am the best bullfighter and you can be the best dog trainer."

Thanks to Hemingway, Tynan, and others, Antonio's story is well told in English. He was the third of El Niño de la Palma's five sons, but the only one born in Ronda, where his mother "gave him to the light," as the Spanish say, on February 16, 1932. He dressed in lights for the first time in June 1948 in Haro, in La Rioja. Three seasons as a *novillero* followed, and then Antonio took his *alternativa* in Madrid on June 28, 1951. That afternoon he signed a contract to be managed by Domingo González Mateos, known as Dominguín, one of the most powerful *apoderados* of that time. Under Dominguín, and with the help of Dominguín's three torero sons — Pepe, Domingo, and Luis Miguel — Antonio became one of Spain's most popular matadors. In 1953 he married Dominguín's daughter, Carmen, thus uniting two great bullfighting dynasties. Then he retired.

Like El Niño and Fran, Antonio had a short apprenticeship, took his *alternativa* in one of Spain's top bullrings, spent three seasons as star, married a powerful woman in his third season, and suffered a professional crisis. Like El Niño and Fran, the young Antonio was talented, successful, brave, and beautiful, and essentially unfinished as a matador. He did not always know how to dominate difficult bulls and, like Fran, had problems killing. But this is where the similarity ends, because when Antonio returned to the ring in 1954 he focused on his shortcomings, learned how to deal with his faults, and blossomed as a star of historic proportions.

The Antonio Ordóñez of legend appeared for the first time in 1958, after he had already been a professional matador for ten seasons. During the late 1950s and early 1960s he was invariably relaxed in the ring, slow, full of elegance, and imbued with the bullfighter's total commitment of body and life that allowed him to take his time with problem bulls, finish off bulls after horrific gorings, and return to the ring with open wounds. This was the classic Antonio, the man Hemingway wrote about and whom Fran knew and revered. Fran always spoke of his grandfather as though he were a genius who had sprung fully formed into the bullring. The evidence suggests otherwise. Like all talented people, Antonio had had to work hard to achieve his promise. Fran possessed all the raw makings of another Antonio; what he needed was the same commitment to grow.

By 1958 most people agreed that Antonio was the best matador, but there was an important dissenter, Antonio's brother-in-law Luis Miguel, Dominguín. Kenneth Tynan described him as a tall, "contemptuously handsome Castilian" who knew more about the handling of bulls than any of his contemporaries. Six years older than Antonio, Luis Miguel had been a professional torero since boyhood. He was an arrogant technician of a matador, a performer who never enjoyed warm relations with audiences, preferring to overwhelm his many detractors with his copious repertoire of passes, his great skill at placing banderillas, and his deadly sword. But he also had a warm side. He attracted women in droves, including the actress Ava Gardner, and he had a wide range of powerful, talented, and intelligent friends, from Francisco Franco to Pablo Picasso.

Luis Miguel took his *alternativa* in 1945 from none other than Manolete himself, and for the next two seasons he pursued Manolete in a serious competition for bullfighting's top slot, driving Manolete to work closer to the bulls and take more chances in an effort to retain his public. Their rivalry ended in 1947 when Manolete, prematurely worn out and drinking hard at thirty, lost his life in Linares. Luis Miguel was on the card that day, and many in Spain blamed him for Manolete's death. For the next six seasons Luis Miguel reigned as the *número uno* of the bullring. Then, in January of 1954, he was badly gored in Caracas, Venezuela, and he retired, which opened the door for Antonio Ordóñez to become the leading star of the ring — although Luis Miguel and his fans continued to insist that Dominguín was the best, with Ordóñez a close second.

Luis Miguel returned to active performing in 1957, and for the next two seasons he and his brother-in-law Antonio avoided each other like heavyweight champs unwilling to fix a date for the big fight. The confrontation finally took place in 1959. They had to do it. Each man was insisting he was the greatest matador, and each was demanding to be paid more than any other matador. There had been bad feeling between Ordóñez and Dominguín since the mid-1950s when Antonio broke his management contract with Luis Miguel's father, accusing the elder Dominguín of dishonesty. But most of all, the public wanted to see

Dominguín and Ordóñez together, and the bullfighters knew this would produce big paydays. That spring Antonio quit his *apoderado* and signed up with Luis Miguel's managers, who happened to be his brothers, Pepe and Domingo, making it easier for everyone to coordinate and to profit.

The Dominguín brothers arranged it so the second half of the 1959 season would be organized around a series of bullfights featuring Antonio and Luis Miguel, first in back-to-back corridas during the same *ferias,* then together in the same corridas with a third matador, and finally in a series of one-on-one, or *mano a mano,* confrontations. In many ways it was a staged event, a cynical moneymaking ploy. But it was also the first serious, protracted head-to-head competition between the two top matadors in Spain since the days of Joselito and Belmonte, and the bull world thrummed in anticipation. To add to the stew, Ernest Hemingway, already afflicted with the physical and mental ills that would drive him to suicide two years later, decided to return to Spain to cover the Ordóñez-Dominguín rivalry for *Life* magazine.

Hemingway's account of what happened was published in 1960 in the three long articles collected in a 1985 book, *The Dangerous Summer.* His reportage was overheated, unbalanced, sharply biased toward Ordóñez. In Hemingway's prose Antonio Ordóñez is a young god who can do no wrong, while Luis Miguel is a conceited, aging talent who chooses to slide by on tricks, and their bullfights together represent "the gradual destruction" of Dominguín at the hands of the superior Ordóñez. Little film footage of these corridas exists, and contemporary newspaper accounts are unreliable, given the old-time practice of critics living off tips from matadors. But the evidence of Hemingway's own words suggests that the rivalry was much closer than he wanted to admit.

From June 27 to August 21, 1959, the brothers-in-law performed together ten times, four of them *mano a mano.* The first five corridas had other matadors on the card, and if you count the ears and tails and gauge Hemingway's descriptions of the crowd reaction, it would seem that overall Luis Miguel got the better of Antonio in them. Then came the one-on-one bullfights. During the first one, July 30 in Valencia, Dominguín took a horn in the crotch, ceding the afternoon to Antonio. But the next day in Mallorca, in a corrida without Luis Miguel on the card, Antonio was gored, and when the brothers-in-law met two weeks later in Málaga, both had open horn wounds. It is often referred to as one of the greatest corridas ever: six bulls killed on six sword thrusts;

eleven ears, four tails, and three hooves cut. (Hooves were cut for exceptional work in those years.)

But Luis Miguel was tossed again in Málaga, and at the end of the day Antonio had come out ahead in trophies cut. After Málaga, it became apparent that Luis Miguel was much worse off physically than Antonio, and the *manos a manos* in Bayonne, France, on August 15 and in Ciudad Real two days later went Antonio's way, especially Ciudad Real. On the twenty-first, in Bilbao, with the matador Jaime Ostos as the third man, Luis Miguel was gored again, ending the competition in Spain and effectively ending it for good. The brothers-in-law did continue their rivalry the next year, in eleven corridas held in France and South America, but these were lackluster affairs off the main Spanish stage.

In retrospect, the so-called dangerous summer of 1959 did not really decide whether Ordóñez or Dominguín was the better matador. Dominguín fought Ordóñez to a standstill in the first five encounters, while Antonio bested an ailing Dominguín in the second five. But Hemingway's title is an apt one, because a lot of human blood was shed that summer, and in many ways the bullfights were a disaster for all concerned. In the short time left to him, Hemingway regretted the way he had written his articles, and his reputation among bullfighting aficionados has never quite recovered from how he handled Dominguín and for some abusive things he wrote about Manolete, who was and is deified in Spain. Dominguín's reputation suffered from Hemingway's condemnation of him, and he was bitter about it for the rest of his life. Antonio was the big winner in print, but it was a pyrrhic victory, because he was tarred as Hemingway's pet, which lost him credit with many in Spain.

Over time, the reputation of Antonio Ordóñez has come to eclipse that of Dominguín, owing to the sheer weight of Antonio's career. From the mid-1950s to his effective retirement in 1971, despite numerous poor performances and lapses of attention and will, Antonio was considered by most serious aficionados to be the best active matador in Spain, and even in his day people acknowledged that he was capable of a kind of bullfighting perfection few others have ever attained. After 1971 he continued to perform, but just one day a year, in his beloved *goyesca* in Ronda. His last *goyesca* as a matador was in 1980. It was a friendly *mano a mano* with his son-in-law Francisco Rivera, Paquirri. In a photograph of that day, Antonio and Paquirri walk around the ring to furious applause with little Fran and his brother Cayetano: grandfather, father, and two sons together in public, perhaps for the last time.

29

·✦·────◄◗◊◖►────·✦·

In the Blood

Ronda, September 7. By midafternoon the streets were packed. Groups of women in flamenco dresses clapped and sang Gypsy songs in front of the bullring gate, and men gathered around the official resale ticket booths looking for a way into the arena. The crowds must have driven over that morning from Sevilla and Málaga—it was a Saturday— because Ronda had been quiet the night before. The day dawned brightly, but darkened as it aged, and a ceiling of dense clouds hovered over the people as they made their way through the clogged Calle Virgen de la Paz and into the *plaza de toros*. Ronda's Maestranza is an unusual bullring. At a full seventy-two yards in diameter, the arena floor is one of the largest in the world. But the Maestranza seats a mere six thousand spectators, accommodated in two covered and colonnaded grandstands, one atop the other, forming a wide wall around the ring with no uncovered seats.

The afternoon began with a parade of antique carriages, drawn by teams of three, four, or five horses, with footmen in eighteenth-century livery. They made their way around the ring to music. Then the toreros swaggered out in their *goyesca* costumes, which were made of the same material as modern bullfighting suits but cut loosely, with longer jackets, decorations in plain black stitching, and bicorn hats of the kind worn by Napoleon's officer corps. Fran was the host and promoter of the corrida, and as such he was determined to be its star performer as well. He'd chosen Domingo Hernández bulls for the occasion—Domecq stock raised in central Spain—and had signed El Juli and Curro Vázquez to perform with him. Fifty years old and set to retire that autumn, Curro Vázquez wasn't going to give Fran much competition. But if Fran wanted to be the story of the corrida, he was going to have to get the better of Juli, a young matador who would do whatever it took to cut the most ears on any given day.

As it turned out, there were no ears cut on the first four bulls of the afternoon, and the mood was almost casual in the ring. Curro Vázquez—who was Fran's uncle by marriage to a niece of Luis Miguel Domínguín's—had little to say for his two bulls, the first and fourth of the corrida. Fran gave his first animal, the second of the bullfight, a standard performance in many ways, but there was also something special about his work, something that peeked out at intervals, like sunlight between clouds. Now and then, Fran was making passes that were slower, smoother, and more forceful than any he had achieved that season. It was just one pass here and one pass there, too few perhaps for the crowd to catch on, but you could see that members of Fran's cuadrilla had noticed and they were excited—and then became frustrated when Fran botched the kill and lost an ear. After his bull was dragged out, El Juli met his first bull, which went on the defensive, and he killed with brutal efficiency.

The trumpet sounded, the ring cleared, and Fran's second bull loped in: a thick black animal with sharp horns, speed, and attitude. Fran stepped out and the bull made for him without encouragement. Fran dropped to his knees, flashed the *capote* over his head, and pulled off a *larga cambiada* that sent the bull out past his left shoulder. "*Olé!*" said the crowd. The bull wheeled. Fran dropped again for another *larga,* this one over the right shoulder. "*Olé!*" Fran stood. Feet together, he made three *verónicas,* bringing the bull back and forth across his body. The bull returned for more and Fran cited for another *verónica.* But this time, as the bull reached Fran, he swirled the outside corner of his magenta and yellow cape back around his hip, folding the fluttering end of the cloth away from the bull's line of sight, jarring its head around, ending the series with a half-*verónica.*

Beauty is in the details. The difference between a lovely face and a plain one can be found in tiny increments, a nose placed just so, a slight plumpness to the lips, a certain clarity to the skin. Fran had made scores of half-*verónicas* that season, and this last one had all the elegance and balance that were typical of his style. But on this little pass he'd slowed the motion of his hand a few beats and had concentrated his effort in a new way, making the pass that much more delicate, more studied, more precise. It was a rounder, fuller, more aesthetically pleasing motion, and it exerted greater control over the bull. All sense of hurry and struggle had been banished from it, and what remained was the emotional effect of it, delivered without any sense of the effort it took to gain that effect. This was inspiration, and if Fran could somehow keep in touch with it for the rest of the performance, he was going to do something that no one who saw it was going to forget for a long time.

The bull took two pics. Then Fran set his feet and gave another series of *verónicas,* and that same tenderness of motion was in his hands, wedded to the same lethargic tempo. The passes seemed to roll like waves meandering over a sandbar, building up into a sluggish fullness before surging over in a gush of released energy. The passes were so relaxed, so devoid of tension, so copious, they almost failed to excite the crowd, until the black peril of the bull swelled in behind the cape, giving the passes a dignity that danger confers on the art of the corrida. *"Olé!"* If Fran had made a series of *verónicas* like that in Sevilla, the people might have stopped the proceedings and given him a lap around the ring. The Ronda crowd was less discerning, however. They didn't realize yet what they were seeing, and they did nothing more than chant *"Olé!"* and await developments.

The sound of a trumpet announced the banderillas, and the crowd was in for a surprise. Fran had decided to place a pair of sticks himself and had offered to share the other two with Curro and Juli. It was an appropriate gesture all around, given Fran's role as host and the festive nature of the *goyesca.* But it was also a maddeningly self-defeating decision. Poised on what looked like a big triumph, he had decided to risk the stamina of his final bull on an act of banderillas that was going to be longer and more wearing than usual. Fran was also giving a big advantage to El Juli, because he never placed his own sticks, whereas Julián was a well-known matador-banderillero and would surely win over the crowd with his work.

The band began to play, as it usually does when matadors place banderillas. Curro Vázquez took the first pair and was almost killed trying to get them in. Then El Juli rammed his banderillas home to applause. Fran walked out to midring and raised his pair over his head. Just then, a wide and flat beam of sunlight broke through the clouds and the gray ring overflowed with light. Fran hopped up into the sparkling air and the bull stormed forward. Fran hit the ground, feet together. The bull came on. Fran waited. The bull got closer. When the bull was within a few inches, Fran stepped wide with his left foot and the bull tilted at the motion of the wayward leg. Just as quickly, Fran popped the leg back to its original position, his feet together, and banged the harpoons into the bull's black hide as it veered, carried away from Fran by its speed and momentum. The audience cheered. The band stopped playing. It was time for the third and final act.

Even casual observers could now sense that something was about to happen, and the audience chattered in anticipation. As Fran emerged with the red cape and sword in his hands, the people hushed themselves quiet. Fran spread his feet apart and cited for the first pass. He extended the cape, shook it hard, and shouted, *"Hey!"* The sound echoed off the walls of the ring. The bull launched and lowered its head, slashing its right horn at the red cloth. Fran stood firm; with his left hand tucked neatly behind his back, he swept the cape away from the bull with an even-flowing bend of his right hand, wrist, arm, shoulder, torso, and leg, making it clear by the beauty of what he was doing that he was on his way to a triumph, as long as the bull cooperated and he could get the sword in on the first try. What the audience didn't know, and maybe what Fran himself didn't know, was that this bull wasn't going to cooperate in any way, and it wasn't going to matter.

Midway through that first pass, the bull came up short. It swayed at Fran and chopped its head. Most matadors would have skipped to safety and no one in the crowd would have blamed them. But Fran stayed with the pass. He knelt into the bull, pushing the cape down into its face, forcing it to lower its head and run into a series of low, controlling passes that hurt its neck muscles and made it take notice of what Fran wanted it to do. Then Fran rose to his feet again, switched the *muleta* to his left hand as he came up, and fanned out a sweet string of velvety *naturales* that resolved into a chest pass, the bull shooting into the air as Fran raised the cape. *"Ohhhhhhhhhh-LAY!"* roared the crowd.

Shouts of *"Musica!"* filled the air. The band began to play a *pasodoble*. Fran stalked forward, eyes on the bull, setting up for the next series of passes. But when he heard the music he broke stride, looked up at the musicians, and waved his sword back and forth at them, telling them to stop playing. The band shut down with a loud drumbeat. The ring was silent for a moment. The bull stared at Fran, its sides rising and falling with labored breath. Then everyone in the stands started talking at once. It took a second for the audience to decide what it thought about this new development, and then the people broke into applause, hesitant at first, then with feeling. Fran had made what Spaniards called a *gesto muy torero,* a gesture that was "very bullfighter." It was as if Fran were saying, "I know we're in my ring and you would like to do me a favor for the sake of my family. But today I would like to show you what I can do on my own terms."

What happened next took less than five minutes. There weren't more than twelve or thirteen passes involved. The bull continued to be recalcitrant. It stopped and started. It indulged in reluctant pauses. Once it came just short of knocking Fran over with a head butt. But on this afternoon in Ronda the mundane problems of bullfighting did not seem to apply to our bullfighter. He moved in a kind of trance, creating a dreamy performance, refining each pass, cleaning its line and tempering its motion one well-designed withdrawal of the cape at a time. Everything was effortless, yet filled to the brim with emotion. Each time the bull faltered in its charge Fran waited, an abstracted smile on his face. Then he took up the pass again and taught the bull where to go, making the bull into more than it was.

Fran was *borracho de toro,* drunk on bull. The indecision and doubt that seemed to follow him into the ring some afternoons was gone. He was playful, heedless, and almost childlike. Two superior sets of passes with the right hand and two more with the left, and somewhere in the middle of it a woman's voice could be heard from the seats: *"Lo lleva en la sangre!"* He carries it in his blood!

Fran paused, cape held out to the bull, looked over his shoulder at the sound of the woman's voice, and nodded broadly in agreement. Fran wouldn't have been who he was without El Niño, Antonio, and Paquirri. His blood had given him everything. But whatever anyone else thought about him, Fran knew that he'd paid for everything he'd been given, and more. He was born into a certain heritage, and sometime in childhood, before he understood the implications of it, he had accepted the challenge of that heritage, with all the advantages and burdens that came with it. But on this afternoon, in this bullring, in his family's hometown, in the place where the terrible business of the bulls took its modern shape, Fran found a way to grasp the whole mess of it and make it his, to take the misery and make it beautiful, which is what great bullfighting is always about.

He arranged his body in profile to the bull, lined up, rocked back, and crashed over the horns, pouring the sword into the bull's body, burying the smooth metal blade between the bull's shoulders, leaving it there, up to the red-wrapped hilt. The bull stood, amazed at being dead. It paced back and Fran followed, eyes on the bull. Then the bull rattled and shook. It swayed. Fran swayed with it, arms outstretched, pelvis thrust forward. Standing on all fours, the bull laid its skull down on the sand and allowed the weight of its dying carcass to tumble after the head and collide with the ground. Fran spun around. His arms embraced the crowd, and the people chanted "Torero!" as Fran knelt down before the bullpen gate, picked up a handful of sand, and kissed it, touching the memory of his grandfather whose ashes were buried there.

The rest of the afternoon was a matter of housekeeping. Fran was awarded his two ears and he took his victory lap. Then El Juli, not to be outdone, got right in the face of a nasty bull and cut his own pair of ears, not so much for art as for lacking a normal sense of self-preservation. After the corrida, Fran and his daughter climbed into a horse-drawn carriage and were wheeled into the streets with the crowd applauding. The cuadrilla had gone to change clothes at an inn across the street from the bullring, and the assistant manservant Antonio Marquez was down in the bar. When I walked in he gave me a big *abrazo,* the loose hug Spanish men greet each other with. Then he hugged me again.

"Did you see him, Eduardo?" Antonio asked. "Did you see how slow he was? The way he made the passes long and smooth? I can't tell you what it means to me. After all these years with him . . ." Antonio had lapsed into sobs. Just then Juani the driver barreled into us, red-faced, and hugged Antonio and then hugged me. "*Me cago en los muertos de su toreo!*" he said. This is an untranslatable Andalucían exclamation; literally, "I shit on the dead of his bullfighting." Normally, it is considered a serious insult to tell someone you are shitting on his ancestors. But in this case Juani meant it as high praise.

The history of bullfighting is studded with examples of matadors who for one special day reached outside themselves and gave a performance that went beyond anything they'd do again in their career. Fran's work in Ronda wasn't like that; it was something much better. It was a glimpse of what Fran might be capable of on a regular basis, as a mature artist, a man who had overcome his faults and fears to be confident in what he wanted to do and capable enough to realize his vision even in the face of adversity. It was also joyous. What was it Fran had said to me on the road to Valencia back in March? "I want to feel happy in front of the bull again." Well, for one afternoon at least, Fran had found that elusive thing he'd been searching for.

I came across Noël in the lobby bar of a big hotel, but he was having a few beers with some friends from the bull circuit and I didn't have the chance to corner him and get his views. After a while we made our way out of the hotel and walked across the bridge to the other side of town. Noël had been invited to a private party that Fran was throwing in the garden of one of the old palaces perched at the edge of Ronda. When we got to the party Noël made right for Fran, grabbed him by the shoulders, shook him, and said in a quiet voice, "You know how good you were today, don't you?" Fran smiled and said, "I am very happy."

It wasn't just Fran and his followers who thought he had done something special. So did Spain's bullfighting critics, and for the next week they showered Fran's performance with praise. "The grandson of Antonio Ordóñez did honor to his family," wrote the 6 Toros 6 critic Paco Aguado, "with an exhibition of bullfighting of exquisite suavity, of absolute ease and naturalness, standing upright, forcing nothing, tranquil, classic. Everything perfect, and better still the final sword thrust."

That evening the cuadrilla bus pulled out of Ronda. They had bulls less than forty-eight hours later in Calatayud.

Epilogue

If Fran's season were the plot of a film or a novel, it would have ended in Ronda, with Fran triumphant and all doubt and gloom washed away. Sadly for Fran, the art of fiction was not at his disposal. He was going to have to continue making his way through the muddle of reality. Ronda had its echoes. A few weeks afterward *6 Toros 6*, the most influential bullfighting magazine in Spain, ran a flattering headshot of Fran on its cover with an interview on the inside suggesting that Francisco Rivera Ordóñez was back and ready for better things. But a triumph in Ronda does not a season make, and Fran's chances to build on his September success were running out. There were four weeks left in the season, eleven corridas, and the days were growing colder once again.

Córdoba, September 24. "Paquirri was a great torero, but he had bad luck," said Antonio Ayoso, who was driving me out of Córdoba in his taxi. "They should never have taken him in the ambulance. They should have taken him in a helicopter. But they put him in that ambulance, and by the time they got to the hospital he was dead."

Seventeen days had passed since the *goyesca* in Ronda, and Fran had performed four more times. He cut two ears in Calatayud on September 9, had no luck in the important *plazas* of Valladolid on the fourteenth and Murcia on the fifteenth, and cut an ear in first-category Barcelona on the twenty-second. That night Fran sped off to Logroño, where he had bulls on the twenty-third, and I flew to Madrid, caught the bullet train down to Córdoba, and arranged to be driven into the mountains to Pozoblanco. In all my travels, I had never been less eager to visit a place. Pozoblanco: the name was bathed in dread and doom.

We were driving out from Córdoba into the Sierra Morena range, taking the very road Paquirri's ambulance had taken the opposite way. "The route was much worse in Paquirri's time," Ayoso said. If so, then it must have been a really nasty road in its day, because it was still treacherous, its coiling hairpin turns so tight the taxi had to slow to a near standstill to navigate them. We ascended through slopes of green pine and burnt grass and turned right at Espiel with its small roadside cemetery; then it was up into the cool high valley of Los Pedroches, with the wind blowing, past fields of grazing sheep and goats, past cement factories and a slaughterhouse, and finally into Pozoblanco. It had taken us close to two hours to complete a trip that Paquirri's ambulance had made in less than one.

The taxi dropped me in front of the Hotel Los Godos, which looked much as it must have in Paquirri's day. One of the hotel's owners, Godofredo Jurado, gave me a glimpse of room 307, which contained the last bed Paquirri slept in. The sheets, pillows, and blanket Paquirri used that night were kept in plastic bags, Jurado said. "If we were in a tourist zone we'd turn this into a museum," he added, opening the door to a modest room with a tile floor, two narrow beds, and a television mounted on the wall. "But we are in an out-of-the-way place, so we just rent it out. More than ninety percent of our clients ask to stay in this room."

Pozoblanco was a nice small town and the people were friendly. Paquirri's death was the biggest thing that had happened there, and most of the citizens seemed eager to talk about it with the scores of reporters who were pouring in to cover Fran's bullfight, on the eighteenth anniversary of his father's death, with bulls from Sayalero y Bandrés, Avispado's ranch. As it turned out, the corrida itself was a bit of a letdown. The emotional high point was the moment of silence in Paquirri's honor. For the record, Fran cut an ear off his first bull and lost an ear to a poor sword on the second. But ears and triumphs weren't really the point of that corrida. Ronda had proven that Fran could match the brilliance of his grandfather, at least for one day. Pozoblanco proved that Fran wasn't doomed to his father's fate.

Bullfighters no longer stay at the Hotel Los Godos when they're in Pozoblanco. Instead Fran and at least one of his colleagues that afternoon put up at the Hotel San Francisco, a modern establishment on the highway outside of town. An hour after the bullfight ended, the lobby of the San Francisco was filled with aficionados, members of various cuadrillas, and journalists hunting for a final quote to round out their stories. Vicente Ruiz, El Soro, the only living matador on the card with Paquirri on the day he died, was also in the hotel lobby. Looking tired, ill, bloated, and prematurely old at forty, he leaned on a cane in front of the elevators and gave his reminiscences to a procession of cameras. Then Manuel Díaz, El Cordobés—who'd performed with Fran that afternoon and who had been the teenager in Pozoblanco, back in 1984, to whom Paquirri had dedicated his penultimate bull—came down from his hotel room and took a few questions.

While all of this was going on, Fran was up in his room with the usual white towel around his waist. A few friends had made the trip to Pozoblanco to be there for him. He chatted with them for a while, and before long he showed most of them to the door. Eventually the only one left was an older gentleman named José. Fran excused himself and went into the bathroom to take a shower. José sat on Fran's bed and watched television. The national news was on, with a story about Fran's corrida in Pozoblanco and a rehash of the sad history that had led up to it. The hotel room was set up in such a way that the TV faced both the bed and the door to the bathroom, and when Fran had finished his shower he came out and was greeted with a slow-motion video sequence of his father being gored by Avispado.

José jumped up to turn off the TV, but Fran had seen enough. He stood there naked, dripping, staring at the blank set. "Oh, my poor father," Fran sobbed. "Why don't they leave him alone. He did so much more in his life than die."

After Pozoblanco Fran's season spilled away to a quiet conclusion. He finished September by cutting four ears in the town of Lorca on the twenty-eighth, but came up empty the following afternoon in the prestigious Feria de San Miguel in Sevilla. Then, on October 5, in the autumn *feria* in Madrid, Fran clicked with Flautista (Flautist), a thirteen-hundred-pound chestnut bull from the ranch of Alcurrucén, giving an exhibition of the kind of pure bullfighting he had shown himself capable of in Ronda. Fran's *muleta* work was notable for one series of passes with the right hand and two with the left hand which had the most severe audience in the bull universe shouting *olés*. Then Fran killed *a toda ley* (completely by the book), and cut an ear that was worth two in most other bullrings.

"If this torero were capable of giving regular performances with passes as fine as those he gave us yesterday," wrote Vicente Ruiz, the critic for the newspaper *El Mundo*, "then we would be talking about a *maxima figura del toreo*. But that is not the situation, at least for now."

In the days following Fran's big splash in Madrid, I traveled down to Córdoba one last time in pursuit of an answer to a question that had nagged at me for months. I wanted to know how Paquirri had died. How could a healthy man of thirty-six die of a horn wound in an industrialized country at the end of the twentieth century? If there was an answer, I hoped to get it from Dr. Elíseo Morán, the man who'd treated Paquirri in the Pozoblanco ring. Fran had made it clear to me that he placed some of the blame for what had happened to his father on the medical care he'd received in Pozoblanco. And he assumed that the doctor in charge had retired. In fact, Dr. Morán still had his practice in Córdoba and in the Pozoblanco ring. Had Fran been hurt in Pozoblanco, he would have been placed in Dr. Morán's care.

Given the nature of my call, I wasn't sure how Dr. Morán would receive me. But when we spoke in his elegant office — he was a courtly man of sixty-eight with a wreath of pure white hair about his head — Dr. Morán answered my every question. He began by outlining the nature of Paquirri's wounds. Avispado's horn had carved three trajectories in Paquirri's thigh, Dr. Morán said: up fifteen centimeters, down ten centimeters, and in eight centimeters. The resulting damage had snapped the tangle of major vessels, including the femoral and saphenous veins and femoral artery, that carry blood to and from the leg.

All of this was well known, but then Dr. Morán said something unexpected: "I never thought Paquirri was going to die. We had controlled the bleeding. He was no longer bleeding and I was calm. I never thought he was dying." There are numerous accounts of Paquirri's final hours. I had studied four of them in detail, and all of them are based on the assumption that Paquirri had been in a race for his life when he was sent down to Córdoba. But Dr. Morán had a different view. He told me that when he said goodbye to Paquirri that night, he thought he was saying goodbye to a patient who was more than stable enough to make it to the hospital alive.

So why, then, did Paquirri die?

Dr. Morán attended a postmortem on Paquirri's body the night of the goring. He said it proved that the medical attention Paquirri had received in Pozoblanco had been effective. The clamped blood vessels and compresses in the wounds had held, and the torero had not bled out in the ambulance. Accepting this, and adding to it the clue that, just before he died, Paquirri had been agitated and had complained that he couldn't breathe, Dr. Morán concluded that the cause of death was a pulmonary embolism. This was probably the result of a blood clot or a bit of fatty tissue that had been dislodged by the horn wound and had made its way through Paquirri's bloodstream to a major vessel in his lung, where it had cut off the supply of oxygenated blood, shutting down the body in short order.

According to various American emergency room doctors I interviewed, an embolism isn't the sort of thing the doctors in Pozoblanco could have predicted or treated, even if Paquirri had been in a hospital. In fact, Paquirri wasn't in a hospital, he was in an ambulance, which is where he should have been, given his medical condition. Paquirri could not have stayed in Pozoblanco. He had to be taken to a big hospital for the surgery and postoperative care he would need to make a complete recovery.

This opinion was affirmed by Paquirri's personal physician, Dr. Ramón Vila, who also happened to be the chief doctor of the Maestranza ring in Sevilla. Dr. Vila was at home on the day Paquirri died. He had, however, been in telephone contact with Dr. Morán in Pozoblanco while Morán was treating Paquirri, and Vila had read the postmortem materials. "The doctors in Pozoblanco did all they could," said Dr. Vila, who is a friend of Dr. Morán's. "In the final analysis, the death of Paquirri was a death from stress, probably a pulmonary embolism."

Dr. Morán and Dr. Vila's diagnosis is a controversial one. Over the years aficionados and journalists have speculated, although without evidence, that Paquirri bled to death from a deep wound that the Pozoblanco medical team missed. When I recounted the known facts of Paquirri's last hours to Dr. James Giglio, a professor at Columbia University's medical school and the director of emergency medicine at New York–Presbyterian Hospital, he agreed the most plausible explanation was that Paquirri bled out. Nevertheless, Dr. Giglio did not rule out embolism, especially if Paquirri had seemed fine just before he died. "If you take as fact that there was a sudden deterioration of a patient that appeared to be stable," Dr. Giglio said, "an embolism is an appealing explanation."

The afternoon was ending and so was my time with Dr. Morán. Long shadows fell across his office. When I asked him what Paquirri's death had meant to him over the years, he did something strange. He leaned over and turned off the lamp that sat on the desk between us. "I never thought he was going to die," he said again, his face hidden in the growing shadows. "When they told me he had died, I was shocked. I felt lost. There is no one in the world, no doctor, who wants his patients to suffer or die. When things don't go well we feel terrible. We spend many nights without sleep." It was only when Dr. Morán showed me to the door that I realized why he had turned his lamp off. He hadn't wanted me to see his tears.

Zaragoza, October 13. The ten-day Zaragoza *feria* is dedicated to *la Virgen del Pilar* (the Virgin of the Pillar), who, along with Saint James, is the most important of Spain's national patron saints. The feast day of this Virgin, and the centerpiece of her *feria,* is October 12, which was also the day Columbus first sighted land in the Americas, as well as the day Spanish-speaking people worldwide celebrate El Día de la Raza (Day of the Hispanic Race). Zaragoza's main square was crowded in the hours before Fran's corrida. People placed bouquets and wreaths on a thirty-foot mountain of flowers being offered to the Virgin outside her church. There were processions of girls in peasant dresses, brass bands, and soldiers marching. Happy Zaragozano families packed the tables of inns and restaurants, munching away on large lunches. That afternoon, with the permission of the government, as bullfighting posters always say, six large bulls would be slaughtered in the town arena.

More than Italy or France, Spain is the country where the culture of the Roman Empire is best preserved in modern form. We were in Caesar Augusta, as Zaragoza was named when the Romans colonized it and made it into a city for retired veterans of their famed legions. If you visit the town during the *feria,* it would not be hard to imagine Caesar Augusta as it must have been during some festival two thousand years ago, when Rome still ruled the known world. Once again it was bread-and-circuses time for the local population, with the parades of citizens and soldiers, the feasts, the offerings of flowers before the temple of the town's most important goddess, and the bloody entertainments of the coliseum as the final pleasure of the day.

Bullfighting is easy to dismiss as an artifact of humanity's savage and uncivilized history. But in its bloody way the bullfight is the essence of civilization, if by civilization we mean humanity's subjugation of the natural world and the development of custom and ritual to replace violence as the governing principle of human interaction. A society that can mount a corrida is an advanced society, one that has tamed nature, met the basic needs of its people (to the extent that entertainment is a priority), and channeled the bloody impulses of its populace into ordered ritual. There is nothing more civilized than a bullfight. It is the sum of humankind's fears and wordless needs contained in a spectacle of rigid control and elaborate ceremony. Spectacles similar to bullfighting were part and parcel of the culture of the Roman Empire, which was the founding culture of Western civilization. Is it any surprise, then, that such spectacles have endured, just as Roman architecture, Roman laws, Roman language, and Rome's adopted religion — Christianity — have?

The afternoon of Fran's corrida was cold, damp, and gray. But the bullring — which was built in 1764 to mount bullfights to raise money for a charity hospital — had a modern tent-like contraption rigged over it to keep out the weather. Inside the arena it was muggy with tobacco smoke and the heat of ten thousand spectators, a packed house. Fran had cut two ears the day before in a small town called Calanda, but on this afternoon, in the first-category ring at Zaragoza, he couldn't get anything going. So he killed his last bull, and with it his season died. When the bullfight was over, Fran and the other toreros shook hands, clapped each other on the back, and walked out of the *plaza* into the chill wet air, some of the audience whistling at Fran as he turned away from what had been a mediocre day.

In the end, Fran performed sixty-two times that season, killing around 120 bulls and cutting forty-nine ears. He'd registered notable performances in Ronda and Linares, cut an ear in each of the first-category *plazas* of Valencia, Barcelona, and Madrid, and had some big afternoons in second- and third-class rings: Lorca, Cartagena, Játiva, and Calatayud. Fran could also take satisfaction in the thought that despite a rough emotional start and an injury that kept him out of action for a month, he'd finished strong, cutting twenty-four ears in his last twenty-one corridas. If the entire season had been that good . . . But it hadn't. Fran finished tenth on the leader board of matadors, a spot that *6 Toros 6* categorized as being the "lukewarm zone." It was a position from which a matador must either move up or move down.

"The season started very nervous, very tense, with many problems," Fran said, "but at the end I really enjoyed being a bullfighter. I was excited waiting for the bull to come out. I was happy in the ring. The end of the season was a personal and professional victory for me. I said, 'I am here, and don't say I am dead. I am still alive and I want to make my dream come true.' "

Fran and his cuadrilla held their traditional end-of-season dinner in the wine cellar of a townhouse that belonged to a prominent businessman and sometime bullfight promoter. As usual, Noël Chandler was invited along. When the dinner of tapas, steak, grilled fish, salad, bread, and wine was finished, Fran sat at one end of the table, a little-boy smile crinkling around the huge Cuban cigar in his mouth. Like everyone else he was a little drunk and very happy. No matter how good or bad a bullfighting season has been, toreros are always pleased to reach its conclusion. They'd risked their lives, done their work, and banked their money, and could look forward to a well-earned holiday. Best of all, they were in one piece. They'd beaten the odds and brought themselves one step closer to an honorable retirement and the telling of tall tales to grandchildren.

The only dissenting voice in the happy chorus was that of the *apoderado*. Pepe Luis Segura was still fixated on the idea that the presence of an American journalist had cursed them all. "You cost us another ear today," he told me as we ate. "You cost us another one."

Then, without preamble, the old picador Francisco López stood up and rapped his knuckles on the table for silence. The room settled down. López spread out his arms, lifted up his head, and began to sing. His song was a fandango, one of the basic forms of traditional flamenco music, the real flamenco that in Spain is called *cante hondo* (deep song). His scarred and ruined voice told the same story of savage beauty and tragic pain that is told over and over in the bullrings of Spain and wherever the deep, old flamenco is sung. He wasn't a great singer. Some of the people around the table snickered a little. But the old picador had a touch of the *duende* that night, and he closed his eyes and lost himself and the dark demon came.

Paco López finished his lament, the party broke up, and the bullfighters strolled out into the autumn night to the big hotel where their cars were parked out front. The season had ended, but the same frantic pace of travel would be maintained for one more night. They were driving home that very moment, eager to get back to Andalucía and their winter vacations. The cuadrilla loaded up the minibus, waved farewell, and pulled out.

Then it was time for Fran to go. He and Noël embraced, and Fran told Noël to call him during the off-season, to plan a trip scouting bulls in the countryside. But everyone knew this was just talk, and that Noël and Fran would probably see each other again in the spring, in some hotel room somewhere after a corrida. Then Fran slipped into his red Chevy van, and Juani drove off.

While everyone said his goodbyes, I was leaning against a car, taking in the scene. When I started to walk away I realized with some embarrassment that the car was Pepe Luis's champagne-colored Mercedes sedan. A few weeks later, in New York, I heard that when Pepe Luis saw this, he began to rage that I had cursed his car just as sure as I had cursed the season. Later that final night of the season, somewhere on the highway between Zaragoza and Sevilla, Pepe Luis and his driver were in an accident and the champagne-colored Mercedes was totaled. Fortunately, neither the *apoderado* nor his chauffeur was hurt.

Appendix: How to See Them

When you first start going to the bullfights, it isn't the specific details that matter so much as your overall impression of the spectacle. For this reason, as a beginning aficionado you should try to attend the best bullfights — that is, those held in major cities during *ferias*. Like sushi, bullfighting loses much of its charm when it is not the best quality: off-season bullfights in big-city rings tend to be drab and poorly attended, and the level of bullfighting in small towns is unpredictable. So the best bet is to go to bullfights during big-city *ferias* when the rings are packed, the atmosphere is charged with excitement, and the bullfighters and bulls are good enough that they won't spoil the day.

Many people may disagree, but for me Spain is *the* country in which to see a bullfight. Hands down, Spain has the greatest number of beautiful and historic rings, the most ferocious and hard-charging bulls, and the most discerning public. Spain mounts the most corridas a year — about eight hundred and fifty — and that isn't counting *novilladas,* horseback corridas, and other bull-related spectacles. The Spanish bullfighting season runs from March through October and unfolds much the same way each year. A complete list of Spanish *ferias* and bullring schedules would go on for pages; the following are some of the prominent ones.

The essential *ferias* of March are the weeklong cycles in Castellón de la Plana and down the road in Valencia. Then comes the April fair of Sevilla, which runs for two weeks, into early May. There are two or three prestigious corridas in Madrid in early May, and then the thirty-day Feria de San Isidro, which spills into June. Granada, Plasencia, Sevilla, and Toledo mount corridas on June 7, the Feast of Corpus Christi. At the end of June, solid provincial *ferias* are held in Alicante, León, and Burgos. The bull-running *feria* of Pamplona goes from July 6 to 14, and later that month there are top-notch weeklong *ferias* in Santander and Valencia. August and September are busy taurine months. The two prestige August *ferias* are those of Bilbao and San Sebastián, with Gijón and Málaga in the second tier; Almería, Azpeitia, Ciudad Real, Huelva, Linares, and Vitoria are among the best that follow behind. The standout September *ferias* are those in Sevilla and Valladolid, followed by Logroño, Murcia, Salamanca, and Ronda; then come *ferias* in Albacete, Andújar, Aranjuez, Guadalajara, Mérida, and Palencia. Zaragoza boasts the key October *feria*, and there is also an autumn *feria* in Madrid and a lovely one in Jaén.

The most important *ferias* of the Spanish season are San Isidro in Madrid in May, the Feria de Abril of Sevilla, the Corridas Generales of Bilbao in August, Pamplona's Feria de San Fermín in July, the Feria del Pilar of Zaragoza in October, and the two *ferias* of Valencia: Las Fallas in March and San Jaime in July. Taking into account the attractions of the host city, the nontaurine aspects of the *feria* itself, the level of bulls and matadors presented, and the ease of finding corrida tickets, food, and lodging, the top big-time *ferias* to attend as a tourist are those of Madrid and Valencia, and, of the second rank, Almería and Logroño. The worst big rings are in Barcelona (filled with tourists), Córdoba (always empty), and San Sebastián (hockey stadium atmosphere). It is likely to rain a great deal in the spring and be boiling hot down south in the summer months. The best weather of the bullfighting season is in September.

France has some thirty bullrings, and of these the best are the ancient Roman arenas at Arles and Nîmes. These rings play host to numerous *ferias*, of which the best are the mid-June cycle in Nîmes and the September *ferias* in both Nîmes and Arles. Worth noting are the *ferias* in Vic-Fézensac in June, Mont-de-Marsan in late July, and Bayonne, Béziers, and Dax in mid-August. Bullfighting is in decline in Portugal, so I can't recommend any *ferias* there. The big ring in Lisbon, the Campo Pequenho, is set to reopen after a restoration, so there is reason to hope.

The bullfighting season in Latin America is the mirror image of the European season, running from October to March, although bullfights do take place during the summer in rings along the Mexican-American border. After Spain, the nation with the most developed taurine culture is Mexico. Mexico has more than seventy rings, a majority of them clumped in the center of the country, in the states due north of Mexico City. The forty-seven-thousand-seat bullring in the capital, the biggest ring in the world, mounts corridas on most winter Sundays. The grandest ring in South America is the Plaza de Acho of Lima, Peru, which was built in 1766 and has corridas on scattered Sundays from October to mid-December.

The best *feria* south of Mexico, from the point of view of matadors and bulls, is in Quito, Ecuador, in the first week of December. Venezuela has close to twenty rings, and the key *ferias* are in Maracay, Valencia, and Caracas. The top rings of Colombia are in Cali, Bogotá, and Medellín.

It is difficult to purchase advance tickets to corridas in Spain, and even though a few Web sites have begun to offer this service, generally there is no need for it. Apart from a few particularly popular corridas and the entire Sevilla *feria*, it isn't hard to get into most bullfights. If you are staying at a good hotel, your concierge will usually be able to scrounge a few tickets for you, but you will probably pay a hefty scalper's price. It's better, cheaper, and more fun to go to the bullring yourself — this is easy to do, since most rings are located in the center of town — bypass the scalpers who will pester you, and head straight to the box office, which will likely have a few tickets left, even on the day of the corrida.

Keep in mind that most box offices observe a generous midday break for lunch and a nap. If the corrida happens to be sold out, ask for the *reventa*, a government-sanctioned dealer that resells tickets at a twenty-percent premium. Typically, the *reventa* booth or booths will be right outside the arena. If the *reventa* is also sold out, you may have to resort to one of the scalpers. Ticket-scalping is illegal, and you may pay dearly for one of the worst seats in the house. But it is rare in Spain to hear of a scalper selling counterfeit or phony tickets, and I have never heard of anyone being robbed by someone posing as a scalper. Of course there is always a first time.

More often than not, however, the box office will have tickets to sell and might even have enough to offer you a choice of seating. In Spanish rings, each ticket, or *entrada,* is printed with the seat number, row number, arena section, and whether the seat will be in sun or shade during the corrida. The first row of seats is called the *barrera,* and the two or three rows behind the *barrera* are called the *contra-barreras.* Rising from the *contra-barreras —* akin to the orchestra seats in a Broadway theater — are the *tendido* seats. Most bullrings have no seats above the *tendidos,* but in larger rings the *tendidos* may be topped with covered *palcos —* like balconies in a theater — and above the *palcos* a covered *grada* section. The biggest rings may have yet another covered section, above the *grada,* called the *andanada.*

All bullrings are divided into large wedge-shaped sections called *tendidos.* Confusingly, this is the same word used for the rows of "orchestra" seats mentioned above. A typical ring has ten *tendido* sections. Four of these are sold as shade (*sombra*), four as sun (*sol*), and two as sun and shade (*sol y sombra*). Ticket prices depend on proximity to the ring and whether the *tendido* section falls in sun or shadow. Generally, a *sombra* seat costs twice as much as a *sol* seat when both are the same distance from the ring. Prices vary widely. *Barrera* seats in *sombra* may cost more than one hundred dollars, while the *gradas* in *sol,* at the same corrida, may be as little as three dollars. It is important to know whether your seat is *sol* or *sombra,* but beware: many bullrings maintain the confusing practice of printing the *tendido* section number on the ticket without identifying whether that section is in *sol* or *sombra.*

In theory, since bullrings are round, no *tendido* is any closer to the action than any other. But in practice, much of what goes on during a bullfight unfolds in the *sombra* half of the ring. It is also the case that when the bullfighters are not performing, they, their servants, and their managers will stand in the *sombra* part of the passageway that runs between the seats and the sand. For this reason, if you want to be close to the action, to the smell of the bulls, to the faces of the bullfighters as they cape the bulls, to the clattering of the banderillas as the bulls run by, and to the goings-on in the passageway as the manservants tend to their matadors, you should try to sit as far down as possible in *sombra.*

But if you are just getting started seeing corridas, or if you have never been to one before, the best place to sit is in *sombra* at least halfway up in the stands. From this elevated vantage you will get the best sense of the pageantry of the bullfight without its gorier aspects shoved in your face. You get the best value for your money in the *sol y sombra* seats, since these are cheaper than *sombra* but are closer to the action than *sol* and will be in shade for at least half the corrida. It is said that the true aficionados in any ring will be found in *sol y sombra. Sol* seats are also a good option for the thrifty, especially if the day is cloudy and the ring is small, where the spectacle is easy to see from every section.

Most bullfights in Spain begin between six and seven-thirty P.M. Plan to get to the ring at least thirty minutes before the scheduled starting time: bullfights begin promptly; the opening parade is something you won't want to miss; it may take quite a while to get to your seat, since aisles and rows in most rings are cramped. Latecomers are allowed to take their seats only between bulls.

As you enter the arena you will see people renting cushions. It's advisable to get one, because your seat is a hard stone step. Programs are handed out free, and all bullrings have a bar selling snacks and drinks, although most rings also have wandering vendors. It is best to use the bathroom before leaving for a corrida, especially if you are a woman; most bullring toilets are nasty and hard to find, and moving around in a vast bullring is always tricky.

If you have purchased good *sombra* seats and are attending a *feria* in Madrid, Sevilla, Bilbao, or San Sebastián and want to blend in, you might consider dressing up. Otherwise it is best to wear comfortable clothes, but keep in mind that it is out of place to wear shorts in Spain unless you are three years old. Women should wear pants: it's most comfortable to sit with your legs open around the back of the person in front of you. Bring a sweater or light jacket, since the temperature drops in Spain as the sun goes down, and umbrellas and raincoats are a good idea for spring corridas.

Thus armed, with drink and cushion in hand, and perhaps a sense of apprehension at what you are about to witness, step into the bullring and take your seat. Oh, and sorry about all the lighted cigars and cigarettes around you, but you'll just have to put up with them. Spaniards haven't heard of no-smoking laws.

Acknowledgments

This book would not have been possible without the unfailing generosity of Francisco Rivera Ordóñez. He had every reason to refuse my intrusive request to spend a year with him, but he said yes on the spot and gave and gave of himself all that year and never asked for anything in return. *Mucha suerte,* Matador.

Thanks also to Fran's cuadrilla: Pepe Luis; Poli, Joselito, and José Maria; Francisco and Diego; Juani, Pepe, and Jesús; Nacho and, above all, Antonio for all his help and for booking me into hotels as Edward Kennedy, the only American name he could pronounce and a real elevation in rank for me.

After Fran, no one made a bigger contribution to the book than Noël Chandler. Private and modest by inclination, Noël overwhelmed me with his learning and his generosity of spirit. He is a great connoisseur of the bulls, and like all great connoisseurs he is an irreplaceable treasure. A big *abrazo,* Mr. Chandler.

My deep gratitude goes to David Black. The *New York Post* calls him a "super agent," and that's what he has been to me, an indefatigable champion with a writer's appreciation for the craft. David handed me off to Eamon Dolan, by reputation and in fact one of the best editors in the business. Eamon was perfect: sure-handed, demanding, and kind. Three years into this project, both Eamon and David have become more than colleagues. They are friends.

Deep thanks also to Jane Lawson and the team at Transworld in London.

My thanks to Leigh Ann Eliseo, Susan Raihofer, Jason Sacher, and Jessica Candlin of the David Black Agency, and Gracie Doyle, Larry Cooper, Lois

Wasoff, Anne Seiwerath, Christina Smith, and everyone else at Houghton Mifflin.

During the creation of this book I amassed debts to more people than I can mention. Those not listed here should know I owe them and haven't forgotten all they did for me.

Thanks to my friends in Spain. Juan Varez brought me to his wonderful country for the first time, sent me to my first corrida, and urged me to learn Spanish. Rocío Barreiros de Arteaga and her many relatives opened doors that I wouldn't even have known about without their help. Manuel Cruz Vélez, Francisco Gallardo, Alicia Mosse, Yun Gallardo Mosse, Lourdes Cosío, and Tom Kallene cheered me, helped me, and made this process more fun than work should be.

The noted aficionados Coleman Cooney and Tristan Wood read the manuscript for accuracy and provided many, many corrections. Various doctors, including Ivan Moseley and James Giglio, helped me wade through some treacherous medical issues.

I'm indebted to the people who let me interview them — those quoted in the book and many who aren't. Thanks especially to the staff at Pozoblanco city hall and to Serafín Pedraza, to Don Francisco de Borja Domecq y Solís and Juan Reyes, to Juan Posada, José Antonio del Moral, José Carlos Arévalo, Muriel Feiner, Julio Fernandez, Dr. Elíseo Morán, Juan Alonso, Salvador Valverde, Fernando Fernandez Roman, Dr. Ramón Vila, Miguel Angel Eguiluz, and Antonio Peña of Onda Algeciras TV.

Many thanks to the bullfighting clubs of New York, to Stanley Conrad, and to the Taurine Bibliophiles of America. Thanks to Roy Shifflett and Wayne Pearce. Thanks also to the entire English-speaking cuadrilla that follows the bulls in Spain; special mention goes to Joe Distler, Jesse Graham, the late Chris Humphreys, Allen Josephs, R. Kelley O'Connor, Imre and Nympha Weitzner, and Lore Monnig.

Michael Shapiro, Ari Goldman, and Sandy Padwe of Columbia University's Graduate School of Journalism showed me what it is to be a reporter. The editors and writers of the *New York Times* made me into one. Above all, thanks to Nancy Sharkey, Joan Nassivera, and my lifetime guru, Dave Smith.

Many friends have been supportive, but Roland Lange, Gian Solomon, Douglas Eklund, and Julian Rubinstein each rendered services above and beyond the call. Thanks also to Ruth Oscharoff.

My wife and I could not survive week to week without the aid and comfort of a combined family that stretches from the Upper West Side to West L.A. I would like to thank especially my father, Milton Lewine, for giving me so much before leaving us too soon, and my mother, Carol Lewine, for having the courage to stay and take care of me. And thanks to Warren Wallace.

My wife, Megan, stayed home and endured a year as a single mother with a baby while I wandered around Spain. She has supported me in ways beyond counting, and so this is her book as much as it is mine. To my children, Noah Milton and Charlotte Sophia: your dad sends each of you a hug with feet and a thousand kisses.

Notes on Sources

This book is the product of more than a decade of following the bullfights as a fan, and of more than three years of professional reporting on the life and family history of Francisco Rivera Ordóñez. I spent close to a year in Spain traveling with Fran and his team of bullfighters, and I interviewed scores of people during that time in English and in Spanish. Scenes involving Fran and his team were witnessed by me or, on one or two occasions, recreated from interviews and videotapes. The historical scenes in the book were drawn from accounts in books, newspapers, and films. My comments on the nature of bullfighting and of Spain come from personal experience informed by reading. Whenever I have used a specific thought or idea of another writer, I have credited that writer in either the text or the notes. I translated the lines from García Lorca's "Song of the Rider." Below is a list of written sources not explicitly cited in the text. I have included only the chapters in which further clarification of sources was necessary. Any inaccuracies or omissions are solely my responsibility.

Chapter 1: Paquirri's last day was reconstructed from interviews and from accounts in two books: José Carlos Arévalo and José Antonio del Moral, *Nacido para Morir*, and Arturo Luna, *La Tragica Cogida y Muerte de Paquirri*, a book that contains reprints of newspaper articles and transcripts of interviews.

Chapter 2: The account of Fran's early career was put together from reviews of his corridas in back issues of the magazines *Aplausos* and *6 Toros 6* and from interviews.

Chapter 3: The technical and philosophical discussion of bullfighting was informed primarily by Spanish bullfighting law, the *Ley y Reglamento de Espectaculos Taurinos,* and by Ernest Hemingway's *Death in the Afternoon,* with much assistance from the writings of Angus Macnab, A. L. Kennedy, José Antonio del Moral, Barnaby Conrad, Kenneth Tynan, and others, and hours of conversation with Noël Chandler.

Chapter 4: John Hooper's *The New Spaniards* and the *Oxford Atlas of the World* gave shape to my own experience of Spain's varied geography and population.

Chapter 6: Don Álvaro Domecq's *El Toro Bravo* was my primary written source for the practices of bull breeding. My history of bullfighting came from Hemingway and from the other books cited in Chapter Three, as well as José María de Cossío's famous encyclopedia, *Los Toros.*

Chapter 8: My take on the role of bullfighting in the development of Spain and on how bullfighting was viewed by historians relied on two sources, Adrian Shubert's *Death and Money in the Afternoon* and Allen Joseph's *White Wall of Spain.*

Chapter 9: See Hemingway, Tynan, and Gerald Brenan for astute commentary on the aristocratic nature of Spanish culture.

Chapter 10: Adrian Shubert's *Death and Money in the Afternoon* contains an excellent section on bullring construction. Statistics on the number of corridas per year and the size and location of bullrings came from the 2001 edition of the *Agenda Taurina* and the Web site of the Spanish Ministry of the Interior.

Chapter 15: Statistics on bullfighters' injuries are drawn from Cossío, *Los Toros;* Francisco Narbona, *Sangre en la Arena;* and Juan José de Bonifaz, *Víctimas de la Fiesta.*

Chapter 17: For a history of pic'ing, see Hemingway, *Death in the Afternoon,* Shubert, and Macnab. Hemingway's discussion of banderillas also comes from *Death in the Afternoon.*

Chapter 18: See Shubert for a history of bullfighting in France.

Chapter 20: For information on Pamplona and San Fermín, I relied on years of personal experience with that *feria* and on numerous books, including James Michener's *Iberia*, Ray Mouton's *Pamplona*, and Javier Solano's essay in Jim Hollander et al., *Run for the Sun*, which also has an essay by Fran.

Chapter 21: Biographies of Hemingway by Carlos Baker, Michael Reynolds, Jeffrey Meyers, and James R. Mellow, as well as A. E. Hotchner's controversial but mostly accurate memoir *Papa Hemingway*, formed the backbone of this chapter.

Chapter 23: The two main sources for the life of Cayetano Ordóñez were Antonio Abad Ojual, *Estirpe y Tauromaquia de Antonio Ordóñez*, and Shay Oag, *In the Presence of Death*. Aside from the general sources already mentioned, the material on Joselito and Belmonte came from the English translation of Belmonte's memoir, *Killer of Bulls*.

Chapter 26: For commentary and statistics on Spanish sexuality, see Hooper.

Bibliography

Abad, Antonio. *Estirpe y Tauromaquia de Antonio Ordóñez*. Madrid: Espasa Calpe, 1988.

Abella, Carlos. *Luis Miguel Dominguín*. Madrid: Espasa Calpe, 1995.

Acquaroni, J. L. *Bulls and Bullfighting*. Translated by Charles David Ley. Barcelona: Editorial Noguer, 1961.

Arévalo, José Carlos, and José Antonio del Moral. *Nacido para Morir*. Madrid: Espasa Calpe, 1985.

Arias, Salvador. *Tauromaquia Lírica: Homenaje a Niño de la Palma, Antonio Ordóñez, Francisco Rivera Paquirri, Francisco Rivera Ordóñez, Real Maestranza de Caballería de Ronda*. Milaño, Spain: Sociedad de Artes Gráficas, 1999.

Ascasubi, Luis de. *Of Bulls and Men: A Traditional Sport*. New York: Thomas Nelson and Sons, 1962.

Baker, Carlos. *Hemingway: The Writer As Artist*. Princeton, N.J.: Princeton University Press, 1952.

Belmonte, Juan. *Killer of Bulls*. New York: Doubleday, Doran and Company, 1937.

Blasco Ibañez, Vicente. *Blood and Sand*. New York: E. P. Dutton, 1919.

Bonet, Eduardo, et al. *Bulls and Bullfighting: History, Techniques, and Spectacle*. New York: Crown Publishers, 1970.

Bonifaz, Juan José de. *Víctimas de la Fiesta*. Madrid: Espasa Calpe, 1991.

Botsford, Kenneth. *Dominguín: The Passionale of Spain's Greatest Bullfighter*. Chicago: Quadrangle Books, 1972.

Brenan, Gerald. *The Face of Spain*. New York: Farrar, Straus and Cudahy, 1956.

Buckley, Peter. *Bullfight.* New York: Simon and Schuster, 1958.

Calleja, Concepción. *Pasión Andaluza: Cayetana de Alba.* Barcelona: Plaza & Janes Editores, 2001.

Casas, Penelope. *Discovering Spain: An Uncommon Guide.* New York: Alfred A. Knopf, 1996.

Castillo-Puche, José Luis. *Hemingway in Spain.* Garden City, N.Y.: Doubleday, 1974.

Cintrón, Conchita. *Memoirs of a Bullfighter.* New York: Holt, Rinehart and Winston, 1968.

Claramunt, Fernando. *Tauromaquias Vividas.* Madrid: Ediciones Tutor, 1999.

Collins, Larry, and Dominique Lapierre. *Or I'll Dress You in Mourning: The Story of El Cordobés and the New Spain He Stands For.* New York: Simon and Schuster, 1968.

Conrad, Barnaby. *La Fiesta Brava.* Cambridge, Mass.: Riverside Press, 1950.

———. *The Gates of Fear: Great Exploits of the World's Bullrings.* New York: Bonanza Books, 1957.

———. *How to Fight a Bull.* Garden City, N.Y.: Doubleday, 1968.

Conrad, Jack Randolph. *The Horn and the Sword.* New York: E. P. Dutton, 1957.

Cossío, José María de. *Los Toros.* Madrid: Espasa Calpe, 1995. Two-volume abridgment of the multivolume encyclopedia *Los Toros: Tratado Técnico e Histórico.*

Domecq, Álvaro. *El Toro Bravo.* Madrid: Espasa Calpe, 1985.

Dominguín, Pepe. *Mi Gente.* Madrid: Editorial Piessa, 1979.

———. *Rojo y Oro.* Madrid: Alianza Editorial, 2002.

Feiner, Muriel. *Las Protagonistas de la Fiesta.* Madrid: Alianza Editorial, 2000.

———. *Women and the Bullring.* Gainesville: University of West Florida Press, 2003.

Fernández, Luis. *Trece Ganaderos Romanticos.* Madrid: Editorial Agricola Española, 1987.

Ford, Richard. *Gatherings from Spain.* London: Pallas Athene, 1999.

Franklin, Sidney. *Bullfighter from Brooklyn.* New York: Prentice Hall, 1952.

Fulton, John. *Bullfighting.* New York: Dial Press, 1971.

García Lorca, Federico. *The Selected Poems of Federico García Lorca.* New York: New Directions, 1955.

Gilperez, Luis. *La Verguenza Nacional: La Cara Oculta del Negocio Taurino.* Madrid: Ediciones Penthalón, 1991.

González Gordon, Manuel. *Sherry: The Noble Wine.* London: Quiller Press, 1990.

Graja, Maria Ángeles. *Va Por Ellas! Las Mujeres de los Toreros: Una Tauro-maquia Sentimental*. Barcelona: Editorial Planeta, 2002.

Gray, Gary. *Running with the Bulls: Fiestas, Corridas, Toreros, and an American's Adventure in Pamplona*. Guilford, Conn.: Lyons Press, 2001.

Hemingway, Ernest. *The Sun Also Rises*. New York: Charles Scribner's Sons, 1926.

————. *Death in the Afternoon*. New York: Charles Scribner's Sons, 1932.

————. *The Short Stories*. New York: Charles Scribner's Sons, 1938.

————. *For Whom the Bell Tolls*. New York: Charles Scribner's Sons, 1940.

————. *The Dangerous Summer*. New York: Charles Scribner's Sons, 1985.

————. *Byline: Ernest Hemingway: Selected Articles and Dispatches of Four Decades*. New York: Touchstone, 1998.

Hendra, Tony. "Man and Bull: Afternoons of a Young Torero." *Harper's Magazine*, November 1996.

Hillo, Pepe [pseud.]. *El Arte del Toreo*. Mexico: Andres Botas y Miguel, n.d.

Hollander, Jim, et al. *Run to the Sun: Pamplona's Fiesta de San Fermín*. Wilmington, Del.: MasterArts Press, 2002.

Hooper, John. *The New Spaniards*, rev. ed. London: Penguin, 1995.

Hotchner, A. E. *Papa Hemingway*. New York: Caroll and Graf, 1999.

Jeffs, Julian. *Sherry*. London: Faber and Faber, 1961.

Josephs, Allen. *White Wall of Spain*. Gainesville: University of West Florida Press, 1990.

————. *Ritual and Sacrifice in the Corrida: The Saga of César Rincón*. Gainesville: University of West Florida Press, 2002.

Kennedy, A. L. *On Bullfighting*. London: Yellow Jersey Press, 1999.

Lalaguna, Juan. *A Traveller's History of Spain*. New York: Interlink Books, 1996.

La Rochefoucauld, François de. *Maxims*. London: Penguin, 1959.

López Pinillos, José. *Lo Que Confiesan los Toreros*. Madrid: Ediciones Turner, 1987.

Luna, Arturo. *La Tragica Cogida y Muerte de Paquirri: Cronica de una Decada*. Pozoblanco: Ayuntamiento de Pozoblanco, 1993.

Macnab, Angus. *Fighting Bulls*. New York: Harcourt, Brace and Company, 1959.

McCormick, John. *Bullfighting: Art, Technique, and Spanish Society*. New Brunswick, N. J.: Transaction Publishers, 1998.

Mellow, James R. *Hemingway: A Life Without Consequences*. Boston: Houghton Mifflin, 1992.

Meyers, Jeffrey. *Hemingway: A Biography*. New York: Harper and Row, 1985.

Michener, James A. *Iberia*. New York: Random House, 1968.

———. *The Drifters*. New York: Random House, 1971.

Moral, José Antonio del. *Cómo Ver una Corrida de Toros*. Madrid: Alianza Editorial, 2001.

Mouton, Ray. *Pamplona: Running the Bulls, Bars, and Barrios in Fiesta de San Fermín*. New Orleans: Quinn Publishing, 2002.

Narbona, Francisco. *Sangre en la Arena: Víctimas del Toro en el Siglo XX*. Madrid: Alianza Editorial, 2001.

Oag, Shay. *In the Presence of Death: Antonio Ordóñez*. New York: Coward-McCann, 1969.

Olano, Antonio. *Dinastias: Dominguín, Ordóñez, Rivera*. Menorca: Promociones Ch. Ass, 1988.

Pérez, Vidal, ed. *Agenda Taurina 2001: España, America, y Francia*. Madrid: Temple, 2001.

Picamills, Antonio. *Dietario Taurino 2002*. Madrid: Dietario Taurino, 2002.

Pritchett, V. S. *The Spanish Temper*. London: Chatto and Windus, 1954.

Reynolds, Michael. *The Young Hemingway*. London: Basil Blackwell, 1986.

Sánchez, Juan Miguel, and Manuel Durán. *Taurina Antologia la Fotografia, 1839–1939*. Madrid: Espasa Calpe, 1999.

Sánchez, Juan Miguel, Manuel Durán, and Ángel Sanz. *Fiestas Taurinas en la Comunidad de Madrid II*. Madrid: Combisa, 1995.

Sanz, Cesáreo. *Historia y Bravura del Toro de Lidia*. Madrid: Espasa Calpe, 1958.

Schoenfeld, Bruce. *The Last Serious Thing: A Season at the Bullfights*. New York: Simon and Schuster, 1992.

Shubert, Adrian. *Death and Money in the Afternoon: A History of the Spanish Bullfight*. New York: Oxford University Press, 1999.

Smith, Rex, ed. *Biography of the Bulls: An Anthology of Spanish Bullfighting*. New York: Rinehart, 1957.

Soler, Pedro. *Oro y Plata: Embroidered Costumes of the Bullfight*. Paris: Assouline, n.d.

Stewart, Chris. *Driving over Lemons: An Optimist in Andalucía*. New York: Pantheon, 1999.

Suárez, José, and John Marks. *The Life and Death of the Fighting Bull*. New York: Putnam, 1968.

Tapia, Daniel. *Historia del Toreo I: De Pedro Romero a Manolete*. Madrid: Alianza Editorial, 1992.

Torres, Begoña. *El Cartel Taurino: Quites Entre Sol y Sombra*. Madrid: Electa, 1998.

Torres, José Carlos de. *Diccionario del Arte de los Toros*. Madrid: Alianza Editorial, 1996.

Tynan, Kenneth. *Bull Fever*. London: Longmans, Green, 1966.

Verrill, Lola. *Goddess of the Bullring.* New York: Bobbs-Merrill, 1960.

Vidal, Joaquín. *Crónicas Tuarinas.* Madrid: Santillana Ediciones Generales, 2002.

Viertel, Peter. *Love Lies Bleeding.* Garden City, N.Y.: Doubleday, 1964.

———. *Dangerous Friends: At Large with Hemingway and Huston in the Fifties.* New York: Nan A. Talese/Doubleday, 1992.

Webster, Jason. *Duende: A Journey in Search of Flamenco.* London: Doubleday, 2003.

Witwer, Kitty. *Divine Addiction: A Book About Bullfighting.* San Francisco: Primate Publishing, 1985.

Index